MARY OF JERUSALEM

BY THE AUTHOR

Rahab

*Merari: The Woman Who Challenged Queen Jezebel
and the Pagan Gods*

MARY OF JERUSALEM

Gloria Howe Bremkamp

1817

Harper & Row, Publishers, San Francisco

New York, Grand Rapids, Philadelphia, St. Louis
London, Singapore, Sydney, Tokyo, Toronto

FIRST HARPER & ROW PAPERBACK EDITION PUBLISHED IN 1990

Library of Congress Cataloging-in-Publication Data

Bremkamp, Gloria Howe.
  Mary of Jerusalem.

  1. Mary (Mother of John Mark)—Fiction. 2. Bible. N.T.—History of Biblical events—Fiction. I. Title. PS3552.R369M37   1988   813'.54   88-45126
ISBN 0-06-061057-3
ISBN 0-06-061060-3 (pbk.)

90   91   92   93   94   MPC   10   9   8   7   6   5   4   3   2   1

To my sister, Lucinda Howe Pennington,
who enriches our kinship with her
priceless gift of friendship.

"—He went to the house of Mary, the mother of John, also called Mark, where many people had gathered and were praying."

ACTS 12:12

In the days and years immediately after Jesus' crucifixion, resurrection and ascension, many of those who had followed him during his public ministry continued to meet together and pray together, to defend and protect each other, and to obey as best they could Jesus' instructions "to love one another." They created the beginnings of what today's Christians know as "the church." Mary of Jerusalem, mother of Mark and a widow, was one of these early believers. This is her story, as it might have been, and maybe, really was.

MARY OF JERUSALEM

1

The Year 36 A.D.

Mary Mark awakened abruptly with a sense of foreboding. For the merest moment of time, she lay tense and still, questioning what had caused her to come awake so rudely, listening for some explanatory sound. The murky dimness of the unfamiliar sleeping chamber was relieved only by a smudge of flame from a tallow oil lamp. She glanced about. Nothing seemed to move in the shadows, and she heard nothing but Rhoda's soft breathing.

She eased up on one elbow and peered in the direction of the servant's cot.

"It's good one of us can sleep like that, I suppose," she muttered, realizing it must be hours yet until daylight. Lying back down, she wondered again about what had awakened her. It was probably nothing more than the vague sense of restlessness she'd felt since arriving at Herod's palace in Tiberias as the guest of her friend Joanna. She really hadn't wanted to come. There was too much to do at home in Jerusalem, but Joanna had insisted. Manaen had urged her to come, too.

And even Barnabas, her own brother, had joined the effort to persuade her. "Jerusalem is unusually cold this year. You should welcome Tiberias' milder climate. Besides, you will enjoy the change," he encouraged. "And Rhoda needs a rest as much as you."

"But what about your trip to Cyprus to check on the copper shipments?" she resisted. "And what about John Mark?"

"If I decide to make the trip before you return, I'll take John Mark with me. Otherwise, I'll see to it that he stays off the streets, and that he's faithful to his studies at the School for Scribes' Apprentices."

So at last she let them persuade her to make the journey. She had relented, as she often did, drawing away from argument, retreating into the silence of her natural shyness—and then after the fact, like now, wishing she had been more firm. The truth of the matter was she never slept well in strange beds, and she found the hot springs and mineral water baths, for which Tiberias was so famous, enervating rather than energizing. Herod Antipas had built the city in honor of the Roman emperor Tiberius, whose favor he so assiduously curried. But he also used it as his own capital in Galilee because his wife, Herodias, enjoyed its hot springs and found it less isolated than Sepphoris, which had been the traditional Galiliean capital for the Herods.

But Mary Mark found Tiberias to be an uncomfortable place. Again, she wished she hadn't come. For an instant, she chided herself for not speaking out boldly against the trip. She had little respect for Antipas, and she thoroughly disliked Herodias, considering her willful and deceitful. Antipas, on the other hand, had a passive quality that weakened him as a ruler. Far too often he allowed Herodias to influence and manipulate his decisions. Feeling such dislike and disrespect made her question her own honesty about accepting their hospitality, regardless of the fact that she was there at Joanna's invitation. She wondered if her state of restlessness was being compounded by a certain feeling of guilt.

She got up, fumbled into a robe, and made her way out of the sleeping chamber onto the broad terrace extending beyond it. She was taller than most women, still slender considering her age of thirty–eight, and statuesque. She moved with the lithe grace of a dancer. Her eyes, a luminous dark brown, dominated her face. The tiniest of wrinkles were beginning to crease the smooth olive complexion, and strands of gray now salted her dark, shoulder–length hair. She did not consider herself a pretty woman. Her features were too strong. But she was pleasant and outgoing with a shy sensitivity that gave her a vulnerable, and very human, quality. There was a quiet, certain steadiness about her, too. Everyone who knew her accorded her that and felt a curious reassurance when she was around.

She came to the edge of the terrace and stopped. It buttressed the east side of Herod's palace like a seawall. And indeed, that's what it was. The waters of the Sea of Galilee lapped at the very footings of the terrace. At its south end, steps led down to a sizable quay where the royal barge was moored. At the north end, the terrace wrapped itself around a corner of the palace wall and blended into an archway that led back toward her own guest chambers. There was a lovely peace about the predawn solitude surrounding her. Her sense of foreboding seemed out of place. She should not feel restless or worried about anything.

In many ways, the peacefulness reminded her of Cyprus, where she and Barnabas grew up. She closed her eyes, remembering the days of her childhood and the wonderful, rambling house of golden–hued sandstone situated a short distance to the northwest of the great port city of Salamis, at the edge of a region known as the Mesaoria Plain. Vast fields of wheat and barley grew in the heart of the plain. Between autumn and spring each year, it was colorful and green with an abundance of wild flowers and flowering bushes and shrubs.

A bit to the south and west of the house, foothills rose to a woodland where eucalyptus, acacia, cypress, and lowland pines grew in abundance. There was a great demand for timber among the shipbuilders in Salamis, and her father and uncles conducted a profitable business by supplying it to them. Timber was a sideline, however, to their copper mining interests. The family had owned copper mines for many generations.

Even before that however, men had mined the minerals, processed the raw ore, and made a livelihood for themselves and their families. Traces of Phoenicians' efforts often turned up as the miners toiled with pick and sledge to harvest the ore from its rock host. More recently, and to the good fortune of her family, the Romans had need of enormous amounts of the reddish brown element. They mixed bluish white zinc with it and turned the copper into rich–looking brass. Or they mixed it with the silver white softness of tin and transformed it into bronze, that durable, versatile metal used for household items, statuary, and weapons of war.

Barnabas still had sizable copper holdings on Cyprus, even though he recently had sold more than half of his mining properties and all of his pasture lands to support the community of Jesus–believers in Jerusalem.

A sudden chill engulfed her. She shrugged it off and envisioned the great sandstone house of her childhood. How she wished John Mark could have lived in that wonderful rambling house and could have known the people who lived there during her childhood: her grandmother and grandfather on her father's side, two of her father's brothers who had never married, two of her mother's sisters who were widowed, Barnabas, and herself. The floor plan of the house had no special rhyme or reason. As the needs of the family grew, her father simply added another room and cut a doorway through an existing wall so the whole thing connected.

It was all quite practical and simple, really. There was a constant string of relatives, friends, and business associates coming to visit. Like most other Cypriots of Greek extraction, her parents were generous with their hospitality. No stranger was ever turned away without a meal and an invitation to stay overnight.

She and Barnabas had inherited their generosity, she thought with an abrupt return to the present. She still used her mother's familiar phrase for her own house in Jerusalem: "Every stranger is a welcome guest." But she wondered sometimes if she had failed to pass the attitude on to John Mark. He seemed to be more like his father, as if he had inherited more of Yonah's quiet, introspective personality than of her own. She wished he could have known his grandparents. He would be a different boy. And she wished he could have lived in that wonderful rambling house. Even for just a little while. He would have liked it.

And he would have liked the nearby woodlands, too, as much as she and Barnabas did when they were young. Deer and wild boar roamed there. Mouflon, the sheep with the great curved horns, grazed on the shoulders of the hills at the edge of the woodlands and in the openness of the valleys. In spring and autumn, huge flights of migrating birds darkened the sky and turned the quiet woodlands into talkative congregations at roosting time.

But perhaps the thing she and Barnabas most enjoyed about their childhood were the summer evenings when family and guests gathered on the flat expanse of roof to catch the cooling breeze from the Great Sea to the east and to watch the mysterious blue–gray mists rise slowly upward at dusk like some enormous curtain.

It was then that the elders would tell the stories of mythical gods and goddesses, heroes and heroines whose deeds of good and evil caused the world to be as it was. And then their conversations would grow seriously reverent as they spoke of the One True God of the Hebrews, the unseen God whose covenant with humankind implanted the quest for justice in their hearts. It was a good time, a protected time, a precious time to hold in reverence in the deepest, and most secret places of her heart. Only in later years had she come to realize that a newer covenant existed between God and humankind—a covenant that touched the human spirit with a need for freedom and courage and for love.

She glanced about, repeating the thought that in the peace of the predawn solitude surrounding her she really should feel no restlessness nor worry about anything. She walked slowly along the terrace trying to settle her restlessness, trying to push away the lingering sense of foreboding.

Before her spread the still-slumbering waters of the Sea of Galilee. In the distance, she now could hear sounds of fishermen preparing their boats for the day's work on the great expanse of water. For them, the lake was a pulsing, living feature of the land. It filled an ancient basin that had the contours of a great heart, and it had nourished all who lived beside it since the predawn of humankind. Its length north to south equalled a full day's walk, and was half that distance from east to west. On the eastern shore, the heights of Gilead crescendoed against the border of Bashan. And somewhere north of that, lost now in the dusky prelight, the river Jordan made its entrance into the great lake. Near its inlet were situated the villages of Bethsaida and Capernaum, where her friends Peter and Andrew, John and James and their families had their homes. And just to the west of Capernaum was the green slope of hills where she personally had first heard Jesus preach.

She brushed the back of one hand across her eyes, as if the gesture would cause the dawn to come faster so she could actually see the green slope of hills. It had been six years since she and Joanna had stood there with the rest of the crowd to listen to Jesus, to witness the miracles he performed in the name of the One True God, and to receive their personal miracles. Joanna no longer suffered the crippling agony in her foot. And for herself, the pain and anguish of widowhood's fearful wounds had been healed.

Since that experience, they both had followed Jesus. They supported his ministry with gifts of food and money, and prayers.

As the wife of Chuza, minister of households and finances for Herod Antipas, Joanna had to be very careful about how she gave her support. But give it she did in discreet and subtle ways that would not jeopardize Chuza's reputation or position.

For her own part, discretion and care were equally important to her household. All of Jesus' followers had to be careful, if they were to do what he asked of them after his resurrection. If they were to spread the word of his teachings, they had to stay alive as long as possible. And that meant staying out of the hands of the authorities as much as possible.

So far, she had been spared many of the hardships others already had suffered. At one time or another, all of the apostles had been arrested and questioned. Some of them had been beaten before they were released. The houses of many believers were regularly raided and their owners cast into prison.

Her own house had been searched after the Pentecost experience of the infilling of the Holy Spirit attracted public attention. But it had been easier for her than for most. She and her household were seldom harassed the way others were. She was grateful for that. Most of the time she enjoyed a position of protected prosperity. She was the widow of Mark Yonah ben Abou, business partner to the influential merchant Joseph of Arimathea. Since Yonah's death some years before, she had continued as an active partner to Joseph. Barnabas moved to Jerusalem and became a third partner. Their business dealings were with kings and princes throughout the eastern provinces of the Roman Empire, including Herod Antipas. So her position of protected prosperity was a well–fortified one.

She moved along the terrace feeling a sense of gratitude for her position in life and wondering whether her courage could withstand deprivation, imprisonment, or even having to move from her comfortable house in Jerusalem.

Imprisonment and hardship were things she didn't like to think about, even though they were all around her as part and parcel of human existence. The strange fact was that she never used to worry about such things. Only after she met Jesus and became one of his followers had she developed a growing awareness for the needs of others. She began to offer to other believers the hospitality of her house and other properties she owned in Jerusalem, just as she had offered them to Jesus himself. She had provided the room where he and his twelve had their last Passover supper together. Later his followers had felt welcome to gather in her house to praise and give thanks to the Almighty God for Jesus' resurrection. And it was also in her house that the faithful were gathered when the Holy Spirit made his visitation on that miraculous Pentecost morning.

The house continued to be open to all those who believed in Jesus and in the fulfillment of his promises. Meals were shared. Sanctuary was given. Prayer gatherings were a daily affair.

If only John Mark could understand the importance of letting the house be used for such things, she thought with a pang of longing. If only he could understand how real Jesus still was, and how alive, and how real the fulfillment of his promises.

Now that he was nearing manhood, he had begun to question many things in a very hard way. His assessment of reality seemed based only on what he could see and taste and touch. At times, Mary Mark thought she even could detect in him a certain embarrassment about Peter and the others and their rough Galilean ways. Once he had thought of them as heroes. But recently it seemed the spirit of Jesus' teachings was growing less important to him. Only a few days before she left Jerusalem to come here with Joanna, John Mark had complained.

"Strife. It's everywhere. Is this what Jesus meant when he talked about peace?"

"The lad's growing up," Barnabas put in before she could answer.

"You tell me Jesus is alive," John Mark charged. "But I haven't seen him."

"You sound like Thomas," Barnabas said. "He had to see the nailprints before he believed."

"What's needed to make you believe?" Mary Mark asked.

"If Jesus is alive, why doesn't he come to see us as he once did?" the boy countered in his blunt, straightforward manner.

"That's the Lord's choice."

"And if he's alive, why hasn't he restored the kingdom, like he talked about?"

"Perhaps you are expecting a different kind of kingdom than he meant."

A puzzled look came across his face.

For a moment, she thought his skepticism was relenting, but then disbelief replaced the puzzled look.

"If Jesus is alive, why hasn't he brought a great army and thrown out the Romans?"

"Would that really settle all the strife, John Mark?"

He stared at her for a long moment before turning away and leaving the room.

Now standing here on the terrace of the palace, a new and upsetting awareness struck her, adding to her sense of foreboding. In spite of the depth of her own convictions about Jesus, she realized she had no answers that would satisfy her son. The search for the reality of life's lasting values was something he would have to do for himself, as she had done for herself. But he was right about one thing—

strife was everywhere. All who lived under the iron fist of the Roman procurator of Judea, Pontius Pilate, were involved in strife and affected by it. Even the generally passive rule of Herod Antipas, tetrarch of Galilee and Perea, added to it.

At this very moment, a war was raging because of Antipas. Or more accurately, because of Herodias. Aretas, king of the Nabateans, had declared war against Herod Antipas to avenge the dishonor to his daughter. A few years earlier in Rome, Herod had divorced her so that he could marry Herodias. At the time, Herodias had been the wife of Herod's half brother, Philip, tetrarch of Batanea and Trachonitis. But Antipas had become infatuated with her. She had engineered it. Antipas had more wealth and larger, more important kingdoms than Philip. The act was both illegal and immoral. Their union was against the customs of society and the laws of God.

But more basic to the cause of strife in Judea was Pilate's harsh rule. It grew more abusive with the years. It was as if Pilate blamed Judea for his own inadequacy against the unremitting process of age.

"He hates growing old," Joanna had once confided to Mary Mark. "His wife tells me of this. She fears for his sanity, so desperately does he hate the advance of years."

In response to Pilate's heavy–handedness, discontent and unrest grew to rebelliousness. Zealots threatened riots in all parts of the Galilee and in Perea. They had petitioned Herod more than once for relief. But concerned as he was over the war with Aretas, he had done nothing to placate them; nor had he complained to Rome about Pilate's roughshod arrogance.

Overlaying these quarrelsome situations were the controversies that continued to erupt over the resurrection of Jesus. It appeared that this single event, with all its overtones of supernatural mystery, had changed the very foundations of people's understanding of reality. Arguments about what was real and what was imagined grew passionate, flamed into suspicion and mistrust, and disintegrated into hatred.

John Mark was right. Strife was everywhere. In the face of it, how could she prove to him that the power of love that Jesus preached was greater than the power that men so roughly wielded? How could she help him to understand that regardless of the world's strife, he could find and keep within himself peace and courage, the kind of courage that would turn opposition into an opportunity for victory? Could she ever help him to understand that?

From the distance the plaintive call of a waterbird broke the stillness. Mary Mark leaned against the rough stone wall of the terrace, considering just how much strife really did surround them all. The view of the lake and hills blurred before her, shimmered without form or delineation. At almost the same moment, she heard footsteps coming toward her from the far end of the terrace. She turned. Even in the half–light, there was no mistaking the tall, athletic figure of Manaen. She brushed at her eyes with the back of her hand. No need to let him see her cry. He could do nothing about John Mark. He could not influence him.

And like most men, he would probably become uncomfortable at the sight of tears. Besides, she did not know him well enough to show such emotion. Joanna and Chuza had introduced him shortly after he returned from Antioch where he had been Herod's representative to the Roman governor, Publius Petronius.

"After all, he's a widower," Chuza said with a wink.

"And you're a widow," Joanna had smiled.

"And you two are matchmakers," she had laughed.

Chuza turned serious. "If you're worried about whether or not he is Herod's half brother, we're not certain."

"Of course we're certain he's not, my husband," Joanna contradicted in a gentle way. "Herod the Great and Malthace had only two sons, Archelaus and Antipas. Archelaus has been dead these many years."

"But Antipas claims him as a half brother. And after all, Herod the Great had ten wives and numerous concubines. He sired well more than fifteen children. Manaen might have been one of them."

"Nonsense," Joanna smiled, coming and taking Mary Mark by the arm in a reassuring way. "Where Manaen is concerned, it is quite doubtful that Herodian blood flows in his veins. And for that, we should all be grateful!"

Mary Mark was glad. Whatever his family background, she was secretly glad he had no Herodian blood, just as she was secretly glad he was so tall. It made her feel protected. Not that she hadn't felt protected with Yonah. She had. Yonah was always very protective, even though he had to stand very straight to equal her own height. Manaen, on the other hand, had a quality of physical authority to which she reacted in a very different way. Even his voice appealed to her.

"Ah, there you are!" He gave a quick, angular smile. He was not a handsome man, except in a rugged way. His brow was craggy and his eyes too deep-set. There was an odd imbalance to his clean-shaven face. "Joanna sent me to find you. We're returning to Jerusalem within the hour."

"What is wrong?"

"Zealots."

"What about them?"

"We've had word they plan to attack the palace."

"Attack—? But why?"

"Herod's army has been defeated by Aretas."

"Defeated?" Mary Mark repeated the word in a whisper of startled disbelief. How could Herod be defeated? Aretas had been justified to declare war on Herod Antipas, but it simply never occurred to her that Aretas could win. A strange dissappointment went through her. Following quickly on its heels came the puzzling question of why she should care. Herod Antipas deserved to be defeated. He had done a dreadful thing. She should feel glad that he was punished for it and that the Nabatean princess' honor had been avenged.

"Destroyed is a more accurate description of what has happened, I guess." Manaen leaned against the rough stone wall and looked out over the lake.

"But, how could that happen? I thought Antipas has the power of Rome behind him."

"Not in this fray. Pilate told Antipas that since it was his wives they were fighting over, it was his war. Now the army is put to rout. Most of his men were killed. The few remaining have been scattered in the deserts of Nabatea. The Zealots learned of it, naturally. They have spies everywhere and are taking advantage of Herod's losses."

"And Herod? Is he alive?" She said it so softly that he turned and leaned closer to make sure he heard her. When she again asked the question, she heard herself stutter a bit, as if his nearness meant more to her than it should.

"Herod's alive," Manaen answered. "He is back in Jerusalem. He sent a special courier with orders for us to return there at once. He fears we are in danger here."

"I'll awaken Rhoda. We'll be ready within the hour."

The return to Jerusalem was without incident, even though the route taken was not the usual one. They traveled west as directly as possible toward Caesarea–by–the–Sea, where Pilate's headquarters were located. As they approached the city's edge, the caravan pulled off the road to give way to a large number of Roman soldiers headed eastward into the heart of the Galilee. After an overnight rest, the royal caravan proceeded southward, through the beautiful Plain of Sharon to Joppa, and then southeasterly through the hills to Emmaus and finally to Jerusalem.

When she asked why they were taking the longer route, Manaen told her, "It is just a precaution. The Romans guard the main coastal road. It's safer than those trails through Samaria."

She found the answer disturbing. But far more disturbing was the troublesome foreboding with which she had started the homeward journey and which continued to cling in her mind. As the journey progressed, she thought much on it. She knew that for all of his passiveness, Herod Antipas was not a man who could accept defeat. Especially this one. The Nabatean victory would be considered by everyone as a major loss of face. Herodias would goad Antipas in subtle ways to redeem himself in the eyes of his subjects. She had demonstrated her vengeful nature on more than one occasion. Mary Mark's mind raced back to the fiendish beheading of John the Baptizer, which Herodias had plotted. No the defeat of Herod Antipas by Aretas was not the end of the war, not even if his army had been destroyed. There would be retaliation. It might not be directed against Aretas, but there would be retaliation. Somewhere. Somehow. And whenever it happened, Mary Mark knew that the results could only be more civil strife, perhaps outright revolt. Then the Romans would get involved. Revolt was the one thing the Romans most feared and, consequently, the thing they most fiercely fought. She shuddered.

Civil strife would endanger her personal sources of income and those of Joseph of Arimathea and of her brother, Barnabas. In turn, the supply of goods and monies for the work of the Lord would suffer. Her friendship with Joanna and Chuza and Manaen might be at risk. Of most personal concern to her was what the effect might be on the agile mind and impressionable heart of her son. All these things were at risk if the foolishness of pride plunged Judea into civil strife and open revolt. She shuddered again, realizing that dread had become the offspring of all her speculations.

Now she wondered if the dread was a real premonition, or merely needless worry.

2

Mary Mark didn't know it, but events were already under way which would prove her sense of dread well–founded, events quite beyond what she would have suspected.

While the royal caravan was still two days distant from the holy city, Caiaphas, Jerusalem's chief priest and president of the great Sanhedrin, made his way toward the residence of Joseph of Arimathea. He was clad in a nondescript robe that hid his priestly identity. Only a matter of urgency caused him to be dressed in that manner or to make such an early trip to see the merchant.

Usually, he summoned those he wished to see to come to him. It was one of the privileges of his rank that he most enjoyed. He had been Jerusalem's chief priest for almost eighteen years, having been appointed by Valerius Gratus, the Roman prefect who preceded Pontius Pilate. Though he sometimes felt the degree of his power had eroded, his possessiveness of the privileges of rank had not waned. But in this instance, summoning the Arimathean to come to the Chamber of Hewn Stone within the precincts of the Temple Mount somehow seemed inappropriate. He needed his counsel. He was going to him. That was, by far, the more politic action.

Regardless of the fact that the merchant was a known follower of the dead heretic Jesus and that he actually believed the Nazarene still to be alive, he had a clear and objective mind, was a shrewd negotiator, and was one of the most respected members of the Sanhedrin. In addition, he had enormous influence with Herod Antipas, a contradiction in loyalties explained only by mutuality of wealth and power.

Caiaphas brushed past the startled servant who opened the outer gate in response to his knocking. "Where is your master?"

"This way, sir . . . " The servant hurried across the unpretentious courtyard toward a large room at the far side of the residence. Once he entered, he stepped aside and motioned in the direction of an enormous wooden table piled high with scrolls, bundles of cloth, baskets containing an array of trinkets, and stacks of small clay lamps. Other baskets, bundles, and bales of assorted merchandise lay nearby on the hardened clay floor. In the midst of seeming chaos, the merchant and two scribes were at the business of taking an orderly inventory of the items.

Caiaphas grimaced at the plain surroundings. He had never understood why Joseph chose to live in such apparent penury when he could afford a palace as big as Herod's, one that could be furnished throughout, including this storehouselike room, with the treasures of every land in which his caravans traded—unless, of course, the plainness was for the benefit of tax collectors. That would be understandable.

He moved on toward the far side of the room. A small dog asleep under the table awakened, began to bark, and charged toward him in a menacing way. Caiaphas abruptly stopped. The men looked up. Joseph called to the dog. It hesitated and glanced around as if to make certain it had heard the right command before returning to its place under the table.

Admonishing the dog, the merchant came forward. He was of medium height, portly, and endowed with a full head of white hair. His eyebrows and neatly trimmed beard were also white, his eyes amber colored.

"Caiaphas, I am honored. Welcome to my poor house."

"This is not the time for such foolish humor, Joseph."

The Arimathean shrugged and feigned a serious look, while noting the pallor of the priest's face and wondering if he was ill.

"I have come on a matter of greatest urgency."

"About what?"

"The tetrarch."

Joseph motioned toward the outer door and led the way back across the big room and out in the courtyard where their conversation could not be overheard.

"What about the tetrarch?"

"He has appealed to Pilate."

"For what?"

"To put down the Zealots' uprisings in Galilee."

"Riots?" Astonishment glinted in Joseph's amber–colored eyes. He wondered why his own people had not sent him word of an uprising and whether or not Mary Mark and the others were safe in Tiberias.

"Since his own army is destroyed, Antipas called on Pilate to put down the rioting for him."

"And what was Pilate's answer?"

"He agreed. And the riots were put down with such brutality that people have been slaughtered by the hundreds. Entire villages have been destroyed. The population is rising up in outrage. Galilee is aflame with vengeance!"

"What about the palace in Tiberias? Was it attacked?"

Caiaphas shrugged. "All I know is that vengeance is spreading throughout all the provinces and survivors from Galilee are streaming through the gates of this holy city seeking sanctuary. We must do something before an open revolt breaks forth." The priest clasped his hands together in a characteristically pleading gesture. "What are we to do? I need your counsel."

Joseph scowled against an abrupt slant of sunlight.

Caiaphas watched him with close-set eyes that were like pinpoints of confusion. "Didn't you hear me, Joseph? We're facing open revolt!"

"I heard you, Caiaphas."

"But we must do something!"

"Give me a moment," Joseph said, continuing to ponder the situation. First and foremost in his mind was a concern for Mary Mark, Joanna, and the rest of the royal party. Second was his concern over why his own people had not reported this uprising to him. For years, his network of information had been swift and accurate. Trading as he did with all the villagers who made crafts of any worth, he was kept informed of all major events. Why not now? But his third concern required first action. What could be done about Pilate? Never a man of soft judgments in the best of times, he recently had grown increasingly harsh. Antipas knew that. For him to seek Pilate's help meant he was desperate. But what about the aftermath? What would Pilate do if open revolt broke out in Jerusalem? The distinguished city of illustrious history would be devastated. That's what would happen. There would be no way to preserve the wide vistas of the Upper City or its pleasant Hellenistic grid pattern of streets and homes. Nor would there be any defense of the Suburb or the Lower City where the houses clung together like beads on a loose string. Open revolt must not break out in Jerusalem. But what would avert it? The most obvious solution would be to get rid of Pilate. That would mean recall, of course. And that would take an imperial order. Would that be possible? Could that be done? The thought caught in his mind.

"What are we going to do?" Caiaphas insisted.

Joseph turned. "We're going to see the tetrarch."

"When?"

"Now!"

"Like this?" The priest glanced at his clothing.

"Now!" Joseph strode toward the outer gate.

A stricken look came over Caiaphas' pallid face. He did not move.

Joseph glanced back and hesitated. "Unless, of course, you'd prefer to go to see Antipas by yourself."

Reluctantly, Caiaphas moved forward.

Herod's palace was only a few blocks from Joseph of Arimathea's residence. It had been built by Antipas' father, Herod the Great, on the highest, most easily defensible point of land in Jerusalem's Upper City, parallel to the city's western wall. The parapets and battlements of the palace served as additional strongholds against any force foolish enough to assault it from any direction. None had in recent history.

Three memorial towers anchored the palace compound on the north. The largest, Phasael Tower, had been named after Herod the Great's brother. Battlements were constructed at its base; and the upper part of its tower was turreted like a palace. Hippicus Tower had been named for one of Herod the Great's friends and generals. Above its base was a deep reservoir for water and a high chamber above that. The third tower was named for Mariamne, the beloved wife whom Herod the Great murdered.

Of the three, Mariamne Tower had the most luxurious residential quarters. Joseph glanced up at it as they turned into the Street of Herod's Palace and remembered something Antipas had once quoted from his father. "The king considers it appropriate that a tower named after a woman should surpass in decoration those called after men." Joseph smiled to himself at the ironic contradiction between the thought and the actions of Antipas' father where women were concerned. In a way, it explained some of the contradictions in Antipas, as if the guilt of his father still influenced his own attitudes. For a man thought to be a strong leader, Antipas had a strangely passive nature. He sought and listened to advice from many confidants on important matters, but he seemed to use the process as a buffer against taking action. He found procrastination comfortable, almost as if he believed that, left alone, all things and time itself would heal.

Directly south of the three memorial towers were the barracks. They were empty now, or practically so, after the defeat at the hands of the Nabateans. And then, stretching south of the barracks for a considerable length, was the palace compound itself.

As Joseph, followed by the reluctant Caiaphas, reached the main gate, the lone soldier on sentry recognized them immediately and passed them through the portal. It opened onto a wide walkway bordering an ornate, beautifully landscaped courtyard. Clusters of trees were situated throughout. Canals and ponds studded with bronze fountains interlaced open walkways. Palace guests and members of the royal court were seated on various stone benches around the gardens, taking the early morning sun.

Bordering the length of this lavish courtyard on both sides was a magnificent peristyle of precise Hellenistic design with colonnades supporting a wide tile roof. On the outside of the peristyle, open walkways connected the two main buildings of the palace itself. Each had its own banquet halls, baths, and accommodations for hundreds of guests, as well as chambers for the members of the royal court.

Joseph hesitated only a moment to cast an appreciative eye at the beauty of the courtyard, then turned south along the outer walkway toward a private entrance in the east wall of the south palace.

"We shouldn't come on him like this. With no warning," Caiaphas muttered, hurrying to keep up. "He will be offended at the outset. And besides, what can we expect him to do?"

Joseph stopped short, surprised at the genuineness of the priest's tone of voice, and searched his face. He looked frightened. Had his own waning power made him believe that Antipas had no power either? It once was different, Joseph thought recalling times past when Caiaphas was a shrewd adversary and worthy representative as president of the Sanhedrin. In those days, Caiaphas would have welcomed an opportunity to demand of Herod Antipas a bold action. It appeared that was no longer true. Something akin to pity went throught Joseph. He clasped Caiaphas' shoulder. It felt thin and fragile under the nondescript cloak. "Come, old friend. For once, Antipas may ally himself with the Sanhedrin instead of the Romans."

"But we have no appointment for an audience, Joseph. You know how he is about things like that."

"Chuza will arrange it. We never need an appointment to see him. Come along."

"You may not need an appointment," Caiaphas complained. "But I do. Chuza's always quite formal with me."

Joseph said nothing more and moved on. Caiaphas subsided into an uncertain silence and followed after him.

Chuza, chief steward of households and finances, sat quite alone and preoccupied in a small annex adjacent to the Great Hall of Audience. Beyond were several long rows of stone benches for citizens who came to make direct pleas to the tetrarch concerning everything from taxes to local neighborhood disputes. This procedure of giving the populus direct access to Herod had been allowed since the days of Herod the Great. Antipas continued it for a number of reasons, most conspicuous of which was the illusion that the common citizen had a measure of control over his own destiny and that the tetrarch was his friend.

"The public audiences lessen the chances of insurgence," Antipas liked to say. "Talking takes away the heat of anger."

On this particular morning, Joseph hoped Antipas was

right. Many of the supplicants were from Galilee. The strange dialects of the region were quite audible. And the subject of their talk was of Pilate's ruthlessness in putting down the riots in Galilee.

Joseph led the way around the edge of the waiting crowd toward Chuza's alcove. Chuza looked up and rose immediately to his feet. He was a short, round little man with a cherubic face. In his pale eyes, however, was a permanent look of wary calculation.

Joseph smiled in spite of himself, remembering Mary Mark's pet name for the husband of her good friend of so many years. "Little Jug should be his name," she had said.

Chuza made a formal salaam to Caiaphas, then turned to Joseph. Worry creased his face. "You have come for news of Mary Mark and Joanna, haven't you?"

"That, and more."

"The women are safe," Chuza said quickly, motioning for them to be seated and returning to his own chair. "They are traveling to Jerusalem now. By the main roads and accompanied by a squad of Roman guards from Caesarea."

Joseph settled back in the chair, eased by that report.

"Manaen is with them, as you know. They should be back within the safety of Jerusalem's gates before tomorrow's sunset."

Caiaphas shifted around in the chair and nervously drummed his fingers together.

"And how can I be of service to you, Honorable Caiaphas?" Chuza asked, giving him a direct look.

Caiaphas cleared his throat and leaned forward in the chair. "I hear there has been a slaughter in Galilee. Are these reports true?"

Chuza nodded. "The reports are true."

Color came up in the priest's face. "What are you going to do about the siutation?"

Joseph put a restraining hand on the priest's arm before

he could speak again and asked Chuza, "Would it be possible for us to talk with Antipas before he begins his audience with the citizenry? Caiaphas and I both are very concerned for the peace of Jerusalem in the days to come."

"I join in your concern, Joseph. And I feel sure Antipas will welcome your visit before he meets with these other citizens. I will tell him you're here." He stood up and made his way down a long corridor in his peculiar rolling gait.

Within a very few minutes, he reappeared at the end of the corridor and motioned for them to come with him. At the end of a circuitous route, they turned into a private antechamber. Antipas stood looking out of the window toward the half–empty barracks at the far north end of the palace compound.

"Your Excellency, Joseph of Arimathea and the honorable Caiaphas are here."

Antipas turned. His swarthy face was lined with fatigue and worry. His eyes had the dull look of cold embers.

Joseph and Caiaphas both salaamed and waited to be motioned forward according to accustomed protocol. For the longest moment, Antipas made no move to welcome them, nor to even acknowledge their presence by a change in facial expression. It was as if he was in such deep thought, he was not really seeing them standing before him.

Chuza moved forward. "Your Excellency, where do you wish your honored guests to sit?"

The question jarred Antipas. He nodded toward Joseph and Caiaphas and, with a wave of his arm, called them forward to chairs positioned near the window. He took the chair facing out across the beautiful courtyard.

Joseph and Caiaphas went to the chairs indicated and sat down. Chuza positioned himself near Herod Antipas and remained standing.

"Joseph, I have been betrayed," Antipas said in a heavy tone. "Betrayed in the most disastrous manner. Have you heard of the devastation Pilate has brought to Galilee?"

"I heard just a short while ago. In fact, that's the matter that brings both of us to see you."

Antipas barely glanced at the priest but gave a questioning look to Joseph. "You're concerned for your trade routes, naturally."

"That's a consideration, of course," Joseph said, "But my greater concern is for the people of Galilee. Such a slaughter must not happen again."

"And my concern is for the peace of Jerusalem." Caiaphas blurted the words as if he could no longer stand having Antipas ignore him.

Antipas turned. "Your tone implies that mine is not."

"You knew Pilate cannot be trusted!" Caiaphas flared.

The dull expression in Antipas' eyes gave way to a flash of resentment.

"It was the least of wisdom to ask his help," Caiaphas charged. "How could you have done it? He is no friend to any of us!"

Antipas' face darkened. Joseph warned Caiaphas with a look.

"Pilate's brutality should come as no surprise to you, Antipas," Caiaphas blurted as if in spite of himself.

Joseph intervened. "Caiaphas' concern for the peace of Jerusalem pushes him, Your Excellency. Forgive his rashness. We are here to help find a solution, not to add to your problems."

"My gratitude goes out to you, merchant! I need help in this matter. I need advice."

"There is a solution, Your Excellency. A rather simple one, really. But it requires a bold action."

"Bold action?"

"The solution has been given to us by Pilate himself."

"How?"

"By his own actions. By the brutality with which he put down the Zealots in Galilee."

Antipas studied Joseph for a moment. Through the open window came the sounds of talking and laughter from the courtyard. Such normal sounds seemed foolish and out of place at the moment.

"We'll have open revolt if we don't do something," Caiaphas muttered, more to himself than to the others. "Open revolt . . . "

"What is this bold action you speak of, Joseph? Is it action you can undertake for us?"

"No, Your Excellency. It is action that only you can take. It is an action that must come from someone with great power and great leadership."

"And what is the action?"

"Ask Rome to recall Pilate!"

A strangle of surprise issued from Caiaphas. Chuza stiffened in astonishment.

Antipas studied Joseph for a long moment with surprise showing clearly in his swarthy face. "Have Pilate recalled?"

"Why not?" Joseph asked in absolute seriousness. "It is not without reason. Your reputation in Rome is of the highest order, Antipas. You are very well thought of. You have kept your contacts with the emperor in good repair. You have served Rome well for many years. You now have just cause to ask for the removal of the procurator."

"But the emperor is old now. And some say he is senile," Antipas countered. "And what if the request is turned down? Pilate will learn of it, and he will take his revenge in some manner, won't he?"

Joseph nodded agreement. "That is the risk you would take, Excellency. But I believe that the emperor will heed your request for the recall of Pontius Pilate."

"You're serious, aren't you?"

Joseph nodded.

"You are really serious!"

"Tell Rome of Pilate's overt brutality in Galilee. Rome will like that less than we do."

"It is a bold move."

"Boldness is needed."

"And timing, Your Excellency," Chuza said, "timing will be all important, too."

"You want me to decide now, is that it?"

"Yes, Excellency."

"It will take a courier many days to reach the emperor and to return with his answer. In the meantime . . . "

"In the meantime, we must not let an open revolt begin here in Jerusalem."

"And how do we stem that? How do we play for time?" Antipas asked.

Caiaphas sat rigidly upright, his eyes wide with a curious shock. Chuza started to respond, then abruptly deferred to Joseph with a look.

"We may not need as much time as we think, Your Excellency," Joseph explained. "The request for Pilate's recall doesn't need to be carried all the way to the emperor. It can be sent to Damascus, to Publius Petronius, the governor. It is much closer. It will save us weeks of time. And . . . "

Antipas began to nod with understanding. "And you will carry the message?"

"There is someone else who can carry it most successfully."

"Who is that?"

"Manaen, Your Excellency. Manaen, whose friendship with Petronius is strong after serving as your court's emissary for so long."

"Manaen? Petronius? Of course! Petronius has the authority to order such a recall himself, hasn't he?"

Joseph nodded.

Antipas turned to Chuza.

"Has Manaen returned from Tiberias?"

"No, sire. I understand the caravan left Caesarea–by–the–Sea yesterday."

"Send word for him to leave the caravan and return here at once."

Chuza nodded and went quickly to a nearby writing desk to prepare the message for Manaen.

A look of satisfaction was on Antipas' face. "This is a good plan, Joseph. I thank you for it. But one thing still remains. How do we cool the tempers of the citizenry until Pilate's recall can be accomplished?"

Joseph rubbed at his beard and thought for a moment. "A whispered rumor about the recall could be started. That would be the best news Jerusalem's citizens could have. And Galilieans would be joyous over it."

"I'd hate for Pilate to learn of it prematurely. I want no trouble with him."

Chuza returned from the writing table. "A suggestion, sire. Why not invite Pilate and his wife to your palace in Jericho for a few weeks. We could be in control of the news that comes to him there."

Antipas considered it for a moment, then stood up, closing the audience and turning to Joseph. "I shall not forget the wisdom of your advice and your concern for the tetrarchy."

They all bowed as Antipas left the antechamber.

Once outside in the street again, Joseph parted from Caiaphas and went his own way. He was pleased that Antipas had agreed to have Pilate recalled and relieved that he had set the plan in motion at once. All that remained now was that the plan succeed. Now there was no other choice.

3

"Come on, Dathan! Onan! We're already late." Frustration was heavy in John Mark's voice. It was the third time in as many days that his friends had stopped at the carver's stall on the way to school; and he knew in his bones it would be third time they would steal from him. "Dathan! Onan!"

They ignored him, continuing to talk to the carver, searching for that moment's distraction that would allow one of them to steal today's chosen object, a small bronze dagger with an obsidian handle.

Nervously, John Mark glanced about the Upper City's Agora. Only a few people were walking about. The market in the Lower City already would be aswarm with people: women from Cheesemakers' Valley arguing over prices, vendors hawking fresh fruits and vegetables, sellers of livestock squabbling over tethering space. It seemed to him that the crowded market would be an easier place to steal something. Here it was so open. It was still too early for many shoppers, but no one else seemed to notice him or his friends. Other nearby stallkeepers were busy arranging their own merchandise.

He looked again toward the carver's stall and saw Dathan grasp the dagger and slip it into the waist sash of his tunic. While he had never stolen anything himself, watching his friends commit the act made him feel as guilty as if he had.

He shrugged off the guilty tremor and started to turn away when a centurion rushed from somewhere behind him and headed straight for Dathan and Onan. Before he could utter a cry of warning, the Roman grabbed Dathan at the nape of the neck, swung him around, and retrieved the dagger.

Dathan struggled and cried out. Onan ran. John Mark stood rooted to the spot, his heart racing, pulse pounding, fear coming up inside him so fast it made him breathe hard.

"What ho, Quinerius?" a second centurion called, striding quickly across the Agora from the other direction. The tall, rough-looking man he had been talking to followed after him.

"I have caught a thief, Cornelius. How should we dispose of him?"

Dathan still struggled, but to no avail, so tight a grip did the centurion have on the back of his tunic. His face had a pale, ashy look to it.

"Should we clap him into our own prison? Or should we turn him over to the soldiers at Herod's palace?"

Dathan's eyes went wide with fear. And fear for his friend raced through John Mark. As the son of Herod's chief scribe, Dathan would be known to Herod's soldiers. It would be the worst possible fate, for the soldiers would turn him over to his father!

"Who are you, thief? Do you have a name?"

Dathan struggled against the centurion's iron grasp.

"Do you have a name, I said?" The centurion shook him like a hound with a hare.

"Yes . . . yes . . . I have a name," Dathan finally gasped.

"Then tell it to me."

"John. John Mark. That's my name."

John Mark's heart thumped precariously. Angry surprise pushed at him. Could he believe his ears?

"My name is John Mark," Dathan repeated.

He started forward to protest but almost immediately thought the better of it. Why get further involved? He would settle with Dathan later.

"That boy is not John Mark," said the tall, rough–looking man. He stepped around the centurions into clear view. "At least, he's not the John Mark I know. The one from the house of Mark Yonah ben Abou. That John Mark is over there. The fourteen–year–old. The tall, thin lad with the chestnut hair."

John Mark looked up. It was Peter!

By this time, a small crowd had gathered. The centurions turned to him. The crowd, too. The carver pointed at him. "He's the one who kept calling to this boy and the other one. Maybe he's a thief, too!"

A sick feeling went through John Mark. He hoped Peter would defend him, but Peter simply looked at him and said nothing.

"What's this boy's real name?" asked the centurion named Quinerius.

He did not answer. How could he tell and still be loyal to his friend?

"You were calling him by name earlier. Who is he?"

"You owe him no loyalty, boy," centurion Cornelius said. "Who does he belong to? At least, tell us that."

John Mark looked at Peter for guidance. But Peter looked away, forcing him to his own decision.

"Who is he, John Mark?" Cornelius urged.

The palms of his hands were suddenly hot and sweaty. "Dathan," he said in a low tone. "His father is Herod's chief scribe."

"Well, that will save the empire the cost of a trial," Quinerius said, glancing at Cornelius. "We shall just ask this crowd what to do with him."

"Take him to his father!" someone yelled.

"Let Herod's soldiers deal with him," called another.

"I agree!"

"Father? Or soldiers?" Quinerius asked playing up to the crowd.

The response was equally mixed.

"Then we are agreed!" Quinerius laughed, as the crowd broke up taunting Dathan. "We'll take you to your father, young thief. It's time he taught you better manners."

"I'll go with you," Cornelius volunteered.

With consternation, John Mark watched them leave. He and Dathan had been friends a long time. How could Dathan have lied so? And Onan—coward!

Peter came to him. "You should pick your friends with more care, John Mark."

"That's what my mother says," he almost whispered the words. Why was it she was always right about such things? It was humiliating. He would like to be right just once, especially about his own friends.

"Are you going on to school?"

He nodded.

"I'll walk with you."

"In case I get in more trouble?"

Peter laughed.

"I can handle things myself, you know."

"Of course you can," Peter agreed, "but real friends help each other in the bad times and in the good times."

"You didn't help me much back there," John Mark said bluntly.

Peter looked at him with surprise. "You needed no help to get into that situation."

"But you didn't have to tell who I was."

Peter slowed his pace. "Did you like it that the boy claimed to be you? Did you like being thought of as a thief?"

John Mark didn't reply, and for a short distance they walked along in silence. As the morning brightened, the streets became more crowded. Vendors hawked their wares loudly. Twice they had to step aside and press against the walls of a house to let Roman chariots pass.

"Dathan's father will be very hard on him," John Mark

finally said. "I wish I hadn't told his name and who his father is."

Peter looked at him, understanding the pressures of disloyalty he must be feeling. They reached the gateway into the School for Scribes' Aprentices and stopped.

"Will you be telling my Uncle Barnabas about what happened?"

"Should I?"

"If you do, he'll tell my mother when she comes back, and she will be upset about it."

"In that case, you do the telling. To both of them."

With a wave of his big, work-worn hand, he moved on along the street toward the Viaduct and the stairway into the Temple area.

It was later that same day when Mary Mark arrived back in Jerusalem. The royal caravan disbanded at the palace. She said goodbye to Joanna. Manaen had not finished the trip with them. He had received an urgent message from Antipas while they were still on the road and had hurried on ahead of them to Jerusalem. But he was not among those who came out of the palace to greet them on their arrival. She was disappointed.

She'd learned a lot about him during the trip to Tiberias. For one thing, he was related to Antipas after all, in spite of what Joanna and Chuza had told her, but not through Herod the Great. Rather, they shared the same mother, Malthace, an Idumean woman who had been Herod's second wife. Manaen's father was a Greek musician from Antioch who came with a roving group of musicians and mimes to play for the royal court.

"He met my mother there," Manaen told Mary Mark. "I am the result of my mother's last romance. The great Herod had found her unfavorable quite some time before my father arrived."

She had sat quietly listening to him, hands folded in her

lap, wishing he had not felt impelled to reveal so much about himself. But at the same time, she was secretly glad to know he had none of Herod's blood in his veins. Whatever their future relationship might become, that fact would make it easier for her.

She again looked around at the disbanding caravan, freshly disappointed that Manaen was nowhere in sight. She signaled for Rhoda to make arrangements with the servants to bring their luggage later and for bearers to carry them on to her house without delay.

As they went south from the palace, Mary Mark could see a part of the roof of her house. A stir of pleasure went through her. It would be good to be home again. And why not? Most of her adult life had been spent here. The large, double-storied house was part of the dowry she'd brought to her marriage. Her father had obtained it some years earlier in exchange for a sizable shipment of copper ore. John Mark had been born here.

By all standards, it was a noble house. It was located at the intersection of the Street of Herod's Palace and the Street of Dyers and only a short distance away from the residence of Caiaphas, Jerusalem's high priest. Like most of the residences in the affluent Upper City, a high wall with gates opening onto the street surrounded the property. The front of the house faced south and was only a short distance west of the city's Gate of the Essenes.

At its back, three alleyways converged in a cul-de-sac at the mudbrick wall of an obscure, palm-thatched courtyard. This was one of the few locations in the Upper City where the streets violated the precise Hellenistic grid pattern. Yonah had devised the cul-de-sac so that stables for the caravan animals could be built nearby. The gate into the courtyard was veiled by an enormous red-flowering bougainvillea. It gave extra privacy to the courtyard and to the narrow stairway leading from it to an upper floor of one wing of the house. That, too, had been deliberately planned, as had the many discreet doorways inside the multiroomed house.

"No man should allow his house to become a trap by having only one entrance and exit," Yonah had often said. "That's as foolish as stumbling through the dark without a lamp."

She agreed with his practical view and had made no attempt to change the big, comfortable house in any way. Yonah had used the west wing of the residence as office and small warehouse. Two gates at ground level faced buildings that housed a leather tanning and dyeing operation across the street. One of these gates was wide enough for animals laden with caravan goods to pass through so they could be unloaded inside. The other was a pedestrian gateway. It was still a house for working as well as living. And, in these troublesome days, it was a house of sanctuary as well.

As a matter of fact, it was more than that. It was being put to unique and revolutionary uses these days, she reminded herself. It was here where women could join men in worshiping and praying. Traditional custom, especially Jewish custom, forbade that. But after she met Jesus, Mary Mark broke with the custom of separatism in worship. Her house was open to both men and women who were followers of Jesus, even though she knew they were thought of as dissidents. She could not do otherwise; she thought of herself as a dissident—a shy one sometimes, when it came to talking about her views, but by her actions a dissident, nevertheless.

The residence of the high priest with its sizable gardens and ornate gateways came into view. In spite of herself, Mary Mark smiled at the contrast between its impeccably attended appearance and the informal, rather nondescript look of her own place. That was as it should be, she decided. Caiaphas' residence was a place for pomp and politics. Her own house, on the other hand, continually opened its doors to believers in need of fellowship or sanctuary.

The bearers turned now into the Street of Dyers and within a matter of seconds were setting down her travel chair. Sallu, her manservant and husband to Rhoda, hurried through the gate to welcome them. He was followed by Kedar, manservant to Barnabas. "How are you, Kedar? Is my son not here?"

"No, m'lady, He's still at the apprentices school."

"And where is my brother?"

"He is away with the brethren, m'lady."

"Away? Away from Jerusalem?"

"No, m'lady. He is with Peter and the others at the house of the Arimathean. He told me to come and fetch him when you arrived. I shall go now, and quickly, by your leave, m'lady."

"Yes, of course, Kedar." She went on into the house to her own private chambers, glad again to be home, feeling the luxury of familiar surroundings, enjoying the ease and peace of this beloved place. She walked to the window opening onto the courtyard and looked out. Bougainvillea and oleander were vivid with color. She breathed deeply, inhaling the fragrance of their blossoms. The acacia tree that Yonah had planted so many years before was now tall enough to cast a filigree of shade over most of the courtyard and its small fountain. She sighed with pleasure and murmured a prayer of thanksgiving for this place and for being safely back in it.

A servant came in with water for her footbath. Another brought a bowl of fruit and a tall pitcher of milk.

Mary Mark turned from the window, removed her cloak and head shawl, tossed them on a nearby couch, and sat down, waiting for the servant to come and remove her sandals. It was then that Kedar reappeared in the doorway with the news that Barnabas wanted her to come and join him at the merchant's house.

"But, I've barely arrived," she complained. "I am tired from my journey."

"Your brother said it is most important. He would not ask you otherwise." There was a certain hint of admonishment in Kedar's tone. "I am to take you there as soon as possible."

"Very well," she agreed, standing and putting on her cloak and head shawl once more. Leaving word with the other servants for John Mark and for Rhoda that she would soon return, she followed Kedar through the streets of the Upper City to the house of Joseph of Arimathea.

Arriving at the merchant's house, she found Barnabas, Joseph, Peter, John, James, Matthew, and Nicolaos, a convert from Antioch, in brisk conversation at a large table.

"Ah, there she is," Barnabas said, rising, coming to her, and giving her a welcoming embrace.

She returned his welcome. His tall frame, once as lean as John Mark's, was beginning to show the weight of his years. He was almost forty now. But he still moved with the ease of a much younger man, a fact that belied the thinning hair and the grizzle of gray in his beard. He was a comforting sight, befitting his name. Barnabas—"son of comfort." He was a kindly man, responsible and mature. He was well named.

"I am glad you have returned," he whispered, guiding her back to the table. "Much is happening here in Jerusalem."

The other rose and greeted her warmly. Joseph's little dog came to her, tail wagging, and stood on his hind legs begging for attention. She leaned down and patted him.

"Your return to Jerusalem could not have come at a better time," Joseph welcomed her with a smile and indicated a place for her on the bench next to him.

She took her place beside her old friend, curious as to

why she had been summoned and suddenly feeling self-conscious. She folded her hands in her lap, defending against the tremble of shyness. Discreetly she assessed the faces of her other friends who by this time had reseated themselves across from her. Peter's weather–tanned, square face and dark, penetrating eyes held a brooding look. James, whose soft features belied his intense idealism, seemed subdued and worried. Matthew, wide of brow and with eyes of piercing blue, drummed gently on the table with the fingers of his left hand. The expression on the clean–shaven face of Nicolaos, the convert from Antioch, was one of sadness and defiance. And John, redheaded and green–eyed, also beardless and youngest of them all, was looking at her with a half smile that cracked into a crooked grin when her eyes met his. She smiled back, trying to feel at ease, but she was uncomfortable at being the only woman in the room.

"We need the careful thinking of a woman, Mary Mark," Joseph said. "Nicolaos has just brought us disturbing news."

Nicolaos straightened and leaned toward her, both elbows on the table. "It's the widows' dole, Mary Mark. It's not working!"

She found it a bit surprising that a custom that had been going on for generations suddenly "wasn't working"! But from the look on Nicolaos' face, she could not doubt his sincerity. She waited, expecting him to say more.

Instead, he simply stared across at her with a scowl of sadness that contained a certain amount of accusation. Her self-consciousness increased. Did he think she was responsible for whatever had gone wrong, or was it that he expected her to already know what the problem was?

For reassurance, she glanced toward Barnabas, but he was no help. He was staring back at Nicolaos. She scrambled quickly through her memory. What did she really know about the widows' dole? It was a part of a traditional and routine custom. Every Friday morning, two collectors went around the market and the private houses to take a collection for the needy. Part of it was in money, part was in food or goods. It was called the Kuppah, or "basket." Those who had only temporary needs were given enough to enable them to carry on until they could once again support themselves. Those who were permanently unable to support themselves, however, were given enough for two meals a day until the next Friday. And for those in pressing need, a special collection was made house to house. This was the Tamhui, or "tray."

She glanced at Peter and the other apostles. Surely they had explained all this to Nicolaos. On second thought, she decided that maybe they hadn't. They were busy preaching the message of Jesus. That was their mission, to preach, to teach, and to heal. And they were being successful. Healings took place every day. The number of believers was increasing dramatically. As a convert, Nicolaos himself was evidence of their success. But the apostles could not be everything to all people and Nicolaos, a Greek, could not be expected to know all about Jewish customs.

"The distribution is unfair, Mary Mark," Nicolaos finally went on.

"Unfair?"

"Unfair!" He gave a curt, emphatic nod.

"Hasn't anyone explained to you about the differences between the distribution from the Kuppah and from the Tamhui?"

As Nicolaos nodded, Peter spoke up, "We've explained that to him. And to many others. Not all, perhaps, but to many of the converts."

"Nicolaos' complaint has to do with language," Matthew inserted.

"Language?"

"To put it plainly, the old issue of the purity of Jewish blood has arisen again," Barnabas explained.

Disappointment went through her. Among the followers of Jesus were both Jerusalem and Palestinian Jews who spoke both Aramaic and Hebrew and who had no mix of blood in their veins. They prided themselves on such purity. They looked down on Jews from other countries who spoke Greek or whose families had intermarried in their adopted lands. Yet all had made the great discovery of Jesus, his message and his messiahship. Many of them had been in Jerusalem on that marvelous Pentecost morning to receive the infilling of the Holy Spirit. Did it all mean so little to them that now, only a few years later, spiritual snobbery was dividing the body of believers?

"Some of our brethren who speak Aramaic think those of us who speak Greek should go hungry," said Matthew with a wry laugh.

Peter said, "The truth of the matter is that this contempt is affecting the distributions from both the Kuppah and Tamhui."

"Widows of Greek–speaking Jews are being neglected," Nicolaos asserted. "I have seen it with my own eyes. After we heard the first complaint, Nicanor and I began to follow two of the men who distribute alms. We saw them give only enough food for one meal a day, instead of two. We saw them bypass some of the houses of Greek–speaking widows."

"That violates the old custom," James said, his face coloring with anger.

"And it goes against what Jesus taught us," John added.

A sinking feeling went through Mary Mark.

"The problem is how to put a stop to this so that it will not happen again when our backs are turned," Peter said quietly.

Joseph turned to her. "Barnabas and I feel that Peter and the other apostles should not get involved in straightening out this difficulty. It will take too much time. Their mission is the preaching of Jesus' message."

"At the same time, we must get this stopped once and for all," Barnabas said. "We want your counsel. How should we solve this problem? What should we do?"

Confronted with a direct question, Mary Mark felt shyness dry up her throat, closing it to words. She thought as Joseph and Barnabas did—Peter and the others should not be burdened with such daily details. But on the other hand, fair distribution of alms was a major practical part of what Jesus had taught about sharing. Hunger and shelter were daily needs. Fulfilling such needs could only come from daily attention. Silently she began to pray for wisdom of judgment and the courage to speak her mind.

The silence in the room lengthened and deepened until the only sound was Joseph's little dog scratching at his ear to shake off some itinerant flea. Nicolaos grew impatient, leaned back from the table, and rubbed at his forehead in frustration.

Mary Mark watched him, weighing once again an idea that had formed in her mind, but one for which she did not yet have words.

Joseph cleared his throat.

Barnabas leaned close and whispered, "What would you do, Mary Mark? Don't be shy. We really need you to tell us what to do."

She glanced at her brother, gathering reassurance, feeling her hesitancy drain away. "There, uh, there might be something I could suggest."

"Good. Tell us," Joseph encouraged.

"I think . . . I think I would do this. I would pick four Greek–speaking men and three who speak Hebrew to oversee distribution of alms on a regular basis. A daily basis. Each man chosen should have known Jesus personally and should have been one of his earliest followers. Each man should know firsthand how Jesus felt about sharing. Each one chosen should be a man of prayer. And each should be filled with the Holy Spirit."

She subsided into silence wondering if they thought she was foolish. Their facial expressions did not change. Judging their reactions was impossible.

"And what of the two men who were known to be cheating the widows?" Joseph asked. "What would you do with them?"

"Oh . . . " She shifted slightly on the bench and reclasped her hands. "I think I would put them to work under the supervision of the seven. Let them experience the fair distribution of alms. Teach them, by example, how it should be done."

"You wouldn't punish them?" James asked.

"Is that what Jesus would have done?" Matthew asked.

James frowned.

"Jesus would have admonished them in love and given them another chance," Mary Mark said quietly.

"Mary Mark is right," John said. "Jesus would not have punished them. He would not have turned them out."

Barnabas sat pulling at his left ear lobe, a characteristic gesture of indecision. Joseph leaned forward, elbows on table, and entwined the fingers of his two hands. "I am in favor of Mary Mark's solution. What is more, I favor Nicolaos as one of the seven, and Nicanor, too. both of them have genuine concern about this matter, or they would not have pursued it as they did and reported it to us."

Nicolaos glanced about with a look of surprise and embarrassment.

James concurred with a nod of his head. "I recommend Timon."

"And I name Prochorus," John added.

"Parmenas will be a good man for distributing alms," Matthew offered. "And Philip, too."

"Stephen should be our seventh man," Peter said. "He is

a strong champion for our Lord with his preaching in the marketplaces. He will be an even stronger champion by doing such a practical service as this for our brothers and sisters."

For a moment, no one moved. No one spoke.

Barnabas stopped pulling at his ear lobe and looked around at each of them. "It is also wise to get Stephen off the streets and out of the marketplaces for a while."

The four apostles looked at him in surprise.

"Stephen is in danger. I'm sure of it.

"We're all in danger," Matthew reminded him.

"But not like Stephen," Barnabas insisted. "He preaches dangerously."

"So did our Lord," said John.

Barnabas nodded agreement and went on. "There now is a man in Jerusalem called Saul of Tarsus. He is always in the crowd that gathers to hear Stephen preach. He baits Stephen. He taunts him and then agitates the crowd to make Stephen stop preaching. The danger is growing. We should get Stephen off the streets for a while."

Apparently ignoring Barnabas' warnings, Peter asked, "Are there any objections to the seven men named?"

No one spoke.

"Then we are agreed that these are the men we will present to the body of disciples for their approval?" He glanced about the group.

No one objected.

"James, you and John find the seven we have named. Tell them of our decision, and what they are to do." He stood up and bowed his head.

Everyone else quickly followed his lead.

"Lord God of all creation, we praise your holy name. We ask your blessings for all of those in need. We give our hearts to you willingly and sincerely."

The soft sounds of amens being said filled the space of

silence that followed the prayer. Shortly, Peter raised his head, thanked Joseph for the hospitality of his house, then turned to Mary Mark. His roughly awkward bow to her showed obvious respect. "Your brother was right. A mother's wisdom is the best way to settle a domestic problem. Once again, the brethren and I are indebted to you, Mary Mark."

A stir of satisfaction went through her. She liked being helpful. And it was flattering to be asked for her opinions. She just wished she wasn't always so self–conscious about it, and she wondered if she would ever be rid of the shyness that left her throat dry and her hands trembling.

On their way out of Joseph's house, Barnabas said to Peter, "The centurion Cornelius tells me you gave aid to John Mark this morning."

"Aid for what?" Mary asked, instantly alert, glancing from one to the other.

An oddly embarrassed look came into Peter's face.

"John Mark isn't hurt, is he?"

"No, no," Barnabas quickly reassured her. "Another boy accused of stealing claimed John Mark's name, and Peter stood witness."

She pressed the big apostle for details.

He avoided a direct answer. "John Mark wanted to tell you about it himself." At the outer gate he moved off quickly in a direction different from the one she and Barnabas needed to take.

As they walked toward the house, Barnabas told her all he knew about John Mark's involvement with Dathan and Onan earlier in the day. Frustration and disappointment welled up. She had influence with other people. She could even help the leaders of the community find solutions to their problems. But it seemed she had no influence with her own son. What irony!

"But, what happened to John Mark this morning isn't all that important."

She glanced at him, ready to argue. Everything that happened to John Mark was important.

"Some other things happened while you were away that are of far greater importance."

"What things?"

"Of first rank is that Herod is demanding that Pilate be recalled to Rome."

She stared at her brother while he repeated what Joseph had told him of the meeting with Herod two days before. They reached the opening to the alleyway at the back of the house. Barnabas stopped to explain further the finer political points involved and how it all would take place.

But her attention wandered. What would Pilate's replacement be like? How would he rule? What changes would take place? Would there, at last, be peace in Jerusalem? She could not remember life in Jerusalem except under Pilate's iron rule; and therefore, she found it hard to imagine what it might be like to have another Roman governor in charge of things.

"Of course, I think Herod's influence with Rome is questionable," Barnabas concluded. "But he does have influence with Publius Petronius, the governor of Syria. Mostly because of Manaen, of course."

Her wandering thoughts stopped. "What about Manaen?"

"He's going to see Petronius with Herod's recall demands." He walked on down the alleyway, pushed aside the red bougainvillea, and opened the gate to the courtyard.

She slowly followed, understanding now why Manaen had left the caravan so hurriedly in Joppa and why he had not met them on their arrival in Jerusalem. "Then he's already gone?"

"He leaves tomorow, I think."

"If you're talking about me, I'm leaving tonight."

Startled, both of them turned to find Manaen grinning at them from inside the courtyard.

"But I couldn't leave without coming to see you, Mary Mark." He glanced toward Barnabas. "I'm sure it comes as no surprise to you that I find your sister quite appealing."

Mary Mark blushed.

Barnabas laughed, excused himself, and went on into the house.

Manaen came to her, took her by the hand, and led her to the small stone bench near the fountain. "So Barnabas has told you of my mission?"

She nodded.

"I wish I could take you with me."

A tremor started through her. She fought it down. "Will you be gone for a very long time?"

"It just depends. If I find Publius in Damascus and if he agrees with our demands, I could be back in Jerusalem within three or four weeks. But if I have to go to Antioch or have to wait to see him, it might be quite a long time."

She glanced away.

"Will you miss me, Mary Mark?"

"Of course. Barnabas and I miss all our friends when they are away from Jersualem." She hoped her tone was casual, for she knew if her hands were not folded in her lap, they would be trembling again.

He leaned over, kissed her gently, and stood up. "Wish me God's speed, Mary Mark?"

"Of course. You know I do."

He grasped her hands, pulled her up onto her feet, embraced her, and kissed her lingeringly. As he released her, held her at arms length, and searched her face, she dared not look at him, lest her heart show in her eyes. He turned, walked across the courtyard, and disappeared through the gate.

"You're in love with him, aren't you?"

Startled, she glanced around. John Mark glowered down at her from the stairs that led to the upper floor of the house.

So hard was he clutching at the stair railing that the knuckles of his blunt fingers were strained white. Fourteen was such a vulnerable age. He was half man, half boy.

Disapproval clouded his thin face. Hurt and anger sparked in his dark, deep–set eyes. "I knew it would happen sooner or later," he accused. "I wish Joanna and Chuza had never introduced you to Manaen!"

4

Anger born of hurt pushed at her. She had every right to enjoy Manaen's affectionate attentions. John Mark had no right and no reason to be jealous. How dare he!

She called out to him and quickly followed as he clambered on up the stairway and into the big upper room. Not having bothered to remove his sandals or wash his feet, he was halfway across it by the time she entered. She, too, ignored the customary ritual, determined as she was to catch up with him. No one else was present, a fact for which she was grateful. She hated family arguments in front of other people. It always made her feel defensive, self-conscious.

John Mark reached the door at the opposite side of the room. She called for him to stop. He barely hesitated.

A spate of angry words rushed into her mind. How dare he ignore her! She called again, sharp and commanding.

This time he halted, hand against the door, ready to open it, shoulders set in a posture of rigid defiance.

She slowed her own pace and fought down the impulse to accuse him of possessiveness, to berate him for his childishly jealous reaction, to demand an apology. A short distance behind him, she stopped and stared at the nape of his neck and the chestnut-colored hair so like his father's.

Silence, alien and resentful, settled between them until the scent of oleander drifted up from the courtyard and brought with it the gentle, plaintive call of a mourning dove.

"This is not the homecoming welcome I was expecting, John Mark."

He remained silent and unmoving.

"I have not encouraged Manaen to like me, nor did I encourage him to kiss me."

"You didn't stop him."

"It was a gesture of friendship."

He scoffed.

"John Mark—!"

"He's not our kind."

"Oh-h-h—?"

"He's Greek."

"He is also a Jesus–believer," she said, making no effort to hide her disappointment at his prejudice.

His shoulders sagged a bit.

"The fact that he, too, is a follower of The Way should make a difference in how you think of him, Greek or not!"

"He's Herod's man," came the sharp disagreement.

A tinge of fresh irritation went through her. "Has Manaen ever been unkind to you?"

"How can you like him?" he countered.

"Has he ever been unkind to you?" she repeated.

He said nothing.

For effect, she quietly added, "Does Manaen steal, like your friend Dathan? Does he run from trouble, like your friend Onan?"

The effect was not lost. He turned halfway toward her. A startled, suspicious look overlayed the hurt brooding in his face. "Peter told you!"

She shook her head, regretting the reference to Dathan and Onan, for it suddenly struck her how really important the relationship with Manaen was becoming. Until she met Manaen she had considered herself trained for and doomed to widowhood. Trained for widowhood? What an odd idea. And yet it seemed to be so true for her. She had watched her mother and two aunts go through so many years of widowhood that it had become a familiar state of existence, one she felt she had learned to live with—and without flaunting the outward show of loss that so many women seemed to do. Not that she took any special pride in her widowhood. She simply had come to accept it as one of any number of states of existence that might have befallen her. This was her lot. She accepted it and bore it with what grace she could muster. Until she met Manaen, thoughts of loving another man never went beyond the question of whether or not she could invest so much of herself in another person again. Would she even want to? But she had met Manaen and she was rethinking many things. John Mark was going to have to understand that.

He turned to fully face her. His demanding tone broke through her thoughts. "If Peter didn't tell you, then who did?"

"Centurion Cornelius told your Uncle Barnabas."

His eyes went wide with surprise, and he seemed strangely relieved.

"But who told whom is not the important point."

"It is to me."

"Oh?"

He started to turn away. She caught him by the arm. "A moment, please. Something else is important to me." She felt his arm tense. "The fact that you have a family who loves you requires, in fact demands, that you pay a special price for it."

"Pay? Price? What price?"

"The price of honesty. The price of responsibility. Like wisdom in the choice of your friends. That's the price required." She let go of his arm. "And so far as Manaen is concerned, he has done nothing to prove that he is not a good man. Until he does, you will have to be more tolerant of his friendship for me." She turned and walked away, leaving her son to stare after her in dismay.

In the days and weeks that followed, Mary Mark thought often of the two events that occurred on the day of her return to Jerusalem. Somehow in her mind, the naming of the seven to administer the widows' dole and her confrontation with John Mark were inextricably intertwined, like cross-weave in fabric that creates different patterns while sharing common purpose. These two seemingly unrelated events intermeshed in an oddly predictive pattern of change for her life. She wasn't sure that she clearly saw it or fully understood it all.

So far as the naming of The Seven, as they quickly became known among the community of believers, was concerned, they performed their duties compassionately and fairly. There were those who opposed them, of course. They claimed there would be retribution against Jewish widows because those appointed were all actually Gentiles. But so careful was the distribution from both Kuppah and Tamhui that all complaints ceased. Cooperativeness prevailed.

But it seemed to Mary Mark that another factor in the appointment of The Seven was even more important, though much less evident. It appeared to be the beginning of a change in basic attitudes and a change in her perception so sweeping that she dared not presume enough wisdom to even let such an idea linger. But linger it did, and with such tenacity that she prayed for more understanding and finally was led by the still, small voice of the Holy Spirit to seek Barnabas' reactions.

They were in the main room of the house waiting for Peter and Joanna and all the others to come for a prayer gathering.

Rhoda and Sallu, with John Mark following, came in carrying braziers of hot embers to be set about on the floor of the big room. The weather had turned chill. Rain threatened.

"I am startled to realize it," she finally confided to him, "that Jews may be 'chosen people' in a way different than we've always been taught."

"How do you mean 'different'?" Barnabas asked, going across the room to help with the braziers.

"I've always thought the meaning of 'chosen people' was that we Jews had exclusive possession of the ear and heart of God, that we were his and he was ours."

Barnabas nodded in a distracted fashion and motioned for John Mark to place another brazier on the floor near the chair where the Mother Mary most likely would be sitting.

"Is that right, my brother? Is my understanding correct?"

He came back to her and sat down in a chair rigidly styled after those favored by imperial Rome, which had been a gift from Herod Antipas to Yonah some years before. "I suppose that your understanding is as clear as mine or any other person who was raised a Jew. But why such a philosophical conversation from you today?"

"It has to do with The Seven, I think."

"What about them?"

"Six of them are Greek-speaking Jews, Barnabas. The seventh, Nicolaos of Antioch, is a Greek—a Gentile. That's why so many people think we elected all Gentiles to administer the widows' dole."

"So? What difference does that make? They're all spirit-filled men of talent and fairness, whether Jew or Greek."

She felt a thrill of excitement go through her. "That's just the point. Maybe we Jews don't own God, after all!"

He stared at her, thunderstruck.

John Mark dropped a brazier. Rhoda scurried about brushing up the loose embers that fell from it. Sallu stood, mouth agape, watching Barnabas.

"Don't you see, my brother," Mary Mark went on. "Instead of owning God, could it be that now we Jews are just people chosen to lead all other people to God?"

A contemplative look spread over Barnabas' face. He stared off into the distance beyond her shoulder considering the idea.

"The question that keeps coming back to me, my brother, is this. Did the Holy Spirit lead us to elect these men who speak like Gentiles as a symbol of this different meaning? And if it did, isn't this the kind of openness and the kind of love that Jesus really preached?"

Barnabas began to pull at the lobe of his ear. But the expression on his face told her she had touched something deep in his spirit that gave substance to her new perception. She began to wonder if the Holy Spirit had led them into a path of understanding more vast than any of them yet realized. And she also wondered if this newer understanding would compound again and again in the spirit of all human beings. How would Peter and the others feel about such a thing, she wondered. And how, in fact, did she herself really feel about it?

Servants came from the rear part of the house interrupting her speculation. They carried cruses of wine and fresh milk, goblets, and trays of breads, cheeses, fruits, and other refreshments. John Mark eyed the food with interest, and followed after them.

Mary Mark directed that the refreshments be placed on the long table across the room and called out to John Mark, "That food is for our guests, my son. If you're hungry now, there's other food in the pantry."

He pretended not to hear and reached for a pomegranate.

Irritation flicked at her. It was a tactic he'd started using after the argument over Manaen. They had not openly spoken of the argument since it happened. But he had begun to show his defiance of her in small ways, pretending not to hear when she gave him instructions, leaving his part of the household chores unfinished, dawdling on his way home from the School of Scribes' Apprentices, missing the evening meal with other members of the household. She sympathized with his confusion and contradiction of feelings about her new friendship with Manaen. But, she reminded herself, he was quickly coming to manhood. Just as she was going to have to let go of him, he was going to have to let go of her! Even so, she more and more frequently sensed this new hostility in him, and she disliked it. She even felt threatened by it.

Why did change always have to be so hard, she wondered. With a nostalgic longing she had not known since Yonah died, her heart cried for a place where she could hide herself and John Mark and Barnabas, a place where she could find sanctuary with the familiar and the safe. Did such a place exist anywhere except in the promises of Jesus, in the Kingdom of God that he preached about? Or was it that the Kingdom of God and her envisioned place of sanctuary were the same and were to be found in her own heart and mind and soul?

She watched John Mark help himself again to some of the fruit on the refreshment tray. Fresh irritation flicked at her. She fought down the temptation to go to him and insist that he leave the food alone. This was no time for an argument. Even now, she could hear Kedar greeting the guests at the front of the house. She got up to go and greet them herself. Barnabas joined her.

Peter led the small group into the room. Behind him came redheaded John carefully attendant on the Mother Mary, as he had been since Jesus entrusted her to his care from the cross. He was followed by his own mother, Salome, who was sister to the Mother Mary, and by his brother James. Thereafter followed Joanna, Matthew, Joseph of Arimathea, Nicodemus the banker, Andrew, Thomas, and Bartholomew. The greetings exchanged were warm with the cordial ease of trust and deeply shared experiences.

Mary Mark moved forward to give special greeting to the

Mother Mary. She was a tense, crisply neat little woman. A special aura surrounded her—indelible, yet not easily describable. Perhaps it was best explained by her continuing puzzlement and sadness over what had happened to her firstborn and by her unremitting efforts to try to understand the newness of life brought by the Holy Spirit.

For the most part, she lived in Jerusalem in the house owned by John and James, but she made frequent trips to Capernaum for long visits with Salome and Zebedee. Only occasionally did she visit Nazareth. Many of her old friends and neighbors there had died or moved away. Those remaining were as unbelieving about Jesus' resurrection as they had been scornful of him during his earthly ministry. She smiled, warmly radiant, as Mary Mark bowed to her and led her to the chair near which the warming brazier had been placed.

Joanna and Salome seated themselves nearby. The men scattered throughout the large room in a random semicircle. Joseph and Nicodemus sat on chairs. The apostles chose to sit on the floor. John Mark left the food table and joined them. As Peter took his position in front of the assembled group, Barnabas motioned for all of the household servants to come and join in the meeting. They did so quickly.

Peter raised both of his hands in a gesture of supplication and acceptance. A hush of reverence fell upon the room. With eyes closed and head uplifted, he began to praise the name of the Lord and give a prayer of thanksgiving.

"We come to you with grateful hearts, O Lord, and in the full knowledge of your ruling might for this earth, as well as for heaven. In trust, we pray for peace for Jerusalem, release from the tyranny of Rome, protection from the divisiveness of evil men."

He paused. His big frame had already begun to sway rythmically and slowly as the Holy Spirit encompassed him. The silence deepened and pervaded the heart and minds and souls of all. Joseph, Nicodemus, the Mother Mary sat quite still, heads bowed, hands folded in their laps. Barnabas, Matthew, Andrew, and Thomas had their hands raised and their heads uplifted in postures similar to Peter's. John was almost bent double, head resting on both his hands. And beyond him, from among the servants, came the first soft murmurings and groanings as the Holy Spirit began to express himself through them.

Mary Mark turned carefully to look at Rhoda and Sallu, and as she did so she felt the wonderful euphoria of Spirit well up inside her own soul. She slipped out of her chair and down onto her knees as the Holy Spirit began to gently move inside her. An enormous sense of peace enveloped her. Softly, the murmurings of tongues came from her own lips. "Our Father God, God of Abraham, Isaac and Jacob, lead us into a deeper knowledge of your will for our lives. Holy Jesus, our Messiah, show us more of the grace of your law of liberty. Holy Spirit, comfort and guide us. Lead us in a walk of obedience for the sake of God the Father, and of our holy brother, Jesus."

She became aware that her voice had trailed off into silence, but the murmurings of the Spirit still stirred within her. She felt the presence of Jesus very near, and a great light of understanding seemed to be coming toward her. She felt herself uplifted, comforted, and reassured, and as the light began to slowly dim she heard someone begin to sing in a language unknown to her.

Now she realized that one after another, all the people in the room were praying aloud from the depths of their beings as they were led by the Holy Spirit and that one prayer followed another in a continuous progression of praise and thanksgiving.

Faith compounded. Time vanished.

A great while later, she became aware of the deep, rumbling voice of Peter once more as he led a closing prayer. It was a traditional benediction familiar since childhood. But it held a much deeper meaning for her now. Her friendship with Jesus colored the words with personal meaning. The infilling of the Holy Spirit graced her with yet another dimension of understanding.

"The Lord bless you and keep you," said Peter.

"The Lord make his face to shine upon you," they all responded.

"The Lord be gracious unto you," Peter concluded.

For several more minutes, the silence of reverence and meditation clung to them. And then at last, someone stirred and stood up. The rustle of robes brushed at the silence and beckoned the body of worshipers to perform one more act of communion with the Holy Spirit.

Mary Mark opened her eyes. Barnabas moved across in front of her going toward the table where the wine and the bread had been placed. Matthew rose and followed after him. Mary Mark got up on her feet to go and help them serve the others.

Each of the worshipers partook of the bread and the wine, murmuring the words Jesus had given them.

"This is my body. Take, eat, in remembrance of me."

"This is my blood, Take, drink, in remembrance of me."

As Mary Mark approached John Mark with the elements of communion, she found him watching her with a peculiar expression on his face that appeared to be an odd mixture of admiration and mistrust. She handed him the bread and the wine and said with him the words Jesus had taught, then turned to move away.

Tentatively, he touched her arm and started to speak.

She hesitated.

But with a shake of his head and a rueful smile, he turned away from her without speaking.

A swift pang of regret went through her. Tears welled

up. She fought to hold them back and moved on to serve Thomas and Bartholomew.

By the time all of the worshipers had shared the communion, the hour had grown quite late. John went to the Mother Mary and helped her out of the chair. Salome and James also stood up, ready to take their leave with them. The Mother Mary went to Mary Mark and thanked her for the hospitality of the house. "As I have told you so many times before, I always feel close to my own son in this house of yours. And I did again tonight."

Mary Mark squeezed her hand and said softly, "He is always with us, isn't he? Please come again. Anytime."

"It will be a while before I return," she offered. "Salome and I leave tomorrow for Capernaum. Zebedee has sent word that we have been away long enough. Especially Salome!" She smiled and held out her hands to Mary Mark. "Bless you, my friend. When I return to Jerusalem, I should like to come here again."

Farewells were said to all the others, the servants retired to their quarters, and finally she made her way to her own chambers. Only then did she realize that she felt more certain than ever that the Holy Spirit was leading them all onto a pathway of newer understanding. There had been no opportunity to discuss the idea with Peter or with anyone else. Nor had there been any opportunity for any exchange of news with Joanna. Tomorrow, she must invite her friend for a visit. Surely by this time there would be news about Manaen and about whether or not Pilate really would be recalled. She certainly hoped so. Maybe then there would be peace for Jerusalem.

But when Joanna arrived for a visit the next afternoon there still was no news from or about Manaen and his trip.

"Surely things will change when Pilate leaves."

Joanna smiled, quizzically indulgent. "Such optimism should have reward."

"Are you saying a new procurator will be no improvement?"

"It depends on the man, of course. But he will still be a Roman!" Joanna reached into the reed basket between them on the bench and pulled out a strand of yellow yarn. Carefully, she began to wind it onto the larger ball of yarn in her other hand. "In the meantime, Caiaphas is openly quarreling with Antipas over who will rule in the interim between Pilate's departure and his successor's arrival. Will it be the Sanhedrin or the palace?"

"Joseph and Nicodemus feel that Caiaphas is not well enough to be an interim ruler."

"Does that mean they will support Antipas?"

Mary Mark shrugged. "Probably. But there will be a fight. You know Caiaphas won't give up without one."

Joanna gave a great sigh and put the yarn into the basket. "It seems to me that the familiar and safe places become fewer and fewer."

Mary Mark's sense of optimism fled entirely. She almost wished Joanna hadn't come.

"Unless our prayers are answered quickly, I fear Jerusalem will see much bloodshed," Joanna concluded.

The rumors about Pilate being replaced held the temper of the citizenry in check for yet a while longer. General revolt did not occur, but minor unrest flared unpredictably all over the city. A brawl in front of Mary Mark's house resulted in the deaths of two men and the blinding of a third. Squads of Roman soldiers roamed the streets of the Upper City now just as frequently and just as rudely as they always had in the Lower City and in the Suburb. Mary Mark no longer allowed Rhoda or any of the household's other women servants to go shopping in the Agora unless Sallu or Kedar or one of the other trusted men servants went with them. She herself no longer felt free to go about unaccompanied in the Upper City or to the Temple to pray in the

Women's Court. It simply was no longer safe for a woman to walk alone in the streets of Jerusalem.

Many other members of the community of believers, of course, had never thought the streets to be really safe. Not since the day of Jesus' resurrection. Now, with the tensions among all factions growing once again, it was worse. John Mark was accosted on his way home from the School of Scribes' Apprentices one afternoon by three street urchins. They broke all the styluses he was carrying, knocked him to the ground, smeared his face with the contents of the ink-pot, and were attempting to stuff a parchment scroll in his mouth when they were chased away by a rabbi and two of his students.

Nicolaos and Prochorus, carrying emergency supplies to a needy widow, were set upon by Zealots who mistook them for Romans. Attempts to disrupt Stephen's street preaching became more frequent and more strident. The Pharisee named Saul of Tarsus, whom Barnabas had warned Peter about earlier, had been identified as one of the most rabid agitators.

Direct assaults against the apostles became a daily expectation—not from the Romans, however, but from the Pharisaic Jews. For next to Zealots, whose impassioned goal was to destroy the Romans, Pharisees were equally impassioned in their quest to destroy all memory of Jesus and his teachings.

"We have only seen the beginnings of such civil strife," Joseph of Arimathea said to Mary Mark as they talked in the obscure courtyard at the back of her house. The first warm touches of springtime had visited Jerusalem. Joseph walked toward the gate where the huge bouganvillea grew and absent-mindedly plucked one of its red blossoms.

"Once Pilate is recalled, perhaps peace will come. We've all been praying for the success of Manaen's trip," Mary

Mark offered in a hopeful tone. He had been gone little more than three weeks.

"We need some definite word soon. The people grow very restless!"

The words had no sooner left his lips than the back gate to the courtyard flew open. Joseph, standing right beside it, was almost knocked off balance.

"A thousand apologies," Barnabas exclaimed, realizing what he'd done. "I had no idea anyone would be standing so close—"

Joseph accepted the apology with a wave of his hand.

"Pilate has been recalled!" He hurried on to explain that he had been on his way to find Stephen when he saw Manaen just returning from Damascus and about to enter the palace gates. "I hailed him. He told me that Pilate has been recalled, that he was going to report to Antipas, and he asked me to find you, Joseph. He's sure Antipas will want to see you. He has sent his manservant to summon Caiaphas."

"My thanks to you, Barnabas. I shall go at once." He turned, bowed to Mary Mark, and disappeared through the gate.

Barnabas came toward her. "Manaen sends greetings to you, my sister. And he asks if he might come to pay his respects later in the day."

Her heart gave an odd thump. The knowledge of his return was as welcome as the reported success of his trip.

"He has done a good thing. All the brothers will think so. It will be good for Manaen."

"I hope John Mark will think he has done a good thing."

Barnabas put his hand on her shoulder and gave her a gentle shake. "The boy will grow to like him. Shall I send word to Manaen that we'd welcome a visit from him?"

She agreed and followed Barnabas into the house to find Kedar.

In the meantime, Manaen, reporting to Herod Antipas, Chuza, Caiaphas, and Joseph of Arimathea, spread before them the official proclamation of recall to which his friend, Publius Petronius, governor of Syria, had affixed his signature and seal.

"This mission was easier than I had expected," he said with a laugh of satisfaction. "Petronius had been uneasy about Pilate for some months. He thinks Pilate has grown much too ambitious. Recently he learned that Pilate has been making more and more frequent use of his father-in-law's senatorial influence in Rome. Petronius sees that as a threat."

Joseph of Arimathea chuckled.

"The request to have Pilate removed could not have been more timely," Manaen concluded. "And the fact that it came as a joint request from both Antipas and the Sanhedrin gave it real weight. Petronius decided to grant the request himself without waiting for the emperor's response. Of course, he doesn't want Pilate to know that!"

A curious smile crossed Antipas' face. "Good! Then it seems all that remains to be decided is who shall govern until the new procurator arrives. Will my palace rule, or will the Sanhedrin rule?"

Caiaphas turned a malevolent look toward the tetrarch.

Joseph intervened before the priest could start an argument. "This is a victory for all Jerusalem—priesthood, Sanhedrin, the palace . . . "

"And for the people!" Manaen inserted.

"Recall means that Pilate has been punished for the slaughter in Galilee," Chuza nodded. "We must spread the news quickly to all the people."

Joseph turned to Caiaphas. "How quickly can the Sanhedrin meet to hear Antipas make this official announcement?"

"By the morrow," the priest said grudgingly.

It was agreed, and then Antipas turned to Manaen.

"Again, my brother, I am indebted to you. How can I reward you?"

"At the moment, Your Excellency, all I require is a bath, some food, and a bit of rest."

"Of course, of course." Herod gave a signal of benign dismissal. "Again, our gratitude."

By the time Manaen had bathed, exchanged his trail-dusty clothing for clean robes, and had food and drink, he no longer felt the need of rest. In response to the message of welcome to the house of Mary Mark, he quickly made his way there, spurred at the thought of seeing her again. He had thought about her a great deal during the journey to Syria, recognized that he was falling in love with her, fantasized about what it would be like to have her as his wife, and, in sharp contrast to such fantasies, wondered whether or not marriage with her really would ever be possible because of John Mark. He had no issue of children from his own ill-fated marriage to Lilia. And maybe that was just as well, since she had died so young. As a result, he felt a distinct sense of ignorance about raising children, especially someone else's children. And especially a child like John Mark who was so near manhood that thinking of him as a child seemed foolish. But he knew it was not an unnecessary thought. Mary Mark's whole life seemed to center around the boy. If he ever seriously expected to marry Mary Mark, he would have to come to terms with her son. But how?

He reached the house, was ushered in by Sallu, and shown through the house to the small, private courtyard where he had kissed Mary Mark good-bye. She was there waiting for him, seated on the stone bench near the fountain. In her hands was a small fold of linen embroidery at which she worked with quick, deft strokes. Excitment pounded through him at the sight of her.

She glanced up, smiled, laid aside the embroidery, and stood up to greet him.

He embraced her tentatively. But when she returned his embrace, he pulled her very close and held her, as aware of her heart's pounding as that of his own. The joy of the reunion was no longer tentative. He kissed her possessively. She did not resist, and for a long, long moment they stood together in the exhilaration of newfound closeness.

At last she pushed away. The faintest tinge of embarrassment had crept up into the warm, alive loveliness of her face.

"I have missed you more than I realized I would." His tone was intimate and low.

She did not answer but glanced around, as if half expecting to see someone else in the courtyard.

He followed her glance. No one else was in the courtyard. Turning again to her, he became abruptly aware that a curtain of reserve now seemed to separate her from him. "Why do you suddenly seem so apprehensive? Has something happened while I was away?"

She sat down again on the stone bench.

He sat beside her, searching her face, his heart growing heavy at her silence and at the glisten of tears in her eyes. "Mary Mark, tell me. What has happened?"

"It's our friendship, Manaen. It has found opposition."

"Opposition? From whom? Barnabas?"

"Oh no," she quickly corrected. "Barnabas is delighted that we are friends."

"Then it has to be John Mark who opposes us."

She nodded and went ahead to tell him about John Mark's reaction to their farewell kiss a few weeks earlier.

His reaction to her report was surprisingly matter-of-fact. He wondered if his feelings for her were not as strong as he'd first thought or if it was just the opposite—that his feelings for her were so strong that no amount of opposition could destroy them.

She dabbed at her eyes with a small linen square. "You don't seem concerned."

"Don't I?"

"No, you don't. But then—maybe I make too much of it. Maybe I shouldn't be so sensitive to what my son thinks of me. After all, he will soon be a man and begin to lead his own life away from me and away from this house. On the other hand, he is my son and I . . . "

"And you do care what he thinks of you. And so do I."

He reached for her hand and enclosed it in his own, wanting to reassure her that all would be well. And yet the very act of holding her hand somehow gave him reassurance. Their friendship and their growing love were meant to be. He felt it deep in his soul. "Is there a way for me to make friends with John Mark?"

A sadly perplexed look filtered into her wide, clear eyes. "I don't know."

"Should I try to talk to him? Try to get to know him better? You know, I really don't know him as a person at all."

"He can be very stubborn. And very blunt."

"If I still believed in the musings of court astrologers and seers, I could claim that our relationship was foretold by the stars or ordained by the destiny of the gods."

She glanced up, quickly questioning.

"But I no longer believe in those things," he reassured her. "I now believe in something much more powerful. Prayer. Prayer will bring us an answer, Mary Mark. The Lord knows the answer. He will share it with us." He pulled her closer and put his arms about her, cradling her as they prayed together in silence.

At last he released her. She straightened and for a long time they sat side by side on the stone bench in the little courtyard talking of things other than their awareness of each other or of John Mark's opposition to their relationship. He told her in some detail of his trip to Damascus to see Publius Petronius, and finally he concluded with the news that Herod Antipas would officially inform the Sanhedrin of Pilate's recall the next day.

"I am proud of you, Manaen. I am glad that we are good friends."

"I want us to be more than friends," he persisted, standing up, pulling her onto her feet and kissing her again.

To her surprise she found herself clinging to him, unwilling for him to leave so soon.

Gently he pushed her away, held her at arm's length, and studied her face. "We will find a way to be together. You know that we will, don't you?"

She looked away, unable to answer, overwhelmed by the reawakening of old emotions, yet incapable of admitting the depth of those feelings even to herself.

"Until later, my love. I must go now." He turned and disappeared through the half–hidden courtyard gate.

The next morning the special meeting of the Sanhedrin did, in fact, convene. But long before Manaen accompanied Antipas to the Chamber of Hewn Stone on the Temple Mount to make the official public announcements, the citizens of Jerusalem and of all Judea had learned of Pilate's recall and that the tetrarch had demanded it. Herod Antipas became an instant hero. There was no further question about who would have the interim rule of Judea. The priesthood had lost one of its last viable chances to reassert its leadership of the holy city.

For the period of time that intervened between Pilate's departure for Rome and the arrival of Marcellus Vitellius, his replacement, government leadership was in the tetrarch's hands. He handled it well. Recruiting for the ranks of his own soldiers increased with such amazing success that he soon had restored his army to full strength. The Romans seemed willing to follow his temporary leadership. The Sanhedrin wisely decided to table their plans to seek a reduction in the portion of Temple tax they were required to pay to Antipas for the maintenance of his palace and his new army.

A few weeks later, during Passover in the year 36, the eighteen-year reign of Caiaphas as high priest of Jerusalem and president of the Sanhedrin ended with his death.

Joseph and Peter brought the news to Mary Mark's house. "Our suspicions that he was not well were true. He simply collapsed while robing for the Passover sacrifice," Joseph explained.

"He died almost at once," Peter added.

"I'm sorry for his widow," Mary Mark said softly.

"Who will replace him, and how will our cause be affected?" Barnabas wanted to know.

Joseph shook his head. "There are two or three good men who could replace him, but until the Sanhedrin meets, the choice of a successor is open."

"Will the new procurator have a vote?" Peter asked.

"And what about Antipas?" Barnabas wanted to know.

"Both of them will be asked to give their approval to the Sanhedrin's choice. But the period of mourning for Caiaphas must come first."

When the choice finally was made some thirty days later, it was Caiaphas' brother-in-law Jonathan who was chosen to succeed him as high priest and president of the Sanhedrin. He was a placid man, surprisingly unambitious, and given to compromise. Perhaps that was why approval was so readily given by Marcus Vitellius, new procurator of Judea, and by Herod Antipas.

And even another twenty days later, at the time of Pentecost, pilgrims coming into the city experienced a period of unaccustomed peacefulness. No one made an issue of the fact that Jerusalem's priesthood now had waning power. Rather, they liked the fact that the city's tranquility was broken only by rabble-rousers who opposed street preachers. But for many of those who lived in Jerusalem, the relative peacefulness was tenuous, temporary, and forebodingly troublesome.

5

The Year 37 A.D.

Near the Sheep Gate, a slight young man called on the scattering of listeners to repent and seek the Kingdom of God. He spoke with power and wisdom. Some among the listeners claimed they had seen him work great signs and wonders, but others were less impressed.

"He's mad, you know," a bedouin said to his companion as they herded a flock of goats past the small crowd and on toward the market just beyond the Fortress Antonia.

"He doesn't look mad."

"But he must be. My cousin says he comes every day and preaches the same message. And every day someone in the crowd tries to get him to stop. Sometimes fighting breaks out and then the soldiers come and make them all move on. Or they take the preacher to prison."

"By what name is this preacher called?"

"Stephen," the bedouin replied, brushing past an intense-looking man who had been jeering the preacher and agitating from the edge of the crowd. His eyes burned with fanatic zeal.

"You're blocking the way there. Move along!" A soldier ordered, coming up behind them. The bedouins did as they were told. But, the man who was jeering refused to move.

"Move along," the soldier ordered again.

"Move the preacher. He's a rabble–rouser."

The soldier frowned in obvious annoyance at the tone of disrespect in the man's voice.

"Heretic! Blasphemer!" the agitator insisted. "Arrest him! He defies the Temple and the Law!"

Some of the other men standing nearby turned in curiosity. The soldier looked across the crowd toward Stephen.

"Arrest him!" the jeering man again demanded.

The soldier turned. "On whose complaint? Yours?"

A snicker of laughter passed among the onlookers.

"Yes, on my complaint. My name is Saul. Saul of Tarsus. I am a student of the great teacher Gamaliel."

"Well, Saul of Tarsus, I'll arrest the street preacher if you can find two witnesses who will agree with your complaint. You know the law."

Saul cast about the crowd looking for two who would be witnesses with him, but the curious onlookers turned their backs to him.

"The preacher is harmless. His preaching convinces no one." The soldier laughed. "I think it is you who should move along, Saul of Tarsus."

Resentment, dark and ugly, flushed Saul's face.

"Move along now."

"You will regret this!"

The soldier laughed again, shifted his spear from his left hand to his right, and made a threatening gesture with it.

Saul stiffened, stepped backward, then turned on his heel and scurried away toward the Temple precincts. He must find Gamaliel. A respected teacher like Gamaliel could stop a heretic preacher. A respected teacher like Gamaliel could persuade a vote of the whole Sanhedrin! That would stop Stephen, the heretic. He took the steps of the great staircase leading up from the street onto the Temple Mount two at a time.

Across the expanse of limestone paving loomed the Temple. Its white marble profile shone in the late morning sun with the luster of fine alabaster. Like arms upraised in perpetual praise, the columns on its eastern facade thrust capitols of golden icanthus carvings heavenward.

Saul hesitated, stunned, as always, by its magnificence, awestruck by the fervency of his own feelings for the traditions he'd learned and treasured since boyhood. The Temple was the residence of God. The Ark of the Covenant rested in the Holy of Holies deep within the heart of the Temple itself. Rituals of sacrifice, support of the priesthood, and strict obedience to the Law were practices–in–adoration to the One True God who lived in the glorious structure before him.

How could anyone deny the reality of the Temple? Who would dare to contradict the power of the Law? No street preacher should be allowed to condemn Temple rituals. Nor should he be allowed to desecrate the Holy of Holies with words claiming a new covenant of the blood, a new covenant of the spirit. "Blasphemy!" Saul spat out. "Stephen must be stopped!"

By the time he reached the entrance to the meeting place of the great Sanhedrin to find Gamaliel, the sun flooded the Temple area with the heat of the harvest season. But inside the cavernous Chamber of Hewn Stone, coolness prevailed. The esteemed elders and priests, bearded and clothed in the raiment of their high stations, were seated in a loosely formed semicircle in five groups of twelve. Each represented one of the twelve tribes of Israel. Clustered at the center of the room were the chairs for six other members who comprised the high council. Beyond them on a raised platform was located the chair of the president. Petitioners, onlookers, and students like himself sat on benches placed against the walls along three sides of the chamber.

The formal session had not yet begun. The place was crowded, and the buzz of voices among the assembled filled the high–ceilinged room with a peculiarly reassuring sound. Saul stood up on his tiptoes looking for Gamaliel and saw him at his usual place in earnest conversation with Nicodemus and two other elders. As quickly as possible, he made his way to his mentor and with careful respect tugged at the sleeve of his robes. Gamaliel turned, a questioning frown settling between his wide-set eyes.

"My apologies to you, Honored Teacher. I must speak with you about a matter of greatest concern."

Gamaliel glanced apologetically at Nicodemus and the other two elders and asked their indulgence.

"It is that street preacher again. The one called Stephen."

"What about him?"

"He continues with his blasphemy," Saul said without attempting to conceal the rancor he felt.

Nicodemus gave him a sharply questioning look.

"Stephen is dangerous. He must be stopped."

"As I have told you before, Saul, he is of no consequence to us."

Saul started to protest.

Gamaliel raised his hand, stopping him. "This Stephen is of much less importance than those other followers of The Way who teach and preach and heal in the Temple precincts. Peter, James, John, and the others. And yet now even they are of no real concern to us."

"Besides, many of them have already left Jerusalem," said one of the elders.

"Jaacov is right," Gamaliel agreed. There was a note of condescension in his voice. "It is as I have told you before. If we leave them alone, they soon will see the folly of their thinking. And even if they don't, they are a minority."

"I should like to make all of them leave Jerusalem," Saul protested.

Gamaliel waved off the protest with a motion of his hand. "So far as the street preacher is concerned, leave him be."

Anger went through Saul, but he tried to hide it by nodding to them and hurriedly leaving the Chamber of Hewn Stone. The heat of the morning hit him with as much impact as his mounting anger. Gamaliel was wrong. Stephen was a threat. No God–fearing, Law–abiding Pharisee could deny that. Yet Gamaliel was denying it. Why? How could he? Not even the Synagogue of Freedmen would allow Stephen to preach there. They had forced him out into the streets because of his blasphemy. Didn't Gamaliel know that? He should get out into the streets himself and learn what a heretic Stephen really was "New covenant of the spirit . . . " Saul said the words to himself with such hatred that they seemed a curse.

In disgust, he kicked at a pebble, and a new resolve settled in his mind. He would do something about Stephen himself. Reaching into the folds of his tunic, he drew forth a small leather pouch, opened it, and poured out the few coins it contained into the palm of his hand. It wasn't much, but it would be enough for paid agitators. And they would be enough to put an end to Stephen and his blasphemy!

He slipped the coins back into the pouch, retied it, and stuffed it back into the folds of his tunic. As he turned toward the great staircase again, he saw the venerable Nicodemus come out of the Chamber of Hewn Stone and make his way toward the Porches of Solomon. The elder was in a great hurry and going straightway through the crowds toward where Peter and John were teaching. Suspicion prodded Saul. He recalled the sharp, questioning look on Nicodemus' face when he'd called Stephen a heretic. Now Nicodemus was hurrying toward Stephen's friends — an odd reaction for a loyal Sanhedrin member. His suspicion growing, Saul followed Nicodemus, keeping as close as possible without being noticed. He was forced to stop too far away to hear their words, but the three men's gestures made it obvious that Nicodemus was warning Peter and John that Stephen was in danger.

What was also obvious was that Nicodemus felt quite comfortable consorting with those heretics. Was he, too, a follower of The Way? Did Gamaliel know? And if he did, why hadn't he forced Nicodemus out of the Sanhedrin? No heretic should belong to the supreme body ruling over Jewish traditions and laws. Fresh, unyielding anger came over Saul, reinforcing his earlier resolve. Without further hesitation, he hurried to pursue his own plans for Stephen.

Mary Mark, Barnabas, and John Mark were at work in the big storeroom in Mary Mark's house when Peter and James came to alert them of the growing danger to Stephen. John had gone in search of Stephen, and Andrew was with him.

"The Pharisee, Saul of Tarsus, once again has complained to Gamaliel. Nicodemus thinks his next step will be to demand a hearing before the Sanhedrin," Peter declared.

"I wish Joseph was not away from Jerusalem," said Mary Mark. "He could prevent such a thing from happening."

"When does he return from Joppa?" James asked.

"Not for several days yet," Barnabas replied. "He will return just before the Feast of Tabernacles."

"We have repeatedly warned Stephen," Peter said in exasperation. "He refused to believe there are times when our Lord is better served with quiet preachings."

"Where does this Pharisee come from?" Mary Mark wanted to know. "What's his background? What makes him such a vindictive, fanatical man?"

"He comes from the country of Cilicia, from the town of Tarsus in the north of that country. His parents are Jewish. His father, a tentmaker of good repute, has been dead some years now. Saul, too, is a tentmaker, I am told. His father's dream for him, however, was that he become a rabbi. And finally he has come to Jerusalem to study with the great teacher Gamaliel to fulfill his father's dream for him. He's fanatical about it. Nicodemus tells me that even Gamaliel is alarmed over him."

"The Pharisee is also very intelligent, but he is more hot—tempered than even John and I," James added.

"And that makes him quite unpredictable," Peter said.

"We have warned Stephen about Saul. And as I said before, we have tried to convince him that sometimes our witnessing for the Lord must persuade and cajole, rather than accuse and condemn."

"The Lord himself told us there would be times when we should witness with discretion," James added. "You remember, don't you, Mary Mark?"

She hesitated, weighing her answer carefully. John Mark was looking hard at her. She did not want him to misunderstand. He was still acting aloof to her, partly because of his dislike of Manaen and partly because of his own skepticism about Jesus' teachings. Now that Stephen, whom he'd always liked and respected, was becoming a target of persecution, she feared that his skepticism would grow even more.

"Do you remember, Mary Mark?" James asked again.

She nodded. "No one should be persecuted for their religious beliefs. That's a personal and private matter, isn't it?"

"Exactly! Yet that's what Stephen's been accused of! Persecution!"

"Persecution?" They all stared at Peter. The look on John Mark's face showed that he clearly thought the apostle had either taken leave of his senses or that he was a traitor to the followers of The Way.

"At the Synagogue of the Freedmen, they believe that Stephen is persecuting them with his preaching that the Temple has outlived its usefulness."

"Why?" John Mark bluntly asked.

"It hits at their business dealings with the Temple. For Freedmen, that's persecution!"

"And you can be sure that Saul of Tarsus urges them to retaliate. They will continue to harass and threaten Stephen," James added.

"They'll do more than that!" Barnabas said. "Unless we can get Stephen to stop, they'll throw more than words at him."

"That's why John and Andrew went to find Stephen, and get him off the streets," said Peter.

A new sense of dread rose in Mary Mark's mind. She leaned against one of the wool bales, not wanting to accept the idea of new danger, especially not danger for Stephen. He was young and bold, yes, but a man full of faith and kindness. He had a wisdom beyond his years that had made him a good choice as one of The Seven to administer the dole. He was spirit–filled and courageous. She dreaded seeing him in such danger.

"Will they do him bodily harm?" John Mark asked.

"They certainly might!"

"It won't matter that he was right," James said, "anymore than such things as kindness and justice mattered when Jesus was crucified!"

The thought startled Mary Mark. She closed her eyes against it, refusing to think further of such a comparison.

"You have grown pale, my sister." Barnabas' strong hand was on her shoulder. "How can I help you?"

"It's just that after these recent months of relative quiet, this new danger is most unwelcome."

"We are all agreed on that," Peter said, coming to her.

John Mark followed close behind, a scared, worried look on his face.

Mary Mark stretched out her hand to him. He clasped it and sat down beside her.

"Can we also be agreed," Peter asked, "that this house of yours is the safest place in Jerusalem to hide Stephen for a few days? We told John to bring him here."

"Of course," she nodded. "But I think there is more to be done than just hiding Stephen."

"And what might that be?"

"We need to bring some pressures to bear against those who threaten Stephen."

"The Sanhedrin is the only group to do that," James

said, his face tense and pinched looking.

"Or Herod Antipas," Barnabas added.

"In either case, won't we need the influence of the Arimathean? Don't we need Joseph here to help us?"

The men looked at each other and realized that what she said was true.

"Barnabas, who should we send to fetch Joseph from Joppa?" Peter asked.

"What about Manaen?"

A look of astonishment and disapproval crossed John Mark's face.

"Manaen has my vote," Peter nodded. The others agreed.

"Very well," Barnabas said, "I shall go at once to the palace and ask him to go to Joppa for us. If good fortune smiles, he may be able to leave this very day and return with Joseph late tomorrow."

But good fortune did not smile. Though Manaen was able to leave immediately, Joseph was not in Joppa when he arrived in the great port city. He sent a messenger back to Mary Mark's house that Joseph had gone up into the Plain of Sharon to inspect a new orchard and that their return to Jerusalem would be delayed several days. The news was not welcome, but they had no choice except to wait. In the meantime, they lodged Stephen at Mary Mark's house with the strict understanding he was not to venture out into the streets until the apostles felt it safe for him to do so.

Though he had reluctantly agreed to their terms, he chafed at being confined to Mary Mark's house. "My mission is to help with the widows' dole and to preach," he complained to John Mark. "It is not to stay hidden here in your mother's house."

John Mark urged him to be patient. "It is only for a few more days. Nicolaos and Prochorus say the Pharisee will soon stop searching the streets for you. He believes he's forced you to leave Jerusalem."

It was the wrong thing to say. Stephen glanced sharply at him.

John Mark tried to recover but only made it worse by protesting, "He's not called you a coward!"

Stephen's face reddened. "If not that, then he scoffs at the Lord. That is all the more reason I should be out of here doing my work — especially now. Pilgrims from everywhere are beginning to come into the city for the Feast of Tabernacles. There will be thousands of them. I should be preaching to them."

And indeed, there were thousands of pilgrims coming into the city. Each day hundreds more came through the city's gates to build their booths in the open spaces at the foot of the Temple Mount to celebrate the second greatest of all Jewish holidays. Next to Passover, the Feast of Tabernacles, or the Feast of Booths as many families still called it, brought the greatest number of visitors to the holy city. Even Gentiles enjoyed it! It featured processions and dancing, exuberance and games and happiness. The "sacrifices" at this event were joyous communal meals of meat and wine.

"I like the Feast of Tabernacles. It's fun!" John Mark said, trying to change the subject, determined to talk Stephen into staying hidden. "It's a great celebration of thanksgiving for bountiful harvests. And Uncle Barnabas tells me it commemorates the ancestral Hebrews' wilderness wanderings. And he says the building of booths comes from the centuries-old custom of using watchtowers during harvest time, especially in olive orchards."

"It also symbolizes the renewal each year of God's covenant with his chosen people," Stephen said. "That, however, is an old covenant."

Mary Mark came into the main room of the house carrying a tray of food. Stephen turned to her. "I've been telling John Mark that I should be out in the streets preaching now.

I should be telling all these pilgrims of the new covenant, the one that Jesus brought us, the one God sent to us through him."

The expression in Stephen's dark, luminous eyes was so beseeching that her heart clamored to help him. Only with great inner effort did she force herself to make no move he could interpret as approval to leave the house. She dared not. It was far too dangerous.

John Mark walked to her and picked up a bunch of grapes from the food tray. "My mother doesn't want you dead any more than I do, Stephen."

His bluntness broke the tension. Stephen threw his hands up in a gesture of apparent surrender.

With a nervous laugh, Mary Mark put the food tray down on a nearby table, grateful that once again Stephen's pressuring for freedom had been put off. Street sounds came soft but compelling through the windows that opened onto the front courtyard. She turned and looked at Stephen and wondered how much longer he could force himself to do as Peter had ordered him and stay in her house.

The answer came early the next morning. Rhoda slipped into Mary Mark's bedchamber with the news that Stephen had left the house sometime before dawn. By the time the sun reached its highest point in the sky, Nicolaos brought word that Stephen had been arrested and taken to the Chamber of Hewn Stone for questioning. With Joseph still away from Jerusalem, they could count only on Nicodemus to defend Stephen during the questioning. Barnabas insisted on going to the Chamber of Hewn Stone as a spectator, and John Mark insisted on going with him. The only other positive factor, if it could be called such, was that the high priest, Jonathan, was a passive man. Now president of the Sanhedrin, his influence might be one of moderation.

But the whole situation was a bleak one. As Barnabas and

John Mark left the house, Mary Mark sent Rhoda, Sallu, and Kedar around the city to gather the women for a prayer vigil. For a while she stayed with them in the big upper room praying for Stephen's safety. But she missed Joanna and her warm loving spirit so deep with faith. Usually she prayed with her in such times of crisis. But she was in Jericho as traveling companion to Herodias.

Mary Mark's own spirit remained restless. Her concentration refused to stay focused on the praying. At last, she slipped away and went to the main room of the house on the lower floor to pray alone until Barnabas and John Mark returned.

By the time she heard the creak of the gate opening and closing at the front of the compound, long shadows shuttered all but the smallest patch of sunlight in the courtyard. She stood quite still, listening for their voices. Instead, she heard only a silence heavy with foreboding. It seemed to creep through the room like some unwelcome guest. Fears began to rise inside her.

When Barnabas and John Mark appeared in the doorway, the looks on their faces confirmed her worst fears. She waited, not daring to ask them for details, yet hoping against hope that she was misreading their expressions.

Barnabas stopped just inside the doorway. John Mark sagged wearily against the wall opposite him. "Stephen called the Sanhedrin stiff-necked people with uncircumcized hearts and ears," Barnabas finally said. "He then called them disobedient and resistant to the Holy Spirit."

"They were furious," John Mark muttered.

"And in the face of their fury, Stephen's face was radiant. He said to them 'I see heaven open. I see the Son of man standing at the right hand of God!'"

"And they gnashed their teeth. And they covered their ears. And they began to yell and scream obscenities at him."

Mary Mark shuddered.

"Then, they rushed him and dragged him out of the city. By the Sheep Gate."

John Mark stared off into a space filled with live, recent, sickening recall. "They stoned him. The blood came from his head and his face . . . "

Barnabas moved away from the door and slowly walked to the window. From far down the street beyond the courtyard came the high-pitched, undulating, unmistakable wailing of women mourning for the dead. "All during the stoning, he prayed for them. He prayed that they be forgiven."

Fighting to hold back his tears, John Mark turned and looked at her. "Why?"

She held out her arms, not knowing whether he would come to her or whether she had an answer he would understand. All she could remember was the image of Jesus hanging on that awful cross and saying, "Father, forgive them, for they know not what they do."

6

The world cried. Great drops of rain gathered together in the early October skies of Judea and wept, their sadness accompanied by somber and steady thunder. A twilight darkness cloaked the morning hours and masked the glow of sunshine that normally would be visible.

Stephen's co-workers in administering the widows' dole—Prochorus, Timon, Nicanor, Parmenas, Nicolaos, and Philip—buried him and mourned him deeply. At the burial place, they were joined only by Peter, James and John, Barnabas, John Mark, Mary Mark, and her household servants. At Peter's orders, the crowd was deliberately no larger. Also at his orders, the other apostles were carrying the news of Stephen's death and a warning to all believers. Matthew, Thaddeus, Jude, and Andrew went to the villages east of Jerusalem. James the Less, Simon Zelotes, Nathanael, Matthias, and Bartholomew went to the villages west of Jerusalem. Barnabas' manservant, Kedar, was sent to the place in Joppa where Manaen had told them he would wait for Joseph. The centurion Cornelius was asked to carry the news to Joanna in Jericho, along with a confidential note from Mary Mark. The note asked Joanna to enlist Chuza's help in obtaining an arrest order for Saul of Tarsus from Herod Antipas.

The note pointed out that Saul's paid agitators laid their cloaks at his feet as he stood watching and giving approval to the stoning of Stephen. It also pointed to the very real possibility that the incident signaled the beginning of hard persecution for all followers of The Way.

Mary Mark's prediction was unfortunately accurate. Saul of Tarsus, his reason enflamed, now saw the opportunity to spread harassment and persecution. The seeds of hatred that he'd planted to get Stephen killed were nutrured now with a torrent of his own violent opinions, with more paid agitators and false witnesses against many other believers. With squads of Temple guards, he led persecutors in house–to–house searches. Wherever they found people Saul assessed as "heretics and blasphemers," they dragged them off to prison.

Believers scattered, fled from Jerusalem in such numbers that only the apostles and a handful of faithful, including Mary Mark's household, were left.

Joanna hurried back to Jerusalem as quickly as she could and tried to persuade Chuza to intercede with Antipas for an arrest order for the Pharisee.

"It will do no good," Chuza told her. "It is not important enough!"

"Not important?" Joanna bridled. "Murdering people is not important?"

Chuza made a placating gesture. "Not to Antipas. Not now. You know what I mean, Joanna."

"I'm not sure I do." She turned from him and went into another room of their apartment in the palace.

Chuza followed her, his round face solemn and worried. "My pet, please understand me. Yes, the murder of people is very important. But . . . right now . . . in the view of our esteemed Antipas, there is nothing as important as strengthening his position of influence and friendship with the new procurator."

Joanna shrugged away from the hand of truce he placed on her arm.

Chuza gave a heavy sigh. "Let me explain. Rumors persist that the emperor Tiberius is not in good health, my love. Should something happen to him, we're not sure who his successor will be. Antipas will need to secure his own position with the new emperor, whoever it turns out to be. The first step in doing that, he feels, is to have a strong bond of goodwill with Judea's new procurator, and with the governor of Syria as well. He is concentrating on that issue, and that issue only."

She turned, hand on hip, to imperiously survey him.

A pleading look was on his face. "I'm sorry, my pet. But Antipas is thinking of his own survival. And we should do the same!"

Joanna let her hand drop from her hip, and her haughty posture changed to one of surprise. "You mean Antipas might be replaced as tetrarch?"

"I don't know. Nor does he. But he is anticipating a defense in case that should happen. Now do you understand why I must show all of my interest in his problem and not ask him to intervene because of some fanatical Pharisee?"

"Yes, of course. I do understand," she relented.

Chuza came to her and took her hand. "Mary Mark's household will not be endangered. Manaen will see to their safety when he returns. You can be sure of it."

Chuza was right, of course, for with the return of Manaen, Joseph of Arimathea, and Kedar to Jerusalem, the house was never without its own security force. Manaen saw to it with such discretion that it was weeks before Mary Mark realized just how closely the house was watched by members of the palace guard.

It was a blessing to have them, considering the great numbers of believers who now sought her house as a haven. It had not been used for such purposes in a long time. Not since right after Jesus' resurrection when the winds of disbelief and persecution blew almost as strongly as they did now.

"If many more believers move away from Jerusalem," Barnabas said one evening after helping a family of six escape Saul's raiders, "we'll need to start a new community somewhere else. In Cyprus or Damascus or Tyre or . . . "

"Or Antioch?" Nicolaos chimed in with a grin.

"Still homesick for that northern city, eh, Nicolaos?"

"It does have its advantages, Barnabas. A few, anyway."

"Saul's not there!" John Mark said in a grim tone. "That's the biggest advanage."

"The danger soon will pass," Mary Mark said. "Saul of Tarsus will be stopped one of these days."

"How can you say that?" John Mark challenged. "He just goes on and on hurting people. He's an evil man. Who will stop him? You? Uncle Barnabas? Me?"

His bitterness did not surprise her. Stephen's death haunted him. With care she chose her words. "A power greater than any of us have will stop him, John Mark. The Lord will stop him. In his own good time, the Lord will stop Saul of Tarsus."

Disbelief etched itself onto John Mark's lean, young face, revealing the struggle going on inside him.

"Your mother tells you true, John Mark. You must have faith!" Barnabas's voice came strongly, brooking no contradiction.

The boy turned and left the room.

Mary Mark looked at her brother. "Someday he will no longer run from the truth. Until then, we must be patient with him. I don't want to lose him."

For the rest of the winter months, the house continued to help those who needed help, offered prayer vigils for many people and many causes, saw many prayers answered and gave praises for that, and served communal meals to the apostles and other friends, both business and personal. Saul of Tarsus still persecuted believers, but his attention was now focused on the villages of Judea and Perea rather than Jerusalem. Another Passover came and went without incident, as did Pentecost fifty days later. And then, on a day touched with the first real heat of summer, news came that the emperor Tiberius had died several weeks earlier.

His successor was a young man named Gaius Julius Caesar Germanicus, third son of the noble union of Germanicus and Agrippina. All who knew him called him by his nickname–"Little Boots." Caligula!

The nickname was deceptive. As a likable child of three or four, he had received a pair of miniature military boots, *caligae*, from one of his father's soldiers. He wore them constantly. The soldiers nicknamed him "Caligula." In his adulthood, however, the likable quality of his personality gave way to deceit and cruelty. The nickname took on a different meaning.

Many of the provincial governors and kings were startled by his emergence as emperor of the Roman Empire, but none was more startled, or more concerned, than Herod Antipas.

"He has a right to be concerned," said Joanna who brought the news to Mary Mark's house on the very afternoon it arrived from Rome. "Caligula is said to be strange and unpredictable. And he has been a longtime friend of one of Herod Antipas' nephews, Herod Agrippa."

"Herod Agrippa?" The name seemed familiar, but there were so many Herods that Mary Mark felt confused. "Nephew?"

"Yes, he is a son of Aristobolus, one of Antipas' half brothers."

Mary Mark hesitated, still confused.

"He and Herodias are brother and sister."

Mary Mark's eyes went wide. "Oh, now I remember. Isn't he the one that Herodias insisted be put in charge of the royal markets in Galilee some years ago?"

"That's the one!"

"And he almost stole Antipas blind!"

"That's the one!" He also was caught taking bribes when he worked for one of the Roman governors. He finally went back to Rome in disgrace. But then he renewed his child-hood friendship with Caligula. After that he did rather well, until he openly expressed his wish for the early death of the old emperor, Tiberius. He was tossed into prison for that." Joanna smoothed her skirt across her lap with the flat of her hands. "But then, of course, Tiberius did die within a few months, and Caligula has become emperor. So now all is forgiven for Herod Agrippa."

Mary Mark knew by her friend's facial expression that there was still more news to come. But the question crossing her own mind dealt with her friend's security, and that of her husband, and, of course, that of Manaen.

Joanna ironed another imaginary wrinkle from her skirt with the flat of her hands and stared off into the distance for yet another moment.

"Come Joanna, I can see by your face there is yet more news. Tell me," Mary Mark urged.

Joanna straightened. "Caligula has given Agrippa all of Herod Philip's tetrarchy and has bestowed on him the title of 'king'!"

"King?" The word escaped on a breath of astonishment. Herod Philip, another of Antipas' half brothers who had died several years earlier, had been tetrarch over a large northern territory. Since his death, no new tetrarch had ever been named. Antipas had sought the addition of the territory to his own tetrarchy. But all his attempts had been unsuccessful. "Philip's territory? After all this time? Given to Agrippa? King?" She shook her head in dismay.

"Can you imagine it?" Joanna's face expressed the scorn she felt. "Agrippa, the troublemaker, is now a king. A king over Batanea, Trachonitis and nearby districts, and the ter-ritory of Lysanius in Syria. That's what friendship with the power of Rome can do for you."

"Antipas must be furious."

"He is also jealous. And he is worried."

"And Herodias? What is her reaction?"

Joanna shook her head. "She may not yet have heard the news. She is still in Jericho. But if I know her as I think I do, she will press Antipas to seek an equal title for himself. She'll not be able to bear the idea that her brother is now called 'king.' "

"And in the meantime?"

She shrugged and got to her feet. "I want your prayers that Chuza and I may not be completely uprooted or banished because of this unfortunate turn of events."

Mary Mark went to her and clasped her hands. "You have my prayers as you have my friendship. Whatever happens."

The thing that happened was the very thing that Joanna predicted. Upon hearing the news of Agrippa's appointment, Herodias immediately returned to Jerusalem and began to insist that Antipas go to Rome to seek an equal title for himself. He resisted her insistence and her persuasions, feeling that to be the wrong course of action. Caligula was too unpredictable. He thought the better part of valor in this circumstance was to sit quietly, strengthen his relationships with the new procurator and with Rome's governor of Syria, and let the excitement of all these changes settle itself.

He also wanted to know what opinions on the matter were held by those men for whom he had respect. He called for Chuza to arrange meetings with Joseph of Arimathea, Nicodemus the banker, and with Jonathan, the high priest. He met with them separately, desiring individual opinions not influenced by others. He sent Manaen to Caesarea-by-the-Sea to arrange a meeting with the new Roman procurator, Marcellus Vitellius. When he completed all these meetings, he called in Chuza and Manaen and told them that each man had advised against his going to Rome.

But Herodias chided Antipas for accepting their counsel. She shamed him for being influenced by two known followers of The Way. Ever ambitious and overridingly jealous, she was determined that her brother, Agrippa, should not outrank her husband. The contest of wills went on for many days. Finally, with the help of the royal astrologer, Herodias persuaded Antipas that the trip to Rome should be made. Her victory, however, was short–lived. Before any preparations for the journey could begin, news of three events arrived that postponed the travel plans indefinitely.

First, Marcellus Vitellius sent a message again urging Antipas not to go to Rome. He reported the city was in a state of great uneasiness about the unpredictable actions of the new emperor. Some talk even suggested that Caligula's mental health was unstable, if not volatile, for in swift succession he had ordered the execution of his principal supporter, the Praetorian Prefect Macro, had imprisoned another of his supporters whom he considered a potential rival, was suspected of causing the suicide of his father–in–law, and was expected to reinstitute the infamous practice of treason trials.

"Stay out of Rome," Vitellius concluded his message. "A new title is not worth the danger."

The second piece of news came from Joseph of Arimathea. Merchants he did business with in Alexandria had sent word that riots among various belligerent factions had erupted. The city was on fire. Even the great library was endangered. The Roman leaders there were asking assistance of men–at–arms from both Herod Antipas and from the troops under the command of Vitellius. To meet the request would leave Judea and Perea vulnerable to attack from any disgruntled neighbor. Antipas was in no mood to be helpful. He still smarted from the defeat given him by Aretas the Nabatean sometime earlier.

But it was the arrival of the third piece of news that settled the question about traveling to Rome. King Herod Agrippa, en route to his new capital of Caesarea Philippi, had arrived in the port of Joppa rather than the more northern port of Ptolemais in order to come to Jerusalem to "pay his respects" to his sister, Herodias, and to his brother—in—law, Herod Antipas. Accompanying him were his three daughters and his son. The courier who brought the message from the ship was a man named Thaumustus. Longtime friend and confidant to Agrippa, he concluded his message by saying, "The ship docked on the morning tide. His eminence, the King Agrippa, and his children should arrive in Jerusalem before the curtain of night descends." He bowed deeply from the waist and then quickly straightened to observe Chuza's reactions.

Chuza returned the bow. "His eminence and his children will be most welcome by the tetrarch of Judea, Galilee, and Perea, his wife, Herodias, and his entire household."

Thaumustus gave a careful smile. "Such hospitality is not unexpected."

Chuza moved around the small writing desk to more closely confront Agrippa's courier. "You, too, of course, are a welcome guest in this place, and your retinue of servants as well."

A quick glint of appreciation for Chuza's matter—of—fact courtesy flickered in the courier's eyes.

"I shall have a servant show you to your quarters and stay near you should you have any needs. I will go to inform the rest of the household of the arrival of his eminence, the King Herod Agrippa." Chuza motioned for one of the palace's most trusted servants to guide Thaumustus to his quarters while he hurried off in another direction to report this startling news to Antipas and to Herodias. On the way, he met Manaen and told him.

"Beyond belief!" Manaen muttered, walking along with Chuza toward Antipas' private antechamber. "What is this Thaumustus like?"

"Affected. Talks about 'curtains of night descending,' instead of 'close of day' or 'nightfall.' But he's also crafty. He misses very little, I suspect. And if you made him your enemy, he would be a worthy adversary."

"That's what I like about you, Chuza, You're reassuring!"

They rounded the corner, accepted the salute of the guard at the entrance of the antechamber, and went in. Antipas was dictating a message to Vitellius. When he saw Chuza and Manaen, he dismissed the scribe.

Chuza bowed. Manaen nodded.

"I bring news from Joppa, Your Excellency. The palace is to be graced with the arrival of very important personages this day," Chuza said.

Antipas cocked his head, suspicious, recognizing the hint of sarcasm in his chief steward's voice.

"Your brother–in–law, sire. He's coming. His children, too, but apparently no wife. I am told to report to you that the King Herod Agrippa is coming to 'pay his respects' to the Honorable Tetrarch Herod Antipas!"

Manaen decided later that shock was the only word that could accurately describe Antipas' stunned reaction to this news.

In fact, as he told Mary Mark much later, it was the first time he had ever seen Antipas actually grow pale underneath his swarthy Idumean skin!

Unfortunately he could not give a firsthand report on the reactions of Herodias. Antipas himself chose to tell her the news. But servants overheard their confrontation and reported it to Chuza. It seems that Herodias blamed Antipas for having to offer the hospitality of the palace to Agrippa and his children. Her reasoning, justified or not, was reported to have gone like this. If Antipas had listened to her and had agreed to make the trip to Rome weeks before, they would have been well on their way. In their absence from Jerusalem, the Romans would have had to supply the hospitality for Agrippa and house him and his children in the

Hasmonean palace, rather than in the palace of Herod! As it was, tradition and custom required them to be their hosts. And what was even more galling to Herodias, they would be required to host a great public reception of welcome.

"Herodias is furious!" Chuza reported to Joanna. "She wants the public reception to be held as quickly as possible in the hope it will shorten her brother's stay in Jerusalem."

"And what about the trip to Rome?"

"She is still insisting that they go as soon as they get rid of Agrippa! Whether or not they go remains to be seen."

7

"A reception of welcome for Agrippa! What hypocrisy!"

"Protocol, Mary Mark," Joseph of Arimathea smilingly chided, "face-saving protocol."

"Thanks be, my household won't have to be involved!"

"Oh, but it will." Joseph handed her a small parchment scroll. "The invitation is a royal command. We are all expected to attend."

She frowned.

"You know the expectations of the court," he countered. "Our business interests will be served best by all of us attending—you, Barnabas, myself, and John Mark."

"John Mark, too?"

"Especially John Mark. Many young people will be there since Agrippa's children are traveling with him."

"I know little of his children. Only that there are four of them."

Joseph seated himself across from her. "The three youngest are within about two years of each other. Bernice is about twelve or thirteen, I should think. Drusilla is about eleven. And young Agrippa is soon to be nine years old. The eldest is a daughter named Mariamne. She is fifteen or sixteen, I should guess—about John Mark's age.

Mary Mark repeated the name softly wondering why it stirred something deep in her memory. "Mariamne."

"The child is named for her great-grandmother, the first wife of Herod the Great, who bore him, among other sons, the ill-fated Aristobolus. He, of course, was the father of Herod Agrippa and Herodias. And if family history and our own observations tell us anything, they both are ill-fated, too."

She nodded, remembering the deep memory now. "The first Mariamne was rather ill-fated, too, wasn't she?"

Joseph's face reflected momentary sadness. "Yes, she was the most beloved of all Herod's wives, it is said. The great Mariamne Tower at the palace is a memorial to her."

"But Herod killed her, didn't he?"

"Or he had it done. He grew violently jealous of her."

Mary Mark rose to her feet and walked rather aimlessly to the far side of the room. The movement was symptomatic. Ever since Stephen's death, any mention of murder or killing prompted a reaction of sadness so acute that only some kind of physical action could assuage it. In this instance, she silently berated herself. Why should this conversation affect her so? She knew none of these people personally.

Joseph got to his feet. "Shall I send my servants around with the travel-chairs to take you and Barnabas and John Mark to the reception?"

She brought her thoughts back to the present but remained silent for a moment longer.

"You will go, won't you, Mary Mark? Like it or not, our attendance is required. It is business!"

She gave a reluctant sigh. It was useless to argue the point. Joseph was right, as he always seemed to be. One of their largest sources of income was centered in the royal court of Herod Antipas. To refuse a royal invitation, let alone a royal command, would be sheerest folly. Besides, there was another important reason to attend. Joanna, Chuza, and Manaen would be there. She should attend for their sakes, if not for her own. The equanimity of the royal court affected them even more directly than it did her; so would any changes that might occur. Joanna had already confided an awareness of Agrippa's covetousness for Antipas' territories and power. So there were two good reasons for not arguing with Joseph about going to the reception. The household was invited; it was involved; it would attend.

John Mark, however, was not as easily convinced when she told him and Barnabas about the invitation. He protested that he did not want to go.

"Then, please change your mind," she ordered as gently as possible. "This invitation is a royal command, my son."

He eyed her suspiciously. "Will Manaen be there?"

Mary Mark stiffened. "Of course he'll be there!"

Barnabas intervened, motioning for Mary Mark to leave John Mark to him. "It would be the height of rudeness to Antipas for Manaen not to be there—after all they're half brothers—just as it is rudeness for you to defy your mother and refuse this invitation."

John Mark stood silent, a brooding look on his face. Barnabas went to him. "You're almost a man, John Mark. You must begin to let your actions show that you understand things as a man would understand them."

Nephew and uncle took the measure of each other for a long moment. It was John Mark who relented. He turned and mumbled, "I apologize, my mother. I will go with you."

As it turned out, the reception was more an acknowledgment of unwanted changes than of welcome. Within the setting of pomp and splendor, ghosts of past enmities appeared in wary eyes and on cautiously smiling faces. Amidst the bounteous richness on display in the great hall of Herod's palace, specters of fears for the future strolled arm-in-arm with invited guests.

Mary Mark and Barnabas stood talking with Manaen and Joanna at one side of the great hall where the music was less noisy. Joseph stood a little beyond them talking with several members of the Sanhedrin. Chuza had stationed himself near two of Agrippa's men—Thaumustus, and a man named

Blastus. They stood behind the royal personages seated on the royal dais. While musicians and mimes performed in front of the royal dais, neither Antipas nor Herodias made any attempt to speak to their guest. Chuza wondered if they'd spoken to him at all since his arrival. The strain between them was clearly apparent.

What also was clearly apparent was Agrippa's boredom with the performers. He fidgeted, glanced restlessly about the great hall, and motioned for a servant to refill his wine goblet again. Next he motioned to Chuza.

Chuza went to him at once and leaned close.

"The tall woman there, near the column, talking with Manaen and your wife, who is she?"

"That is Mary of Jerusalem, Your Excellency."

Chuza carefully used Mary Mark's public identification, rather than the familiar name given to her by Jesus and his disciples.

"Who does she belong to?"

"What's that, Your Excellency?"

He repeated it in a louder tone.

Herodias frowned at him.

"Does she belong to Manaen?"

"No, Your Excellency."

"Who's she married to?"

"Ah . . . . she is the widow of Mark Yonah ben Abou, a business associate of Joseph of Arimathea."

"Then she is wealthy?"

A resentful look flashed momentarily in Chuza's eyes. His answer was careful and oblique. "The woman's brother and the merchant see that she is provided for."

Agrippa dismissed Chuza and continued to look across the room in Mary Mark's direction until his son and youngest daughter came running up to him with a plea to be allowed to sit on the royal dais so they could better see the performing mimes.

Herodias again frowned in his direction, annoyed at the intrusion of his children. But Agrippa ignored her, and welcomed his children to sit on the edge of the dais.

As if his master's actions required some explanation, Thaumustus confided to Chuza, "His excellency is quite devoted to his children."

"So I see."

Thaumustus covered his mouth with one hand, careful not to be overheard. "He is particularly devoted to the younger two children. He blames himself for the death of their mother, I think, although everyone knows he is not responsible in any way."

A questioning look came over Chuza's face. Thaumustus went on to explain that the children's mother had died during the time Agrippa was in prison in Rome for having declared his allegiance to Caligula while the emperor Tiberius still lived. "If anyone other than the woman herself were to blame for her death, I suspect it to be one of the men close to Tiberius. Certainly, it was no one close to King Agrippa!"

"Then her death occurred not too long ago?" Chuza asked in surprise.

"Correct."

Without warning, Agrippa stood up, stretched backward with his hands at his waist as if to remove a kink in his spine, and gave an unceremonious yawn. The expression of boredom was overt.

Musicians stopped playing. Performers hesitated, bowed toward the royal dais, and then withdrew. Assembled guests turned from their conversations to stare in puzzled uncertainty at hosts and honorees.

Herodias hissed at her brother from behind her face veil. "Is there nothing you will not do to embarrass us?"

Agrippa ignored her and instead announced to Antipas, "I wish to walk among your guests. I wish to talk with them, to hear about conditions in your territories from someone other than your own ministers."

Antipas' face darkened.

"For my report to the emperor," Agrippa added.

He might as well have added that someday he expected to rule Judea, Galilee, and Perea in place of Antipas. The implication was clearly obvious. Its effect was not lost to any of those on the dais. A gasp of dismay escaped from Herodias. Chuza's round face took on a look of disapproval. Smugness momentarily altered Thaumustus' impassive features. Blastus pretended not to have heard.

Fighting to control his anger, Antipas got to his feet, motioned the musicians to resume their playing, and led Agrippa off the royal dais toward the assembly of guests. But rather than trailing after his brother–in–law, Agrippa moved off independently into the groups nearest the dais, a maneuver that forced Antipas into the role of a follower.

Joanna nudged Mary Mark. "It is already happening, as I told you it would. Agrippa has started his public campaign for Antipas' power and position. He is using every conceivable small device to humiliate Antipas."

Mary Mark responded only with a half–attentive nod. Of far greater interest to her were Agrippa's two oldest daughters, Bernice and Mariamne, who had just entered the great hall with John Mark and his friend Dathan. They all stood together laughing and talking near one of the food tables at the far side of the royal dais in obvious enjoyment of each other's company.

A mix of reluctant reactions went through her. She was surprised at John Mark's association with Dathan again. Since the incident in the Agora, no mention had been made of him nor of the other boy, Onan. Dathan's father had dealt harshly with him and made him come to apologize to John Mark. She wasn't sure she approved of the renewed association, but perhaps it was only temporary while Agrippa and his daughters were in Jerusalem.

The girls were attractive and from this distance seemed to be well mannered and orderly enough. John Mark appeared to be particularly attentive to the older girl, Mariamne. She was dark–haired with a pretty face and laughing eyes. A regretful warning traced through Mary Mark. She pushed it aside, asking herself what harm there could be in the acquaintanceship and reminding herself that she needed to let go of John Mark as much as he needed to let go of her.

"She reminds me of you when you were that age," Barnabas spoke up beside her.

"Does she really?"

"She does, indeed."

He turned to Manaen and Joanna. "Would you ever believe that this woman who is my sister was once as coquettish as that?"

"I would believe it," Manaen teased.

Joanna made a clucking sound.

"Coquettishness was never one of my traits," Mary Mark objected with a laugh. "I was, and am, much too shy."

"And I would believe that, too," Manaen teased again.

Mutual laughter welled up, lingered an instant in the flickering orange–gold of a nearby torchiere, then fled as Agrippa pushed his way through the crowd and came toward them. Antipas, looking agitated, trailed behind him.

Joseph turned from his conversation with the Sanhedrin elders to greet both rulers. The others followed his example.

Antipas introduced the elders. Agrippa acknowledged the formality in a stiff manner. Then, ignoring everyone else, he turned to Mary Mark. With a half smile playing about his lips, he gave her a searching look of such length that it began to be embarrassing.

Mary Mark struggled to meet the look with one equally searching and irritating, while at the same time memorizing what he looked like. The family resemblance between Agrippa and Antipas was clear. He was a bit shorter than Antipas, a few years younger, and a good deal more handsome simply because he was not as swarthy–looking. But there was a great difference in the eyes. Antipas' eyes held a look of calculation and caution. But the look in Agrippa's eyes reminded Mary Mark of the cold, relentlessly hard look of a man bent on total self–gratification. In spite of herself, she shivered.

"An introduction, brother–in–law," Agrippa finally said. "I have not met this guest."

Antipas obliged.

She acknowledged the introduction, but felt her face grow hot at the unwanted attention as he continued to stare at her. "Is that your son over there with my daughters?" he asked abruptly.

"It is."

"It meets with my pleasure that they are together."

Mary Mark said nothing.

"Does it meet with your pleasure?"

"Your daughters are quite pretty," she demurred.

Her indirection caused him to smile more openly.

She found his reaction irritating. She wished him to approve of absolutely nothing about her or about John Mark.

"If our children are becoming friends, then we, too, should become friends. Don't you agree?"

She glanced across the great hall at the group of young people, wishing to share absolutely nothing with him.

"By what name is your son called?"

"His name is John Mark ben Yonah."

"My two daughters are Bernice and Mariamne. The younger children on the dais are Drusilla and Agrippa. We shall be here in Jerusalem for quite some time, I expect. Perhaps Antipas or Manaen will arrange another visit for us."

Resistance, backed by a sense of fear, went through her.

Manaen stepped forward. "That's thoughtful of you, Your Excellency, but that may not be possible. I understand the lady expects to travel away from Jerusalem very soon."

A pause of astonishment dropped over the group. Agrippa narrowed his eyes in suspicious calculation. Mary Mark stood quite still, lest the slightest movement betray the protective lie.

"That is correct, isn't it, Barnabas?" Manaen urged confirmation.

Barnabas nodded, smiled, and explained with surprising smoothness. "Cyprus is our original home, Your Excellency. My sister and I expect to journey there quite soon."

"And the boy—your son, m'lady—will he be going to Cyprus with you?"

Before she could answer, Joseph stepped forward. "Yes, the boy will be going, and so will I."

"You?"

Joseph nodded. "Barnabas ben Levi and his sister have copper holdings on Cyprus. Since we have joint interests in the trading of the copper throughout Rome's great empire, we often make inspection trips together."

Agrippa's look of disbelief disappeared. "I see. Well, once I am established in my palace in Caesarea Philippi, you must come to visit me, merchant. I understand that my brother-in-law already does business with you. I may want to do business with you, too."

Joseph salaamed.

Agrippa glanced again toward Mary Mark. "It seems we have yet another thing in common."

An involuntary shudder went through her.

He bowed slightly, and moved away to visit with other guests. Antipas followed after him.

When they were beyond hearing distance, Barnabas slapped Manaen on the shoulder. "You have a quicker head than I ever imagined, my friend."

"Thanks be." The tone of relief in Mary Mark's voice brought a chuckle to the others.

"How long will Agrippa and his children stay here?" Barnabas asked Joanna.

"At least another month or maybe two."

"That long? We shall have to make certain our lie about the trip to Cyprus is not found out."

"That's an absolute truth," Joanna agreed. "Agrippa can be far more vengeful than Antipas."

"None of us will tell," Joseph chuckled. "But what about John Mark?" Joanna insisted. "He seems absolutely smitten with Mariamne."

"Don't say that," Mary Mark implored.

"But he does. And you know he'll want to see more of her. And he'll talk and . . . " Joanna went on.

"He doesn't know about all of this," Manaen reminded her.

"Exactly," said Joanna. "And if questioned about his mother's whereabouts by Agrippa or by Mariamne for her father, he will quite innocently tell the truth. That she is here. In Jerusalem."

A ripple of laughter started among them, as the irony of their situation came clear in Joanna's rushing words. Here they were, five responsible adults, all professed followers of the The Way, which had its foundation in truth, anxious and arguing about how to handle a social untruth of their own making.

Mary Mark smiled wanly. "We might really have to make that trip to Cyprus."

"Nonsense," Manaen said. "John Mark will tire of Mariamne soon enough."

For the next three weeks, it was easy to preserve the lie they had told. Antipas became their unsuspecting aide by taking Agrippa with him to inspect the pitch diggings near the southern end of the Dead Sea. He hoped to strike a trading deal: pitch from the Dead Sea for timber from the northern forests. From there, they went further down into the southern desert to a mining site.

But Manaen's prediction of John Mark's quick loss of interest in Mariamne was a poor one. He was enchanted with Mariamne. He found time to be with her every day. She was impressed with his skills at reading and writing. He doubled his efforts at the scribal school and hurried through his home chores so that he could spend time with her. They walked in the palace gardens and played the Egyptian gambling game of "bones" that Mariamne had taught to him and Dathan. And they spent countless hours in the quiet spots of Herod's vast palace talking and being alone together in the sweetness of first love.

The growing relationship now began to seriously worry Mary Mark. She hoped for the best, but expected the worst.

"That's because you're his mother," Joanna consoled as they walked together in the palace gardens. "But John Mark is a good lad. He will do nothing to hurt you."

Mary Mark shook her head. "Unless it is out of his own hurt, Joanna."

"What do you mean?"

"His jealousy."

Joanna's eyes went wide. "Jealousy?"

"He's jealous of my friendship with Manaen. It might cause him to do something foolish. That is my fear."

"Have you prayed about it?"

Mary Mark nodded.

"Have you called together the other women to pray with you?" She shook her head.

"Why not?"

"Pride, I suppose."

Joanna made no clucking sound of disapproval, but her face clearly showed it. "Our Lord promised to answer prayers. And you and I both know that he does."

Mary Mark paused to pick a blossom from an oleander bush, not really liking the direction of the conversation.

Understanding her friend's discomfort, Joanna walked on a few paces, saying nothing more.

"I thought of asking Peter to send John Mark to Samaria with Philip when he goes to minister to those who have fled there," Mary Mark said, catching up with her.

"What a wonderful experience for John Mark!"

Mary Mark brightened. "You really think so? It's very important that he doesn't view the trip as a deliberate separation from Mariamne, although, of course, that's excactly what it is."

"Go and talk to Peter," Joanna urged. "I'll go with you, if you like."

The distance was not far from Herod's palace to Peter's house near the Viaduct at the top of the street that led down into Cheesemakers' Valley. Peter's wife answered their knock at the gate and led them across the narrow courtyard into the main room of the small, plain house. Peter and his mother-in-law were just finishing their midday meal. At the sight of the two visitors, Peter stood up, welcomed them, and bid them come to the table.

They did so, exchanging greetings with his mother-in-law but declining the invitation to have a meal.

"I have come to ask a favor, Peter," Mary Mark said, getting right to the point of the visit.

"I hope it is one I can grant."

"Do you still plan to send Philip to Samaria?"

Peter nodded. "He leaves two days hence."

"Will you ask him to take John Mark with him?"

Peter leaned back and studied Mary Mark's face for a long moment. Then with gentle gruffness he asked what prompted her request.

Joanna interceded and explained the situaion. "It's important to separate them."

"That's an important need," Peter conceded, "but, the mission to Samaria will not be a safe one, not even for Philip, a grown man with much maturity in the Lord. Even for him, this will be a dangerous journey."

Mary Mark waited. Peter leaned forward on his elbows. An unhappy frown creased the space between his eyes. "For his years, John Mark is still very young."

"You are saying no?"

"I am."

She knew his decision was the right one, but her heart felt heavy at hearing him say it.

"It's with regret that I say no, but I must. Aside from the obvious dangers, there is the question of John Mark's uncertainty about our Lord."

Sadness filled her heart.

Peter reached across the table and took her hands in his own big rough ones. "You have been so kind to all of us, Mary Mark. It troubles me to say no to you. But to say yes would be neither kind to you nor fair to John Mark.

She searched his eyes. There was no deceit in them. "And the trip is dangerous. No matter that it is the believers who have fled from here who have asked us to send Philip to them. It is still dangerous. Philip is not even taking his wife and daughters, and you know how strong in the Lord they are."

"I understand, Peter. I really do." She pulled away from him and stood up. "Please don't tell John Mark I have asked this. I wish not to embarrass him."

Peter agreed and stood up, as did his mother–in–law and Joanna. Peter's wife came to them embraced first Mary Mark and then Joanna, and led them back through the house, across the small courtyard, and through the gate.

Once they were outside the gate and walking back in the direction of the palace, Joanna said, "He is right. But what bothers me is how John Mark will ever mature in the faith unless his faith is tested."

"It will be," Mary Mark said moodily. "Perhaps it is being tested already, his faith *and* mine."

8

Within the next few days, the question became not so much a testing of John Mark's faith in his beliefs about Jesus as about his faith in his mother and her feelings for Manaen. He'd thought about it a lot since the day he saw Manaen embrace and kiss her. And he was still trying to sort out his own feelings that had made him react with such anger. He wasn't sure he'd succeeded, even though quite some time had passed since the incident.

Now he brought the thoughts to the forefront of his mind again as he sat at his writing table in the School for Scribes' Apprentices. The copywork he'd been assigned was dull. He laid aside his stylus and looked around the plain room. It was long and narrow, and also dull. The boredom of its limestone–plastered walls was broken on one side by crude wooden racks stacked with pots of charcoal, sheets of papyrus and animal skins waiting to be made into scrolls, and clusters of styluses.

Randomly occupying the room's central space were a half dozen or so fellow students sitting on flat, hard benches before other writing tables like his own. He found them dull, too. All except for Dathan, who was sharing his enjoyment of being with Agrippa's daughters and talking about them when he was away from them. Both girls were full of fun and teasing. It was easy to talk to Dathan about them. It was even easy to talk to Dathan about the feelings he had for Mariamne.

He wished he could talk to Dathan about his mother, too, and her growing interest in Manaen, but he couldn't.

He didn't dare. Those feelings were too close, too personal to talk about. It bothered him too much to see his mother look at Manaen with that expression of total approval reminiscent of the way she used to look at his father. There was a closeness, a camaraderie in the look that left him feeling apart, alone, unwanted.

It was a new sensation. He never felt that way about Joseph of Arimathea, or his Uncle Barnabas, or Peter, or any of the other men who were close friends to his mother. He never felt pushed aside for any of them. Was this feeling of resentment toward Manaen just a part of growing into manhood? He'd asked himself that question often and without any satisfactory answer. Or was he, as Mariamne told him, too sensitive where his mother was concerned?

Not that he had discussed the specific situation with her. He hadn't. As close to her as he already felt, as influenced by her as he was beginning to be, this feeling of reserve about his mother's friendship with Manaen restrained him. Rather her comment had come during one of the times they had hidden away from Dathan and Bernice in order to be alone. They sought these times of being by themselves more and more frequently. This particular time, they were sequestered in a far corner of the palace gardens where a small grouping of oleanders and young acacias provided both shade and privacy.

They sat on the ground, leaning against the sturdy litheness of the young trees, holding hands. Their talk had drifted to the sense of loss each of them felt at the death of a parent.

"Since I am the oldest, I have to be the strong one," Mariamne confided to him in a sad tone. "But I miss my mother."

John Mark looked at her, trying to decide if he thought she really was strong. There was such a delicate quality about her, the small face framed in its cascade of dark curls, the look of sensitivity reflecting from her lavender eyes. A feeling of protectiveness went through him. He took her hand and gently raised it to his lips.

"Do you miss your father?" she asked.

He nodded automatically. "But of course, he's been dead much longer than your mother has."

"Does that make a difference?"

"It might. I was just a small boy when my father died—four or five years old, I think. I barely remember him. But you were nearing womanhood when your mother died. You should have many memories of her. That might make a difference."

She nodded. "We shared a lot. We did so many things together." Suddenly a mist of tears shimmered in her eyes.

John Mark let go of her hand and shifted his position. Watching someone cry made him nervous. His mother never cried. At least, not in a long time. In fact, the last time he remembered her crying was when his father died. He could still remember how it frightened him. To his mind, nothing else about his father's funeral had seemed to touch him, neither the priests, nor the ceremony, nor the crush of friends and family—not even the undulating wail of the mourners. But when he saw his mother sob with desolation, the meaning of the day took hold of him with fear.

He panicked, ran to her, and clung to her skirt, resisting every effort of Barnabas and Joseph to separate him from her. And she had understood. She motioned them away, leaned down, gathered him close to her, and let her tears mingle with his own. His panic fled. His fears vanished and were replaced by a sense of being protected and of protecting, a sense of close sharing, a sense of belonging. Now he realized those feelings never had been disturbed until Manaen came into their lives.

"You are very far from me, John Mark," Mariamne said softly, brushing the mist of tears from her eyes.

"I was thinking of my mother."

"Oh?"

"Yes."

"She influences you greatly, I think. In fact, you are very sensitive where she is concerned, I think—perhaps too sensitive."

He reached up, snapped off an oleander blossom, studied it for a long moment, and wondered if he could bring himself to discuss his feelings about his mother and Manaen with Mariamne.

"Once more you seem very far away from me, John Mark. Is even an oleander blossom more interesting than I am?" She smiled, innocent and teasing.

His heart gave an unexpected thump at the vulnerability of the smile. She moved closer to him. His throat went dry, and his pulse began to race. He had never wanted her so much as in this moment.

She reached up, took the oleander blossom from his fingers, and placed it behind his left ear. Swiftly, he encircled her with his arms and pulled her very close. She yielded to his strength without protest until he kissed her with a passion that surprised them both.

Her look of teasing innocence fled. She pushed at him, but he insisted. She struggled against him and pushed at him, dislodging the oleander blossom from behind his ear. "It cannot be!"

"But I love you!"

Determined, she scrambled free of him, clambered to her feet, and ran toward the palace.

Breathless and shaken, he stood up and watched her disappear into a side door just as Dathan and Bernice, arm in arm, came into the garden from an outside gate. A peculiar, bitter feeling of unfulfillment went through him. He straightened and brushed at his robes. The oleander blossom lay where it had fallen. He glanced at it; then he crushed it under the heel of his sandal and left the garden.

From across the dull, plain school room, Dathan abruptly glanced up from his work and looked at him questioningly. John Mark realized with a start he had been blindly staring at his friend while his mind retraced the memories of recent days. He had not seen Mariamne since that day in the palace gardens. Nor, until this very day, had he heard from her. But today Dathan brought word that Mariamne wanted to see him and would meet him in the palace gardens when his work at the school was finished. His reaction had been a mix of delight and caution, but he knew he would go. In fact, thinking of it now, he realized he could scarcely wait until the master scribe called an end to the day's work.

By the time he and Dathan reached the palace gardens, the day was well spent. But Mariamne was there, waiting with Bernice on one of the stone benches quite near the gate. At the sight of her, his heart gave that unexpected thump, and he could feel his throat going dry. He stopped in his tracks, cautioning himself to be aloof. He would not let her make a fool of him again.

Mariamne got up and quickly came toward him. Dathan bowed to her and moved on toward Bernice, leaving the two of them alone. She stood before him quietly, eyes downcast, as if she expected him to speak first. But he said nothing.

Finally, in a soft, sad voice, she said, "My father and Antipas have returned from their journey. And my father is now quite anxious to leave Jerusalem and proceed to his own capital in Caesarea Philippi."

A sinking feeling went through him.

"It is very far from here, John Mark. I probably shall never ever see you again."

He stood silently looking at her, his heart heavy with disappointment.

"I want you to have this." She took his hand and opened it so she could place in the palm a small amulet carved from amethyst.

He stared at it for a long moment. How could he take it? Everything he'd ever been taught forbade idols of any kind. Yet, how could he not take it? To refuse would be to offend Mariamne in the harshest way. And he had already done that by trying to make love to her. So he closed his hand over the amulet and slipped it carefully into a fold of his tunic.

She looked up at him, a pleading look in her eyes. "Have you nothing to say at all?"

"I don't want you to go."

She glanced away.

He clasped her hand and held it in both of his. "Perhaps you can stay for a while longer. Perhaps your Aunt Herodias will arrange it."

Mariamne shook her head. "She and Antipas leave tomorrow for Rome, I am told. When we leave for Caesarea Philippi, they leave for Joppa to sail to Rome."

John Mark felt defeated. He let go of her hand and walked away.

Mariamne followed him. "I have had such joy being with you, John Mark. I wish it could last. Our being together, I mean. I've never had such a friend as you. Not ever before."

He hesitated, thinking hard. Tomorrow was so soon, and without her it would be so empty. There must be something he could do to be with her longer. What would his Uncle Barnabas do in this situation? Or Peter? Or Joseph? They would gather their friends together to influence the situation. That's what they would do. But what friends did he have that could influence Agrippa?

"You don't believe me, I suppose," Mariamne finally said in a disconsolate tone, "or else you don't care."

John Mark wheeled around. "Oh no, Mariamne. I do believe you. And I do care. I care very much. In fact . . . "

Her sadness faded into curiosity as she looked at him, and saw that excitement had replaced his worried frown. "John Mark! What are you thinking?"

"Chuza!"

"Chuza?"

"And my mother!"

"Your mother?"

"She is a very hospitable woman. In my whole life, I have never known her to turn away someone in need of shelter!"

"But, John Mark, I don't . . . "

"Leave everything to me. And . . . please . . . wait here."

He turned and ran toward the south wing of the palace where Chuza's offices were situated. The more the idea whirled in his mind, the more he liked it. With Mariamne as a guest in his mother's house, he could be with her every day for hours and hours. Whether it was for another week, another month, or another two months didn't matter. What did matter was that tomorrow and its emptiness without her would be shoved aside, at least for a little while.

The very thought of it exhilarated him in an unaccustomed way. Not even Chuza's doubtful reception of the idea dampened his spirits. Finally, though quite reluctantly, the rotund minister agreed to seek King Agrippa's permission for Mairamne to stay on in Jerusalem if Mary Mark agreed to let her stay in her house. John Mark's joy was unbounded. He hurried back to the gardens to tell Mariamne of his success with Chuza and then rushed through the deepening twilight toward his mother's house.

The torches at the front gate already were lighted. Cooking fires at the side of the courtyard added their orange light to that of the torches, casting great shadows. The smell of roast lamb and pungent herbs came to him, making hunger pangs rise in his belly.

From inside the main salon of the house, he heard music

and voices. "Guests again," he murmured. "One more should be no trouble. Mariamne eats very little."

Rhoda came out from a side door, issuing instructions to the cooking servants.

John Mark called to her. "Who are guests this night?"

"Five merchants from the east, the honorable Joseph, the lady Joanna."

"Is that all?"

"Your uncle and your mother are with them, of course."

He hesitated, debating whether or not to broach his wonderful idea in front of the guests or to somehow get his mother alone to speak with her about Mariamne.

Rhoda sighed impatiently. "Are you going to join them, young sir?"

"In a moment." He waved her off, still undecided exactly how he was going to put this to his mother. Somehow, standing here at the entrance to his own home, the idea was losing its gleaming, wondrous quality. The reality of what he was asking formed itself much more clearly. He moved slowly on through the entrance to the house and hesitated again just inside the entryway.

Beyond in the main room, his Uncle Barnabas and Joseph were seated with the five merchants at the large table at the far side of the room. Their conversation was muffled, indistinguishable. But Joanna and his mother were nearer the entryway at a Roman type dining couch. He could plainly hear their conversation. And what he heard made him stand stock-still, eavesdropping, rather than going on into the room.

"It's heartening to learn that Agrippa and his children will be leaving tomorrow." The relief in his mother's voice was so obvious it wrenched at him.

"I thought you would find that news comforting. I know how concerned you've been about John Mark's interest in Mariamne. What would you do if they were not leaving tomorrow?"

"John Mark would go with Barnabas to Cyprus."

"Is Barnabas planning a trip to Cyprus?"

"No, but he would if I asked him to, under these circumstances, especially since Peter did not want John Mark to go to Samaria with Philip."

The heat of humiliation rose inside him. Samaria? Philip? Not wanted? Cyprus?

"My first interest is that Agrippa's daughter is no longer close at hand to further influence John Mark."

He clenched his fists against a tide of angry hurt.

"I know it sounds awful. But that's the way I feel. With all the persecution from the Pharisees, our community of believers fleeing, and the skepticism John Mark is already showing about the teachings of Jesus, he doesn't need the influence of a girl who believes in Roman gods."

John Mark flinched and pulled from the fold of his tunic the small amulet Mariamne had given him earlier. The carved stone felt as warm to his fingers as the joy she brought him was to his innermost being. For an instant, he hated Mary Mark and her prejudice against Mariamne. The intensity of the emotion was akin to what he'd felt when he saw Manaen kiss his mother. He took a deep breath, fighting off the sick feeling draining through him, and a curious resolve curled its way into his mind and settled there. He would not be separated from Mariamne. He would not.

Quickly he turned and left the house, snatches of the conversation he'd just heard jumbling through his mind. Chuza must have known all along that getting Agrippa's permission for Mariamne to stay on in Jerusalem didn't really matter as long as his mother felt as she did. Chuza must have known. "I'll seek Agrippa's permission if your mother will allow Mariamne to stay in her house," he had said. How he must be laughing, John Mark thought bitterly. And no doubt Joanna had already brought the message to his mother that he wanted Mariamne as their house guest. If he'd been a few minutes earlier, he probably would have heard her. More than that, how could he ever tell Mariamne she was not welcome in his mother's house? Fresh resentment pounded through him. He felt foolish, betrayed. How could he ever trust his mother or her friends again?

As he approached the Gate of the Essenes, he hesitated and considered the idea of leaving the city entirely. It would be easy enough to slip past the Roman sentry. But even if he did, where would he go? The night wind had sprung up, turning the air chill and promising an uncomfortable night for those without shelter. He shrugged off a sudden shiver and pulled the lightweight robe he was wearing over his tunic more closely about his shoulders. His sense of futility deepened.

He moved on, wandering aimlessly through the streets of the Upper City, still unnerved by what he had overheard, trying to sort through his jumbled thoughts and letting the heat of his humiliation burn itself out. When he reached the Viaduct, he stopped and leaned against its stone retaining wall, still undecided about what he should do. He couldn't go home. He didn't dare face his mother now. He would say something he might regret. He glanced about. Peter's house was just a short way off at the top of the street that led down into the Cheesemakers' Valley and the Lower City. But he couldn't go there either. Whatever made his mother ask Peter to let him go with Philip to Samaria, anyway?

He thought about going on across the Viaduct toward the Temple area. He turned, in fact, and looked across the Viaduct in that direction. No one was on the arching pathway. The early evening street silence was broken only the faintest sound of a lute being played inside some nearby house. Behind him and to his left, the prominence of the Hasmonean palace loomed darkly, blocking out the night's star cover. He was quite alone. And the more he realized it, the less he liked it. Slowly he turned. At its far western end, the broad avenue he was on abruptly ended with the forbidding wall of Herod's palace. Torchieres burned at its gates, revealing sentries rigidly pacing back and forth. Frustration rose inside him so fiercely that his breath came in quick gasps as if he had been running hard. He spat to relieve the awful tension and whispered, "Mariamne, I cannot lose you. But how can I stay near to you? Who can help me to do that?"

Dathan! He straightened as the thought came to him. Of course! He would help him. In fact, he was the only one who would be in a position to help him. He should have sought Dathan's help in the first place. Why hadn't he thought of it before? Quickly now he hurried forward toward the imposing walls of Herod's palace. As he reached the point where the intersecting street paralleled the palace walls, one of the sentries called out for him to stop and identify himself. He did so promptly, volunteering that the purpose of seeking admission to the palace grounds was to see his friend Dathan, son of Umeh, chief scribe to Herod Antipas. The second sentry came up, recognized him, and waved him through the outer gates.

Once inside the palace gardens, John Mark made straightway for the northernmost building of the palace complex, which was mostly used as a barracks for Herod's soldiers. Part of the lower level of the building had been turned into an apartment for Umeh and Dathan. It was large, comfortable, and easy to find. John Mark had come here often to see Dathan. He reached the entrance to the building, paused long enough to pick up a small clay lamp from a shelf and set a flame to it from a nearby torchiere, then proceeded down the long, dark hallway toward the apartment.

The main room, large enough but sparsely furnished, appeared to be empty. John Mark stepped inside. Softly he called out Dathan's name, hoping not to disturb Dathan's father, who was a hard, bristly, impatient man. And besides, he preferred that no one but Dathan be aware of his need.

Again he called Dathan's name. In response, a shadowy form moved near the firepit. John Mark stepped in that direction, squinting against the glare of the small lamp in his hand. The shadowy form was Dathan. He was curled up like a cat on a hard reed mat near the firepit. "Dathan! I need your help," he whispered, shaking his friend awake.

Dathan responded by turning over.

"I need your help," he said again, going on to explain what had happened, what he had decided, and what help he wanted from his friend. "Now, I have decided if Mariamne can't stay here in Jerusalem for a while longer, I shall travel to Caesarea Philippi to be near her!"

The words brought Dathan to full wakefulness. He sat bolt upright and peered at John Mark in disbelief.

"You can help me."

Dathan shook his head.

"Yes, you can!" John Mark insisted. "You know how to hide me away in the royal caravan. Or you know someone here in the palace who can do it."

Dathan cursed. "Have a care."

"I am determined."

"You are dumb!"

"If cases were reversed, I would help you."

"I would not ask such a foolish thing!" Dathan clambered to his feet. "Even if I could do what you ask, sooner or later King Agrippa will know what has happened. He's already been full of questions to my father about you and Mariamne and me and Bernice while he was on the trip to the Dead Sea."

"We did nothing wrong. None of us."

"Not that we didn't want to." Dathan gave a broad wink.

John Mark ignored him. "He didn't seem to mind that we entertained his daughters at the palace reception."

"That was different."

"How different?"

"You hadn't lost your head over his daughter then."

John Mark stiffened. "You didn't tell him!"

"I didn't have to. Mariamne is walking around in a daze of springtime. She's as foolish over you as you are over her."

John Mark's heart seemed to jump into his throat.

"Not only that," Dathan went on. "She has confided to Bernice that her heart is lost to you!"

His own heart began to pump hard. He felt the color creeping into his face.

"King Agrippa finds it amusing. He says she can't be serious. But at the same time, that's the real reason he abruptly decided to leave tomorrow for Caesarea Philippi!"

An ember crackled in the firepit, interrupting the silence that so quickly settled between John Mark and his friend. Agrippa would never make such a decision, he thought. Agrippa might decide to travel early to his new capital for political reasons. But for this? Dathan had lied to him and about him before. Why not now?

"You should know better, John Mark." Dathan chided. "King Agrippa wants his royal daughters to marry royal husbands! You should know that."

"Marriage?" Until Dathan's hard words came hurtling at him, he had not considered marriage with Mariamne. Marriage was a thing apart, a dimension of living for older people and only for him in some future passage of his life. What he wanted now was only to be near Mariamne, to walk with her hand in hand, to talk together as friends, to laugh and share the tenderness and sweetness of being together. "If you won't help me, Dathan, then, I shall find a way myself to stay near Mariamne." He turned and hurried away from Dathan's laugh of disbelief.

Before sunrise, Agrippa's royal caravan departed Jerusalem. It was not an especially large caravan, and in surprisingly quick time it covered the distance to where the road divided at the north end of the Dothan Valley. To the left was Shechem. To the right, another road led the short way to Sychar. Overnight the caravan encamped at nearby Jacob's well.

It was here that Manaen caught up with the caravan, searched out John Mark from his hiding place among the royal drovers, and forced him to return to Jerusalem.

"Let go of me!" John Mark jerked and twisted, trying to pull free from the rough hands of Manaen's two burly servants. "Let go! Do you hear?" But the more he struggled, the tighter they held onto him.

Aroused by the commotion, the chief drover got up and came toward them. "What's the trouble here?"

"A runaway," said Manaen.

"Slave, eh?"

Manaen stepped forward, blocking the drover from coming any closer.

"No!" John Mark protested. "I am no slave. There are no . . ." One of the servants clapped his hand over his mouth. The rest of the protest was lost in a strangling sound. He began to gasp for breath.

"Don't bother yourself," Manaen said to the drover. "We have our runaway well in hand now."

The drover glanced past Manaen's shoulder.

"You're certain I can't help?"

"Quite certain. But my thanks to you anyway."

The drover turned back in the other direction. But not until he was well beyond hearing distance did the servant take his hand away from John Mark's mouth.

He spat. Anger flooded him. He spat again as Manaen came toward him.

"Give me your word you'll not run from us again, and my men will let go of you."

"I'll give you nothing!"

"Very well." Manaen nodded to the servants who half

carried, half dragged John Mark to where four swift Arabian ponies were tethered.

He struggled again, but to no avail; he found himself being thrust up onto one of the horses, tied to the saddle, and having his wrists bound with a length of rope just long enough for him to be able to rein the horse.

It was obvious that Manaen wanted to return to Jerusalem within the shortest possible time. Conversation was sparse and limited to essentials. None of it was addressed to him and that was just as well, John Mark decided. The bright, hot anger that had flamed through him at his capture had banked itself into a stubborn, smoldering resolve to escape and to seek vengeance at the first opportunity. Already he'd pulled against his bonds so often that his wrists were rubbed raw. One of them had bled sometime during the night. The wetness had soaked the rope making it tighten, adding to his pain and discomfort. Now that the light of morning was brightening the sky, he gave up thoughts of escape, knowing that Manaen and the two servants would watch him too closely.

Within another hour they crossed the invisible boundary near Gophna that separated Samaria from Judea. Once well inside Judean territory, Manaen pulled off the trail, turned to the servants, and said, "We'll stop for a while for food and rest."

They tethered the horses and came to untie John Mark. As they did so, one of the servants noticed his wrists, pointed to the wounds, and called for Manaen to come and inspect them for himself.

It was the closest John Mark had ever been to Manaen, and he found his height surprising. He had never noticed Manaen's being taller than he was before. And there was a strength about him that he'd never noticed before either. He wondered if that was what his mother liked about him. Dislike abruptly overtook his momentary surprise. He stepped back away from him, wishing he could hide his wrists, not liking being this physically close to his enemy.

Manaen took hold of his hands and carefully moved the rope bonds to better see his wrists. "That must be quite painful."

John Mark stood silent and unmoving.

"Even for a stoic like you."

He forced himself to stay unmoving, even though his wrists throbbed with fresh new pain.

Manaen turned to the servant. "There's a small bit of aloe wrapped in muslin in my saddle pouch. Bring it to me, please."

The servant obeyed. And within another moment or two, Manaen had cut and removed the rope and applied the soothing balm of the aloe to his wounded wrists. Almost instantly his pain and discomfort began to abate. He stood looking at his wrists trying to decide if it was the healing power of the aloe or being free of the rope that had such a quickly beneficial effect.

"That should help." Manaen rewrapped the small piece of aloe stem in the muslin and handed it back for the servant to replace it in the saddle pouch.

John Mark knew he should at least acknowledge that it was indeed helping. Instead, he held out his unbound hands and asked, "Aren't you afraid I'll escape?"

Manaen gave him a narrow look but said nothing.

One of the servants approached. "My master may trust you. But I'll be the one that will have to chase after you." He slipped a longer tether of rope around John Mark's waist and attached the other end around his own waist.

When they once again started their journey, the servant removed the waist–to–waist tether and retied John Mark to his saddle for the rest of the journey to Jerusalem. Before darkness had settled once more over the land, the gates of Jerusalem were in sight.

"What do you intend to tell your mother?" Manaen asked reining his horse closer to John Mark's.

The question surprised him. He had assumed that Manaen already had done all the talking. Up to this point, he'd been totally in control, trussing him up like a criminal, giving orders like a captain of the guards.

"You'll have to tell her something about where you've been for the past two days."

"Doesn't she already know where I've been?"

"I think not."

"Then how did you know where to find me?"

"Dathan."

Irritation pinched at him.

"And you didn't tell my mother?"

"No, that's your responsibility. She doesn't even know that I went after you." Manaen reached for the reins of John Mark's horse and simultaneously reined in his own mount. Pulling a short dagger from a scabbard hanging from the pommel of his saddle, he leaned sideways and with a deft flicking motion cut the rope that tied John Mark to his saddle. "What you tell your mother about the past two days is your responsibility. She'll hear nothing from me."

John Mark blinked in astonishment, not so much at what Manaen had just said as at the fact that he had cut him free. Here. Outside the gates of the city, he was free. He could flee. There was nothing to stop him. He could make his way to Caesarea Philippi and Mariamne if he wanted to. Or he could go home. But why should he?

"Don't misjudge your mother," Manaen said.

John Mark glanced at him.

"She has a great capacity for understanding the pain of a broken heart." Without waiting for him to answer, Manaen nudged his horse forward toward the gates of the city. The two servants followed without even bothering to glance toward John Mark as they passed.

He watched them go with a more uncertain mix of emotions than at any time during the past two days, as if some rare opportunity was about to be missed. He was alone, free to make his own choice, free to make his way back north to Mariamne or straight ahead to the place where . . . Memories flooded in on him.

Manaen and the two servants looked very small now as they neared the massive city wall. He spurred at his horse and raced to catch up with them.

9

The Agora in the Upper City was crowded. It was market day. Men and women from all the surrounding villages had come to sell their goods and livestock and to visit with friends from other parts of Judea. Mary Mark and Rhoda walked through the noisy crowds, shopping carefully and not daring to get separated. Abundance was everywhere. Fresh stocks of salted fish had been brought in from Joppa. Great baskets of wool from the flocks near Bethlehem stood piled and leaning against each other. Beyond them, scattered about in an indistinct pattern of plenty, were the wares of merchants from Egypt and the southernmost parts of Cush and Nubia. Across the way were booths where bolts of cloth from the northern seacoast city of Tyre were displayed.

When Mary Mark saw the beautiful Tyrian purples and blues cascading from their hampers, she motioned for Rhoda to come and inspect them more closely. The woman selling the cloth salaamed to her, inviting her to buy.

Mary Mark ran her fingers over one piece of fabric testing it. The weave was smooth, almost silky. She crimped the cloth between thumb and forefinger, testing it again. The color was like that of sapphires, glistening and shimmering in the morning sunlight. The quality of the cloth was as excellent as its beauty was fascinating. She turned to show the fabric to Rhoda. As she did so, they both became aware of three men standing quite nearby in tense conversation.

"Saul the Pharisee is back in Jerusalem."

Mary Mark stiffened. A worried look flashed into Rhoda's eyes.

"But I thought he left Judea!" one of the men went on.

"Would that he had!"

"Anyone disagreeing with him is in danger."

"More than that. He openly boasts of his plan to kill Peter and John."

An awful look of fear came over Rhoda's face.

Mary Mark dropped the cloth she was holding. "We must go to the Temple Mount and find Peter and John. We must warn them."

But Rhoda resisted, holding her back. "We can send Sallu with the warning, my mistress. Let us return to the safety of the house."

But Mary Mark was adamant. "Go home if you must, Rhoda, but I'm going to warn Peter and John."

She set off determinedly through the Agora toward the Viaduct and the Temple area beyond. She knew Peter and John would be somewhere on Solomon's Porches on the Temple Mount. It was their regular place to preach and teach and heal whenever they were in the city.

Reluctantly Rhoda followed, refusing to let Mary Mark go alone through the crowded streets.

Arriving at the portico on the Temple Mount, it was not hard to find them. Crowds of people were always near them. Besides, Peter towered above most men, and John's red hair was like a signal fire. Mary Mark waved, caught John's attention, and motioned that she needed to speak with him.

He came toward her, grinning. "Is it well with you?"

She shook her head. "I bring disturbing news."

"What news? What about?"

"About Saul. He is back in Jerusalem. He openly boasts of plans to kill you and Peter."

A strange look came into John's face. "Wasn't Stephen's death enough for him?"

Mary Mark went on to explain how she and Rhoda had overheard the news and urged John to tell Peter quickly.

"As soon as he is finished preaching, I will tell him."

"You must tell him now," she insisted. "I feel a dreadful urgency about this."

John still hesitated, as if he didn't believe her.

"Why do you doubt me?" she asked impatiently. "Have I ever given you cause?"

A conciliatory smile spread across John's face. "No, Mary Mark, you have given us no cause to disbelieve you. Wait here."

He moved toward Peter, carefully signaling that Matthew, Jude, and Simon, who were at the other edge of the crowd, should go to where Mary Mark and Rhoda waited. Presently he returned with Peter. All of them moved a short distance away from the rest of the crowd where they could talk.

Mary Mark repeated what she had overheard in the Agora and again expressed her deep concern for their safety.

Matthew spoke up. "Why not take this time to go to Samaria? Philip has been asking you to come. You need to check on his conversions. Why not go now, Peter? You and John both."

The others agreed.

"All the rest of the disciples will agree with us. They'll want you to go," Jude said. "There may be no time to lose."

Farewells were said then and there, and each person went in a separate way down off the Temple Mount. Matthew escorted Mary Mark and Rhoda back to the house in the Upper City.

For the next several days, it seemed that unwanted forces of change were more active than ever. They invaded the very air of Jerusalem. Even though Mary Mark was kept quite busy managing the household, the strange foreboding had once more filled her mind. In idle moments, her thoughts drifted to some dangerous corners of doubt. For

Peter and John's safety. For the escape and rescue of those other believers who were once more targets of Saul's persecution. She even caught herself entertaining thoughts of self–pity, especially where John Mark and Agrippa's daughter were concerned.

John Mark had made a clean confession of his attempt to go to Caesarea Philippi with the royal entourage. And he had informed her of Manaen's part in returning him to Jerusalem. To her surprise, there had been a tinge of new respect in his voice when he spoke of Manaen's part in the incident.

Her reaction to the escapade was what neither of them expected. She'd had the good sense to listen and to forgive rather than to judge and condemn, grateful that John Mark had returned unharmed and aware of his changed attitude born of the experience. He had been quieter than ever, more introspective, since his return. She knew he pined for Mariamne. And she knew he had written to her, sending the scroll northward on the most recent of their trade caravans. But he was also studying and working harder. She found that aspect of his behavior comforting. She wished she could feel more comforted about his attraction to Agrippa's daughter, but she knew that was a vain hope.

It was as vain a hope as her continuing hope for peace and tranquility. What would life be like with only peace and tranquility, she asked herself as she sorted a stack of reed mats that needed airing. Since the house once more had become a haven to many of those who had decided to flee their own homes, she often helped her overworked servants with household chores. She lifted an armload of mats and crossed the room toward the opening onto the roof. As she passed the window, she glanced down into the courtyard and saw Chuza's messenger with Barnabas. She could tell that something was wrong by the very way they spoke with each other. She was tempted to call down to them, but restrained herself, realizing that the news might be something the household servants shouldn't hear. Instead, she put down the mats and went to the main floor of the house. By the time she reached the entryway, Chuza's messenger was leaving, and Barnabas was making his way into the house.

"It isn't Joanna, is it?"

"Not directly." He walked past her into the house.

She followed. "Manaen? Chuza?"

"All of them are affected," Barnabas said. "Herod Antipas has been banished."

"Banished?" The word stung. "Antipas? Banished?"

"The emperor Caligula was offended by Antipas' request for a title equal to that given to Agrippa."

"Offended?" She suddenly remembered how Joanna had described Caligula to her. "All who have met him say he is strange and unpredictable. Even the new procurator says he is mentally unstable."

Barnabas nodded. "Apparently Caligula felt that for Antipas to make such a request meant that he secretly disapproved of the emperor himself!"

Mary Mark shuddered, recognizing a deep and dangerous mind-sickness in the reaction.

"So he has banished Antipas to Spain. And, as you might have already suspected, he has named Agrippa as tetrarch of Judea, Perea, and Galilee." He paced away, rubbing his hands together in a gesture of irritation. "Do you realize, my sister, that this makes Agrippa ruler over more territory than anyone since Herod the Great?"

She sank down on a couch, overwhelmed by the enormity of change that now would take place. Joanna, Chuza, and Manaen—what would happen to them? Were they to be banished, too? But though her thoughts were of their friends, her next words revealed an even more personal concern. "Our trade routes. They will all be affected, won't they?"

"I sent Chuza's messenger to tell Joseph and to ask him to come here as quickly as is convenient."

"What will become of our friends?" She said it softly, almost to herself.

But Barnabas heard. "We can help them. We will find a way to help them."

"I have always feared this day. For a long time, I have known that life does not stand still, that it cannot stand still. Relationships change and grow and change again, just as our physical bodies change and grow and change again. But, deep in my heart, I have feared losing Joanna and Chuza and—" She hesitated, as if to mention Manaen's name would be to indict him for banishment, too.

"Manaen may have more choices than you think, Mary Mark." Barnabas' voice was reassuring in its matter-of-factness. "In spite of his close ties to Antipas, he is one of us. If for no other reason, the fact that he is a believer makes him our responsibility."

She turned and looked at her brother, considering his words, recognizing as never before his understanding of love. Their Greek friends had a special word for it—agape—love of friends, love for others, love that goes beyond self-interest.

Tentative sunlight crept into the room, pushing back the shadows of doubt, firmly insisting that the darkness of fear could no longer occupy its space around them.

Or so she thought. When Joseph arrived, however, he brought additional bits of information that made doubt reassert itself. In fact, he already knew all about Antipas' exile. And as he explained it, her doubt turned to a fear of real danger.

"In the first place, Antipas' trip to Rome was doomed from the start," Joseph said. "His banishment had already been decided. Agrippa caused it."

"Agrippa? How?" She and Barnabas exclaimed at the

same time, glancing at each other in dismay.

"I'm surprised he has that much influence with Caligula," Barnabas said.

"Frankly, so was I," Joseph went on, "but apparently he has. Long before Antipas ever left for Rome, Agrippa had sent a letter to Caligula stating that Antipas was not loyal to Rome, that he was too passive to be a good ruler, that his sixty years of age made him too old to govern an important area like Judea and Perea."

"What rot!"

"Unbelievable!"

"There's more!" Joseph paced about as agitated as Mary Mark ever remembered seeing him. "The letter went on to point out that it would be in Rome's best interest to combine all the lands in this part of the empire under the governance of one ruler—Agrippa himself, of course, being the one ruler."

"Incredible!"

"Devious and quite dangerous, you mean," Barnabas corrected.

"Yes, quite devious and quite dangerous," Joseph agreed. "It means that the man is to be trusted in nothing, absolutely nothing. And yet, we will have to do business with him. We will have to be cautious about every small detail. We shall have to assume that every transaction with Agrippa's court will be a dishonest one. Caution. We will have to take every caution!"

"How did you learn all this, Joseph?"

He hesitated, then looked at Mary Mark and smiled. "I have learned all of this from Manaen! He is truly our friend, Mary Mark."

"And he now will be in great danger, won't he? Right along with Joanna and Chuza, Manaen, too, will be in danger as long as he remains in Agrippa's court. Isn't that right, Joseph?"

The merchant nodded. "There is one advantage that Mana-en has, though. Not even Chuza has such an advantage."

"And what is that?"

"His friendship with Publius Petronius, the governor of Syria.

"Of course."

"You think that will be enough protection?" asked Barnabas. "Damascus is a long way from Jerusalem."

"True," said Joseph, "but the political ties Petronius has to Rome are many and very strong. Agrippa will become aware of that fact, if he isn't aware of it already."

"So you're saying that for the time being you think Mana-en is safe enough?"

"I think so."

"And how safe is Chuza? And Joanna?"

"I've already told her that we will take care of them," Barnabas inserted.

"Of course. We shall want to see to that if it becomes necessary, but at the moment, there is a more immediate concern." Joseph pulled a small parchment from the sleeve of his robe and brandished it like an ensign of war.

"What is that?" Mary Mark asked.

"A personal message from Agrippa to me. It announces, among other things, that he plans to move into the palace here in Jerusalem."

Mary Mark exchanged a quick, wary look with Barnabas. "What's wrong with the palace at Caesarea Philippi?"

"The climate of Caesarea Philippi does not suit him," Joseph said with a wry smile.

Mary Mark didn't feel like laughing. John Mark would once again be with Mariamne.

"But there is more. Agrippa expects a great feast of welcome to be given for him since he is now the new ruler of so many important and varied territories." Uncharacteristic sarcasm clouded Joseph's words.

"By whom?" asked Barnabas.

"By us. You, Mary Mark, and me."

The surprise Mary Mark felt was mirrored in the look of dismay on her brother's face.

"We are chosen, he says, because we do so much business with and for the royal palaces throughout the territories he now rules and because we have so many contacts with the people of influence, including the Roman leadership in all the regions surrounding. But we are not the only ones to whom Agrippa has given such a high honor!" Joseph brandished the parchment again, mimicking Agrippa's bravado. "The Sanhedrin and the priesthood of Jerusalem are also being asked to pay their homage in this same way."

"Not with us, I hope!" Barnabas exclaimed.

"No, not with us," Joseph agreed. "I will speak with Nicodemus and Gamaliel and Jonathan later today."

"Antipas never asked such a thing of us!" Mary Mark complained. "This is dreadful!"

Agrippa is a different kind of man entirely," Barnabas frowned.

"Do we have any choice?" Mary Mark asked in a tone more resigned than questioning.

"None," said Joseph. "We can count on nothing from Agrippa but insult and possible injury. He is a devious and greedy and dangerous man. We must be very careful from now on."

In spite of their unwillingness and their resentment at being put in such a position, they nevertheless were generous in their planning for the celebration Agrippa had demanded. They arranged for three full days of festivities and feasting. When they learned that hunting with falcons was one of Agrippa's favorite sports, they added that, along with a day of games of skill. Hundreds of guests were invited. And hundreds came from all the regions now under Agrippa's rule and from the surrounding territories as well. Every person of influence was included.

Special arrangements were made for Publius Petronius because he was a friend to Manaen and because his mandates still affected the economy and the peace of the entire middle region of the empire. This in turn, of course, affected the continuing success of their far-flung trading business. One of the most important of the special arrangements was accomplished with the help of the procurator Marcellus Vitellius. To put the entire Hasmonean palace at the disposal of Petronius, he temporarily moved his entire garrison of legionnaires into the Fortress Antonia. It was all done without Agrippa's knowledge.

On behalf of Mary Mark, Barnabas, Joseph, and procurator Marcellus Vitellius, Manaen sent a personal letter of welcome from them, along with one of his own, to Publius Petronius. Both letters made it quite clear that they would be his hosts while he was in Jerusalem and that every arrangement had been made for his comfort and enjoyment by them — not by the priesthood, not by the Sanhedrin, and not by Agrippa.

As a result, of course, he arrived in Jerusalem with a very large entourage of his own legionnaires and happily turned the Hasmonean palace into his temporary headquarters. The commodious suites prepared for him in the palace of Herod Agrippa went vacant!

"It is an insult, of course," Chuza told Barnabas in all innocence, not having been alerted to the prearrangements made by Manaen. "Agrippa is annoyed beyond belief. But to be truthful, Barnabas, I think it is hilariously funny. And it serves the braggart right!"

Barnabas chuckled at Chuza's obvious enjoyment of the situation. "It does insult Agrippa, doesn't it?"

"Absolutely! How better could Petronius tell Agrippa to keep his distance?"

The three days of festivities went swiftly and, for most of those attending, enjoyably. John Mark spent nearly every waking hour with Mariamne. Barnabas mingled with men from Cyprus and from Antioch, which culminated in trade agreements and contracts for the sale of additional copper ore. Joseph conferred with men of influence from the far provinces, both east and west, reinforcing trading contacts. Manaen and Chuza spent the three days attending Herod Agrippa, at his request, as he attempted to establish a better relationship with Publius Petronius.

For Mary Mark, the three–day celebration went even more swiftly. With the help of Joanna, she oversaw a myriad of details for the hundreds who accepted the invitation, fussed with cooks over last minute menu changes, instructed the palace banquet master on special seating arrangements, consoled visiting wives whose husbands strayed into dalliances with Agrippa's courtesans, and worried about John Mark spending so much time with Mariamne.

By the time the evening of the third day approached, she realized that the gala had gone much better than anyone might have anticipated. There had been no overt quarreling among the guests of such diverse backgrounds and attitudes, no fights. Special requirements for food and accommodations had been handled. Now if the final banquet went as well, she, Barnabas, and Joseph could consider the three-day welcome for Herod Agrippa a success.

Whether or not Agrippa had that perception of it was something else. But for her part, she was glad that the entire event was about to be completed, for she had quickly tired of all the veneer, the smiling and making conversation with people she barely knew, people who spoke of their allegiance to pagan gods. She hungered for the sanctuary of her own house and the company of those who believed as she did, those with whom she shared her love of Jesus and his teachings.

She glanced about the great banquet hall. This last great feast had gone well. She felt a small tremor of relief go through her and realized how tired she was. But it was almost over. Only one or two more customary speeches of appreciation and acceptance needed to be made, if she had calculated right. She watched Publius Petronius get to his feet. In his hand was a small scroll. He unrolled it carefully, waited for the noise among the guests to subside, and read the announcement.

"By this Imperial Proclamation, I, Gaius Julius Caesar Germanicus, Emperor of all the lands under the benevolent protection of Rome, do hereby order Publius Petronius, *amici principis* and Governor of Syria, to commission a statue of my Royal Personage in the guise of Jupiter, who also is a god. And further, that upon completion, this statue of my Royal Personage is to be set up in the Temple in Jerusalem of Judea."

Silence, utter and astounded, greeted the pronouncement. Petronius surveyed the hall with equal silence.

Mary Mark felt as if her heart were standing still.

In the Temple? A statue of Caligula, a Roman emperor? In the Temple of the Jews? Never! It would mean national rebellion and mass martyrdom! She glanced toward Barnabas and Joseph reclining on one of the dining couches in front of her. They were as unmoving as statues themselves, their eyes riveted on Agrippa. His face was a mask of distorted disbelief and dismay. So stunned was he, in fact, that his look bordered on one of terror. But seated next to him, Manaen's face was oddly unmoved. There was no surprise, no stupefaction showing. His face was absolutely expressionless, as if he had known ahead of time what was on the scroll and welcomed the pressure it placed on Agrippa. But across the great hall, near the couches where Agrippa's children were, John Mark stood up, took his leave of Mariamne and left the hall.

10

The general reaction to Petronius' reading of Caligula's decree was rejection, immediate and total rejection!

A hue and cry went up from all the people of Jerusalem. Every religious faction, every political persuasion threw aside traditional differences. Sadducees, Pharisees, Zealots, conservatives, and nonpartisans, Jews and Gentiles alike agreed in their disapproval and rejection. Rebellion threatened.

But Publius Petronius turned deaf to all protests. He stood firm in his warnings against rebellion. "There will be travail and tragedy if rebellion is pursued!" he declared, ordering the legionnaires he had brought with him to bolster the Roman troops already in Jerusalem. Then he went searching for a Greek sculptor to create the statue Caligula wanted. "It will save the cost and drudgery of transporting it from a sculptor in Damascus or Antioch," he explained when Agrippa tried to dissuade him by warning again of a national revolt.

But he remained adamant. "It is the emperor's order to have the statue made and placed in the Temple. I am the emperor's consul and governor of Syria. I shall obey the imperial order."

Agrippa later complained loudly over this to Manaen in the presence of Thaumustus and Chuza. "I thought your friend Publius Petronius was a sensible man!"

"Ordinarily he is," Manaen answered.

Agrippa cursed.

"This may not be an ordinary circumstance for Petronius, Your Excellency." Manaen suggested.

"He seems to have all power," Agrippa contradicted.

"Only because he heeds the order of his emperor," Manaen said carefully. "In this instance, Petronius may be obliged to protect his own position with unquestioning obedience while someone else finds a way to change the emperor's mind about this statue business."

"Who can change Caligula's mind?" Agrippa fairly snapped out the question.

"You, sir!"

"Me?"

"Yes, Your Excellency."

"Why me? What about protecting my position? Why me?"

"Because of your friendship with the emperor."

Agrippa narrowed his eyes in appraisal of Manaen.

"We have heard that he holds you in great esteem, that you have been friends for many years. And we have also heard that you have great influence with him."

Agrippa continued to watch Manaen as though uncertain of his sincerity. Manaen returned the searching look.

Thaumustus stepped forward. "A suggestion, Your Excellency, if I may."

Agrippa gave approval with a glance.

"No one wants a national revolt, especially not now at such an early date in your reign, sire. Chuza has suggested that you might call together the leadership of the Sanhedrin along with four or five other leaders here in Jerusalem and ask their help in finding a solution to this situation."

Agrippa arched an eyebrow in skeptical interest.

"This whole thing has many ramifications, sire. The support of Jerusalem's leaders, whatever you decide should be done, will be of value to you."

"The men I have in mind don't want a national rebellion

any more than you do, Your Excellency," said Chuza.

"But how can they be helpful?" Agrippa asked.

"There often is strength in numbers, Your Excellency."

"For what? To outfight the Romans?"

"Persuasion, sir."

"Persuasion?"

"Yes, persuasion. Without it, what hope is there to get Caligula to change his orders? And yet, if he doesn't, we surely face a national disaster."

"Chuza is right, sire," Thaumustus urged. "The emperor's statue simply must not be placed in Jerusalem's Temple."

And so it was that a meeting was held that would be a turning point in all their lives. Included in the meeting were the procurator Vitellius, Jonathan representing the priesthood, Nicodemus, Joseph of Arimathea and Gamaliel representing the Sanhedrin, Barnabas, and James from the community of Jesus-believers in the absence of Peter and John who were still in Samaria. James' presence may have been a mistake. It was the first face-to-face meeting between him and Agrippa. Their reaction to each other was mutual—instant dislike. Perhaps the dislike was generated by the naturally skeptical look on James' face or the rashness of his comments. Or perhaps it was Agrippa's open scorn for those "who believed a dead prophet had come back to life and had the power to rule the world." Whatever the reason, the dislike between Agrippa and James was immediate and obvious, as if it had been foreordained.

Gamaliel tried to ease the tension by opening the meeting with a subject he knew everyone agreed on: a reminder of the riots in Alexandria that had been ignited by attempts to deny the Jews of that city of their full rights to citizenship. Though it led directly to the heart of the matter they had all come to discuss, it turned out to be an unfortunate choice.

Agrippa nodded, recalling the incident in full detail. "Later, in fact just a few months ago, the emperor once more attempted to place statues in the Jewish places of worship. A contingent of Alexandrian Jews went to Rome to explain their customs to the emperor."

"I remember that," Vitellius confirmed. "I was in Rome at the time. The Jews tried to explain that their beliefs would not allow them to sacrifice to Caligula, but that they would be very glad to sacrifice for him."

"And how did you assess Caligula's response?" asked Agrippa.

"I assessed his response as quite negative."

Agrippa began to laugh.

The men looked sharply at him.

"In fact, it would not surprise me to hear that Caligula would think any Jew failing to recognize his divinity a lunatic." He laughed louder. But the humor of it escaped all his visitors.

Color rose in James' face. Joseph's look turned hard. The merest flicker of dislike flashed in Manaen's eyes. "It's not a question of lunacy," Gamaliel firmly interceded. "It's a question of honoring what you believe. Jews believe there should be no statues in their synagogues."

"I agree with you, rabbi. If for no other reason than to keep the peace, I agree with you!" He threw up his hands in mock surrender. It was a gesture unneeded and condescending; it served only to strain the situation more.

Joseph narrowed his eyes.

"Is that your only interest?" James asserted, spitting out the words as an indictment. "Keeping the peace?"

Agrippa swiveled in his chair. "What other reason do I need?"

James made a further indictment. "None, I suppose. You have never worshiped as a Jew anyway!"

Dark splotches of anger appeared in Agrippa's face. "And

I understand that these days neither do you!"

The elders of the Sanhedrin cast worried glances at each other. Barnabas shot a warning glance toward James.

"Where his excellency worships is not the question," Chuza said quickly. "The question is how far Herod Agrippa is willing to go to honor the customs of the Jews in these troubled times."

The tension eased a bit.

"He would not have asked you to come here if he was not sincere in his search for a solution."

"Manaen!" Agrippa called out, turning abruptly. "As half brother to my uncle and having served for so many years in the royal court, what do you think the solution is?"

"It is as I've said before. I think you should go to Rome and persuade Caligula to change his mind. You are the man who can get him to rescind this inflammatory order."

"And you, Chuza? What solution do you see?"

"You are probably the only man in the empire who can get Caligula to change his mind, sire."

"And you, Thaumustus, what is your opinion?"

"The same, m'lord."

"And I presume the rest of you have come here to add numbers to these opinions, is that it?"

The others, with the exception of James, nodded agreement.

Agrippa shook his head. "And what do I get out of it?"

Jonathan, the high priest, straightened in his chair and gave a wan smile. "We have a proposition for you, m'lord Herod Agrippa."

"A proposition?"

"It is a simple plan in which each group represented here achieves something it wants."

"Go on."

"The plan is this. If you will go to Rome and persuade Caligula to change his mind about having his statue placed in our Temple, we of the priesthood and of the Sanhedrin pledge to you the greatest prize of all."

"And that is?"

"Civil peace in Jerusalem." He said it in an even, quiet, placid manner.

But it had a jolting effect on Agrippa. He straightened and leaned forward tensely. "Civil peace? No extra tax tribute? Just civil peace?"

Jonathan nodded. "Rome desires such peace in its provinces, almost even more than additional wealth."

"And the credit before Rome's powerful senate will be all yours, Agrippa," Joseph inserted. "That kind of credit can do nothing but add to your reputation in both senate and the imperial court."

There was a moment of hesitation; then Agrippa gave a great laugh. "What do you take me for? A total buffoon? You know as well as I that you can't guarantee civil peace. You've never been able to, and certainly you can't now. Not with that rebel Pharisee from Tarsus back in Jerusalem!"

Gamaliel's eyes went wide.

"And not with all the public preaching of the Jesus-believers, like your friend James here. Civil peace? Guaranteed? That is no proposition. That is foolishness." He gave another scornful laugh.

James started to argue.

Manaen stopped him. "It may be different now. The Sanhedrin has made a solemn bargain with the Jesus-believers."

"What kind of bargain?"

"The Jesus-believers will stop their public preaching on the Temple Mount and in the streets. They will restrict their preaching to individual homes. In turn, the Sanhedrin will put a stop to the harassment and the persecution of the Jesus-believers. Most of it has been spurred by the Zealots and Pharisees, including Saul of Tarsus."

For the first time, Agrippa looked as if he might take the proposition seriously. "Is this all true, Joseph?"

The merchant nodded. "Furthermore, the Sanhedrin also agrees to patrol and to contain the actions of all Zealots and Pharisees with its own Temple guards and soldiers. There will be no added expense for the royal court."

"And this includes the rebel Pharisee, named Saul?"

"It does," Joseph confirmed.

Agrippa leaned back in his chair, considering the proposition. The expression on his face was set and unchanging, making it impossible to read his reaction.

Gamaliel stood as still as a statue. James shifted impatiently from one foot to the other. Joseph rubbed at his beard, and Jonathan gave a wan smile as if such a simple act might move Agrippa to speak.

Finally, Agrippa got out of his chair, paced to the one long window in the meeting room and stared out for several moments. When at last he turned back to them, he looked at each man in turn as if assessing whether or not he could really do what he promised.

"So you pledge to keep the peace, do you?"

No one said anything. No one moved.

"Very well, I will go to Rome. But I warn you, civil peace is the price you must pay to me. If your part of the bargain is not kept, I shall exact a different kind of price. From each of you." Closing off any further discussion, he abruptly turned and left the room.

"Where can we find your student Saul of Tarsus?" Joseph asked, turning to Gamaliel.

"Somewhere on the Temple Mount, I suspect."

"Then, let us be about finding him. If we intend to keep our pledge of civil peace, we must first get Saul out of Jerusalem. And keep him out!"

They bid farewell to the others and went in search of Saul. As Gamaliel had suspected, they did indeed find him on the Temple Mount and very near the entrance to the Chamber of Hewn Stone. Joseph excused himself and walked away while Gamaliel told Saul about the bargain just made with Agrippa.

"Why do you tell me all this?" Saul demanded.

"Because we want no more of your persecution and troublemaking where the Jesus–believers are concerned."

Saul spat.

"This is not just my personal wish. The entire Sanhedrin wants you to stop your persecution of them."

"Agrippa will never keep his bargain with you!"

"We're not talking about Agrippa. We're talking about you, Saul of Tarsus."

He shook his finger in Gamaliel's face. "And I am telling you I am not bound by this so–called bargain. I'm not a member of the Sanhedrin."

Gamaliel refused to let anger overtake him. "But surely, Saul, as a good Pharisee you would not want to see a statue placed in the Temple. Surely, your views have not changed so much that they cannot appreciate civil peace."

"You are foolish, Gamaliel."

"I must agree," Joseph said, coming up behind them, accompanied by two Temple guards.

Both men turned. Gamaliel appeared to be surprised at his old friend's apparent disloyalty. Saul was genuinely gleeful at this unexpected support.

But the reactions were sifted and winnowed like chaff from wheat by Joseph's next words. "You are foolish, my friend Gamaliel, to think that a hardhead like this Pharisee could have a thought wider or deeper than his own prejudices."

Astonishment washed Saul's face. The high forehead wrinkled resentfully.

"He thrives on persecution and harshness. You know that. He has proven to be of that attitude."

"It has ever been so," Gamaliel agreed.

"But it is more so now." Joseph stepped closer and pinned Saul with a penetrating gaze. The Temple guards moved closer, too, watching Saul in a predatory way. "We are giving you two choices, Saul of Tarsus."

"What choices?"

"The choice of going to prison or the choice of leaving Jerusalem — for good!"

Saul looked stunned.

"Your days of persecuting people who believe differently than you are over. There will be no more persecution of the Jesus–believers in Jerusalem," Joseph said, clearly threatening. "We have pledged our word that the persecution will be stopped! One way or another, it will be stopped. You Saul, will be stopped."

Gamaliel confirmed it. "He speaks for the entire Sanhedrin, Saul. It is our part of the bargain with Agrippa to keep Caligula's statue out of the Temple. If this bargain should fail, you will see a bloodbath unlike any you have ever imagined. It will destroy good Jews and bad, Sanhedrin and priesthood, Sadducee and Pharisee."

Saul's eyes went wide with disbelief.

"It will even destroy you, Saul of Tarsus! As I said before, you have two choices — prison or leave Jerusalem."

Saul now sought relief from Gamaliel, but there was none. The two Sanhedrin elders stood united in their resolve to rid Jerusalem of him. Finally he shrugged and raised his hands in a gesture of surrender. "I . . . I . . . I choose to leave Jerusalem, but . . . "

Not yet convinced, Joseph asked, "Where will you go? And when will you go?"

"Why, I'll go to . . . to . . . Damascus, I suppose. Yes, to Damascus. And I'll leave at once. But . . . "

"But, what?"

"I'll need letters of introduction."

"To whom?"

"The leaders in Damascus. The teachers. I know no one in that city. And I should like to continue my studies."

"Your studies? Or your persecutions of those who don't agree with you, like you did with that boy Stephen?" Joseph's accusation came hard and sharp.

Saul's face went white.

Gamaliel interrupted. "That is past, Joseph. Leave it. Let it go. Let's give Saul his letters and be rid of him."

11

The Year 39 A.D.

Agrippa succeeded in persuading Caligula to change his mind. The statue was not placed in the Temple. National rebellion was avoided; civil peace prevailed.

The community of Jesus–believers, as promised, held all of their gatherings in private homes. The Sanhedrin held tight security on the Zealots and other fanatics. Even the Romans seemed to enjoy the unusual quiet and relaxed their rough ways. Except for the occasional theft by a street urchin or a family argument somewhere, the holy city was peacefully at rest.

In the impressionable mind of John Mark, it was a miracle, one he could see and hear and feel. And it was all because of Herod Agrippa. "He's a great king! Mariamne is so proud of him. I think he should be acclaimed a national hero!" he enthused one day to his mother and uncle as they inventoried a caravan newly arrived from eastern lands.

"His greatness as a king will depend on what he bargained with," said Barnabas.

"What he bargained with?" John Mark's eyes were wide with a puzzled expression.

"Yes, what he bargained with."

"But—"

"You surely don't think he just walked in and told Caligula that he couldn't put his statue in the Temple. Or do you?"

"Well, I—"

"Well, he didn't. He had to have something to offer to

Caligula in exchange for his changing his mind."

John Mark's eyes widened even more, enhancing the naive expression on his face.

"Oh come, John Mark!" Mary Mark cut in rather sharply. "Don't put on such an innocent face. You are man enough to know the basic dealings of a good trade."

"But what would Agrippa trade?"

"That's my question," said Barnabas.

Mary Mark turned back to the basket of goods she was inspecting and began to count.

"What would he trade?"

Barnabas shrugged. "It could be any number of things."

"Like what?"

"A promise of more tax tribute. The naming of a city for him. A gift of several new slave girls to become his concubines. Any number of things."

"But whatever it turns out to be," Mary Mark put in, "you can be certain it will not benefit anyone but Agrippa and Caligula."

"He may be a better man than you think, my mother!"

She glanced at him, trying to guess the depth of his hero worship, and decided not to push him. "You may be right. In fact, I hope you are right."

He looked surprised.

"As long as you persist in seeing so much of his daughter, I must persist in my hopes that he is a better man than I think he is. Otherwise . . . " She raised both hands, palms upward, in a familiar gesture of maternal resignation.

John Mark's face darkened. He mimicked her tone and gesture. "And I must persist in my hopes that Manaen is a better man than I think he is! Otherwise . . . "

"Don't speak that way to your mother!" Barnabas ordered.

"It's all right, my brother," Mary Mark contradicted. "It is time we talked this out. Here. Now."

"There is nothing to say, my mother."

"There is everything to say."

Adamant, John Mark shook his head. "I dislike your friendship with Manaen as much as you dislike my friendship with Mariamne. There. It is all said."

Persisting, she went to him. "It is precisely because of those dislikes that we must talk this out."

He stood his ground, looking her squarely in the eye.

The thought went through her mind that she was face to face with a grown man, not with the child she still often perceived him to be. "We must not let these dislikes come between us."

"Does that mean I must give up Mariamne?"

The bluntness of his candor was more than she had expected.

"If it does, then you must give up Manaen."

"John Mark!" Barnabas cautioned. "You're being foolish. Your mother is no mere child toying with someone's affections!"

John Mark wheeled. "And I suppose you think I am."

"Not necessarily. The situations are entirely different."

"In what way?"

"I think Mariamne is toying with your affections," Barnabas said.

Dismay flooded John Mark's face. "You don't even know her!"

"I don't have to. I see the changes in you made by her influence."

"And so do I," Mary Mark agreed.

John Mark made a swearing sound.

"That's one of the changes I see in you. You have never sworn, ever. But you do now. You have never given your allegiance to someone so removed from your family and the beliefs you have been taught. But you do now."

His eyes clouded with defensive anger.

"I don't ask you to give up Mariamne as a friend." Mary Mark went on, her voice persuasive in its sincerity. "But I do ask you to keep a tight rein on your heart where she is concerned. I fear for you. And I pray for you."

Faced by such unyielding love, he could not answer. He wanted to run to her, to feel her strong embrace, and have her tell him that everything would be all right as she always had when he was a boy. But he was a man now. He could no longer afford such displays of affection. She might see it as a sign of weakness. If she didn't, Barnabas certainly would. He turned and walked away, not knowing what else to do.

Barnabas called after him that the inventory was not yet finished.

"Let him go, my brother. Let him go." Mary Mark said, putting a restraining hand on his arm. "He has much to think about."

"I hope he'll think of what I said about the girl toying with his affections."

"Do you know that for certain?"

He gave her a funny, surprised look. "How certain do I have to be? Logic tells me how this 'friendship,' as he calls it, will end."

"And what else does logic tell you?"

"Logic tells me that sooner or later, he will want to marry the girl. Agrippa will not allow it. John Mark is not royalty. The girl already understands this, yet she leads him on. She toys with his affections."

"You may be right."

"And that makes him vulnerable beyond description." A hurt expression came onto Barnabas' face, as if some nostalgic memory stirred in him.

Mary Mark pretended not see the look, knowing it would embarrass him. She pulled a short, three-legged stool from one of the baskets and sat down on it. "How do we help John Mark?"

The hurt expression disappeared. He straightened. "Maybe this is the time for me to actually make that trip to Cyprus and take him with me."

But Mary Mark shook her head. "We'll have to find some other way to help him. There are just too many things to deal with here. How could I manage without you, Barnabas? And without John Mark, too, for that matter."

The unprecedented peace in Jerusalem had encouraged many conversions for it had created a climate of freedom for people to learn more about the teachings of Jesus. Peter and John were back in Jerusalem. John had returned directly from the extended stay with Philip in Samaria. Peter, on the other hand, had gone westward to the coast and then south where he visited several coastal cities preaching and teaching and healing Greeks as well as Jews. But at last he, too, returned.

"We're especially glad you're back," Mary Mark told him, explaining how rapidly the number of believers was growing. "With Saul and his fanatical friends gone, there is peace in the city. We can scarcely keep up with the new converts. Those who were fearful have come to us now."

And indeed they had come in such numbers that the safe houses were filled to overflowing and more were sought out. Not a single day passed now that Mary Mark's house was not in use for teaching and prayer sessions. Joanna was spending so much time away from the palace that Chuza was beginning to complain that he never saw her. Manaen, Barnabas, The Seven, and all the leadership of the community were teaching new converts. Even Joseph of Arimathea was pressed into service as a teacher from time to time.

During one such session, a courier came looking for Joseph to tell him of a new outbreak of riots in Jamnia. A statue of some sort had been set up in the entrance of the documents repository, where the rabbinic and historical documents of the Jews were stored. They had been transferred there from Jerusalem and from the great library in Alexandria because the village of Jamnia was considered more peaceful and thus safer for these important records. Now they were threatened by the rioting and fighting between a band of fanatical Greeks and some Jewish Zealots.

"Why do you bring this news to me?" Joseph asked the courier. "Why not the high priest? He's the president of the Sanhedrin."

"It's not prayers we need, Honorable Joseph, nor a judgment of law. We need camels and other pack animals to remove all the documents to a still safer place. The chief keeper of the documents told me to tell you that!" The courier paused to catch his breath and then hurried on to explain. "He also says he needs men to put down the riot and that you would know whether or not to bring the Romans with you."

"No Romans," Peter said emphatically when told about the courier's message. "Having just come from there so recently, I can guess who's behind this. Let's take only men from among our believers and from among your caravan men. If we can contain this ourselves, so much the better. The peace has been too good to have it ruined by a handful of hardheads."

And so it was that Joseph and Peter rounded up a hundred men and dozens of animals and made their way to put down the riots in Jamnia before the Romans could mix in it. Barnabas remained behind with John, James, Matthew, and Manaen to lead the ever-growing band of faithful in Jerusalem. He even called on John Mark to help him with the teaching, considering the experience might have a good effect on the boy. "It will be good for him to have to read from the Torah to those who cannot read and to new converts," he said, when Mary Mark asked why he did it.

John Mark found himself so busy that the time he could

spend with Mariamne was sharply reduced. He fussed about it, but he was faithful to the chores Barnabas gave him.

Mary Mark noticed it and said a prayer of thanks. She realized that he would have to learn his own lessons of life and that family protection had only limited boundaries. But this diversion of his attention and his energies to something other than Agrippa's daughter gave her an unmistakable sense of relief.

Within days of the departure of the group for Jamnia, a second courier came to Mary Mark's house looking for Peter. He was from Damascus. In Peter's absence, he gave the news to Matthew, James, and John—news none of them believed.

"Saul has been converted!"

"That Pharisee claims to have been infilled with the Holy Spirit!"

"It can't be true!" James exclaimed. "No matter how reliable the courier."

"No matter how reliable his source in Damascus!" John agreed, running his hand through his thick red hair. "Can you believe such a wild story?"

"Who is the source in Damascus?" Barnabas asked.

"Ananias."

"He is a true brother."

"I know . . . but, Saul? Converted?"

"Please, tell us the whole story. Start at the beginning," Mary Mark said.

"You start, Matthew. It was the courier who talked to you first."

Matthew nodded and swiveled around on the bench to face them directly. "This is what he told me. As Saul neared Damascus, a sudden light from the heavens flashed around him. He fell to the ground, and he heard a voice saying, 'Saul, Saul, why are you persecuting me?' Saul wanted to know who was asking. And the voice said to him, 'I am Jesus whom you are persecuting. But rise and enter the city, and it shall be told what you must do.'

"The men who were traveling with Saul stood speechless. They heard the voice, but they saw no one.

"Saul got up from the ground, and though his eyes were open, he could see nothing. So the men who were traveling with him led him by the hand and took him into Damascus.

"For three days, he neither ate nor drank, and he had no sight.

"Now Ananias said the Lord spoke to him in a vision and told him to arise and go into the Street Called Straight and inquire at the house of a man named Judas for a man from Tarsus named Saul. He told him that Saul would be praying. While he was praying, he saw in a vision Ananias coming and laying hands on him so that he might regain his sight." Matthew paused and glanced at James and John to see if he should continue or if they wished to finish the report.

"What did Ananias do?" Mary Mark asked as James and John motioned for Matthew to continue.

"He argued with the Lord!"

"He argued?"

"He argued with the Lord by saying he had heard from many people of all the harm Saul had done to the believers here in Jerusalem, and other places, too, and that he carried papers to the priesthood in Damascus to persecute believers there."

"And what did the Lord say?" Barnabas wanted to know.

"The Lord told him that Saul was his chosen instrument to bear his name before Gentiles, and before kings, and before the sons of Israel! And further the Lord said he would show Saul how much he must suffer for his name's sake."

"And so," John picked up abruptly as Matthew paused to consider the gravity of the word of the Lord, "Ananias did as the Lord told him. He went to the house in the Street

Called Straight. He laid hands upon Saul, and said to him, 'Brother Saul, the Lord Jesus who appeared to you on the road by which you were coming has sent me so that you may regain your sight and may be filled with the Holy Spirit.' And immediately there fell from his eyes something like scales, and he regained his sight. He arose and was baptized, and he took food and was strengthened."

Mary Mark took a deep breath and sat back. It was an incredible story—but not so incredible that it surpassed the power of the Lord, she reminded herself.

Barnabas, ever the thorough one, asked, "Where is Saul now? Is he still in Damascus?"

"He stayed there for several days," James answered, "preaching in the synagogues. If you can believe it, he preached the word of Jesus in the synagogues. He gave his testimony. And he confounded the Pharisees and Sadducees by proving that Jesus is the Christ!"

Barnabas nodded, a smile playing about his lips.

"But he incensed the Jews."

"I can well imagine!" Mary Mark put in.

"They plotted to kill Saul. But our brothers there helped him escape, and they think he went into the deserts of Arabia."

"Let us pray he stays there," James offered.

"Shouldn't we send word of this to Peter and the others in Jamnia?" Barnabas asked.

"They won't believe it anymore than we do."

"Thomas and Bartholomew will think it's a trick of some kind dreamed up by Saul. And I may agree with them," James declared. "What do you think, Barnabas?"

"Ananias would have no reason to lie to us."

"The Lord works in myriad ways . . . " Mary Mark said almost to herself.

The apostles looked at her searchingly.

"You sound as if you believe this story!" said James.

John leaned toward her, his youthful face earnest with questioning. "Mary Mark, you're a very special woman. But knowing what you do about Saul of Tarsus, having seen firsthand what he has done to so many of our brothers and sisters, and knowing what he did to Stephen, do you really believe that a man like that can be reformed?"

Abrupt self-consciousness came, drying up her throat. She glanced about at all of them. Shyness tempted her to shake her head and say nothing when almost beyond her will and through the dryness of her throat she heard herself say, "When you and Peter were the Lord's instruments for the healing of the man lame since birth, did you really believe that?"

12

The controversy that arose over the genuineness of Saul's dramatic conversion grew in direct proportion to the number of people hearing about it. Most of the Sanhedrin and all of Jerusalem's priesthood publicly scoffed at the event. Privately, they congratulated each other over being rid of a thorny fundamentalist who had proved to be a dangerous embarrassment to them. Whether or not the conversion had actually happened did not matter. The important thing was that Saul of Tarsus had publicly aligned himself with the heretical followers of The Way. "Good Jews," they said, "no longer have to claim that fanatic as one of their own."

The irony and treachery inherent in that reaction was not lost on those who were sincere followers of The Way. They felt Saul's conversion was yet another trick of some kind, one that might even have been perpetrated by the Sanhedrin. They found the reported conversion demeaning to Jesus and to their adoration of him. Saul was their enemy, a persecutor hated and feared. Why should they believe he had changed? And why, on the remote chance the report was true, should Jesus forgive such an angry and evil man? Forgiveness was a gift Saul would never deserve. The report of the conversion had to be a treacherous lie.

The same fear and mistrust prevailed among the leaders of the community of believers. To a man, the twelve apostles agreed that the conversion was a diabolical trick.

Among The Seven however, Prochorus, Nicanor, and Nicolaos believed that Jesus just might use such a man as

Saul who was so well schooled in the traditional laws and rituals. Why not choose the persecutor Saul of Tarsus for such a dramatic conversion, they argued. But Timon and the rest believed none of it. They were adamant in their rejection of Saul's conversion.

Joseph of Arimathea expressed no opinion but rather sat and listened to all viewpoints. Only Barnabas and Mary Mark believed the reports and kept their minds open.

When John Mark questioned his mother about her views, she explained, "To doubt that Jesus has the power to make such a change in a person is to doubt the healing he wrought in me, and in Joanna, and in so many others."

"But you were never an evil person like Saul of Tarsus!" John Mark protested. "You never persecuted anyone. You never killed anyone!"

"Then the need to heal Saul of his evil thoughts and actions was even greater than the need to heal me of the wounds of widowhood, wasn't it?"

He looked bewildered.

She went to him. "The great miracle of Jesus is his capacity to turn every obstacle into an opportunity for victory."

He searched her face, trying to comprehend.

"Saul, by his own choice, was an obstacle. Now, by Jesus' choice, he is the opportunity for victory with the Gentiles."

"Does that mean that men like Saul will quit putting statues in holy places? Does that mean the Gentiles will quit making riots, like in Jamnia?" John Mark asked.

"It means that more and more people will begin to learn about Jesus, and the power of his teachings will change their lives. They will act differently."

"If Saul does make the Gentiles stop their rioting, he might even become a national hero. Like Agrippa," John Mark grinned.

She considered her son for a long moment, uncertain whether he was trying for humor or if his understanding of things spiritual was more shallow than she'd ever realized. If it was the latter, her prayers for his understanding needed to be more frequent and more specific. She turned away and walked out into the small courtyard at the back of the house.

John Mark followed her. "Is the comparison between Saul and Agrippa a valid one, my mother?"

"It gives me an unsettled feeling," she said, realizing that it was a natural enough comparison for him to make. He'd been raised, as she had, in a setting where politics and religion were almost one and the same, where ritualism often overshadowed the spirit of attitudes and actions it was intended to honor and symbolize. Until Jesus came along. He taught a different theme. Would John Mark ever recognize that new theme? Would he ever take it for his own to shape his life? How strange that such distant occurrences could affect her household. Saul and Agrippa. National heroes, indeed!

"Isn't that what everybody is always so concerned about?" John Mark pressed. "Stopping the riots? Keeping the peace?"

She nodded. "But there is more to it than that."

"What more?" he wanted to know, coming to sit down with her on the bench near the fountain.

She looked at him carefully, wondering if this was a time he would be receptive to her words, or if he would scoff impatiently and turn hard and unhearing as he so often did these days. "What more?" he asked again.

"Do you remember one time when you were a very little boy, maybe only six or seven? You had a toy camel that had been broken somehow."

John Mark nodded. "I remember. I loved that toy. Father brought it home with him from one of his journeys. He'd had Kedar carve it for me from a small piece of olive wood."

"That's the one," Mary Mark smiled.

"I was very sad when I broke that toy."

"Do you remember who mended it for you?"

He thought for a moment, then glanced at her with a sharply quizzical expression.

"Do you remember?"

He nodded. "Jesus did."

"Yes, on a visit here in this house. With skilled, strong hands, he mended the toy. But in the doing of it, he also mended something else, something far more important. He mended your broken heart. He took away your sadness."

"Yes . . . but . . . " he slowly shook his head. "I don't see the connection."

"The connection is this. By converting Saul, Jesus is mending many broken hearts. He is taking away the sadness and the fear from many people. His purpose is more far-reaching than making Saul a national hero, John Mark. Just as his purpose in mending your toy was much more far-reaching than the toy itself. He has but one purpose—to teach the ways of the Kingdom to all people. Even to Saul. And through Saul, to hundreds and thousands of Gentiles that you and I will never know, and in places that you and I will never go. Do you see the connection I make? And do you see why it's important to you and to me?"

He looked at her for such a long moment without saying anything that she decided she'd once more had no effect on him, that he thought she was silly, too serious, or foolish. But within another moment, he leaned toward her and gently kissed her brow. "I do see the connection, my mother, and why it's important to you." He stood up, ready to leave, then hesitated. "And it's important to me, too, even though it is such a distant event."

Another distant event, unknown to either of them, was occurring at that very moment a thousand miles to the west. It also would affect them both.

The emperor Caligula had just learned about the riots in

Jamnia and the destruction of his statue. He considered it a personal offense. In the first place, he had allowed Agrippa to talk him out of putting his statue in Jerusalem's Temple. Later regretful of that action, he had sent word by swift couriers to his coastal commanders in Palestine that his statues were to be placed in holy places all along Palestine's coast.

Since there were no statues of the emperor in Palestine, not even in Roman headquarters at Caesarea-by-the-Sea, all the existing busts of the Greek god Zeus had been bought in order to obey the imperial command. They felt quite comfortable with this ploy. It was well known that Caligula fancied himself the reincarnation of that most ancient and powerful of Greek gods. It further seemed appropriate that bands of disgruntled Greeks should be pressed into service for the task of physically placing the statues in those places the Jews held in highest esteem. Jamnia had been their first choice because of the importance Jews placed on the documents of their written history.

But now word had come back to Caligula that his likeness, his image, had been destroyed. "Those damnable Jews!" he raged. "They've destroyed my statue! Desecrated my godhead! "Where's Agrippa?" he demanded.

"He's on his way back to Jerusalem, sire!" answered the royal consul. "He was sailing to Sidon and then going by land. He wanted to visit Tyre and other cities, and . . . "

"I should have known he couldn't keep the peace in Palestine. I should never have believed he could. I should never have let him talk me out of putting my statue in Jerusalem's Temple. I have been betrayed!"

"But sire, Agrippa only promised to keep the peace in Jerusalem, not in the entire land," the consul attempted to remind him.

"Do you suggest that I have a faulty memory?"

The consul apologized, reckoning that defense of an absent potentate was not worth having Caligula's unreasoning anger turned toward himself. Then he attempted to appease Caligula by turning the conversation to subjects known to be more pleasing to him: gossip of whose wives were being unfaithful among the members of the senate, which husbands had new concubines, and a recitation of the latest ribald stories.

The attempt failed. In the middle of the recitation, Caligula rose from his couch, shouted for a scribe, and began dictating a royal edict concerning the fate of Agrippa and the promotion of Publius Petronius to procurator of Judea. Agrippa was reduced to a mere tetrarch of Judea, Galilee, and Perea, the same title and territories his exiled brother–in–law had held. Marcellus Vitellius was demoted to second–in–command under Petronius, even though he was to remain in Palestine. Petronius remained as governor of Syria with his headquarters in Damascus.

So far as the followers of The Way were concerned, this newest change was welcomed. It was a blow against Agrippa. It limited his power. Manaen was one of their own, and his continuing friendship with Petronius could always be helpful.

"But let us not crow too loudly," Peter warned those who gathered in Mary Mark's house to discuss the matter. "There is always danger for us in changes like this."

"Aye," Thomas concurred. "Agrippa can turn meaner than normal and start his own persecution."

Anger shot through John Mark. Agrippa wouldn't do such a thing. Why was Thomas always so negative and skeptical?

"One good thing has come out of it, if you ask me," James said. "Agrippa has been put in his place."

"But he doesn't know it yet, most likely," Manaen reminded them.

"Unless a messenger has caught up with him somewhere on his return journey," Joanna said.

"Either way, he'll be the last to know he's been demoted."

"That's even better!" The malevolent glee in James' face

underscored his dislike of Agrippa. "It adds more insult to it all!"

John glanced at his brother and frowned. "Deserving or not, he still has power. Agrippa is still a man to be careful of."

"Aye!" John Mark muttered under his breath, interpreting John's words as being in support of Agrippa. He was glad that someone else recognized that Mariamne's father was still a person to be reckoned with. It reinforced his own sense of loyalty toward him. He was truly sorry that Agrippa had been demoted, that the territories he ruled over had been reduced from seven to three, and that most of his mother's friends thought of Agrippa as a monstrous pagan to be feared. Maybe, in a way, John did, too. Everything else he'd heard lately was against Agrippa. That kind of talk had been going on all over the city. Even Mariamne had heard it. She was hurt by it and had asked him about it. He'd softened things as much as he could. And now, he could tell her the good thing John had just said. It would help to cheer her up.

And he needed for her to be in a good mood when he saw her next. It would make it easier to talk to her. His heart pounded in sudden anticipation of what he had determined he would say to her. The question he intended to ask her was so important to both of them.

Of course, he'd have to talk first with his mother. He glanced across the room to where she sat between Manaen and Joanna, and for the hundredth time reminded himself that it was custom and courtesy to talk to his mother first. He had started to talk to her earlier in the day before all these friends came. He shifted around on the plain wooden bench, fighting off an onslaught of impatience, wondering again why he didn't just go to his mother now and tell her he had to talk to her. He wanted yet this night to go to the palace to see Mariamne. He had tried before to tell her what was in his heart, but the right moment simply had never presented itself. Tonight, though, he intended to find the right moment. He wanted so much to see Mariamne, to talk to her and tell her of his love.

Once more, he glanced across the room toward his mother. Peter was now leading the conversation and had brought up the question of whether or not the apostles should return to the Temple Mount for their preaching. Her interest in the conversation seemed to flag, for she was glancing about at their friends in a detached way. When her eyes met his, she smiled briefly and appeared to reinterest herself in the conversation.

John Mark got to his feet, carefully made his way to her, and leaned close to whisper. "I must speak with you, my mother."

She questioned him with a frown. "Right now?"

He nodded. Manaen and Joanna both turned to look at him.

He felt suddenly hot, embarrassed that he had so completely interrupted their attention. He regretted his impetuousness, fearful now that his mother would be irritated over the interruption and that the irritation would cast its shadow over what he so desperately needed to talk to her about. He straightened, waiting for her to get to her feet, and then led the way out of the room.

"All right, John Mark," she began once they were in an adjacent room with the wooden door firmly closed. "You've been acting strangely for the last three days. And now this interruption . . . "

"I apologize, but what I . . . "

"What you have to say better be important."

"It is."

"Well—what is it?"

He took a deep breath, gathering his courage, wanting his voice to sound steady and strong.

"What is it, John Mark? What is so important that you take me away from our guests?"

"I . . . uh . . . I need to talk to you."

"Yes?"

"I . . . uh . . . What would you . . . What I mean is . . . "

She stepped close to him and took his hand. "Whatever you need to ask, please do it. I cannot read your thoughts."

"It's Mariamne, my mother."

"Oh?"

"I want to marry her. I'm old enough. I'm almost seventeen now. I'm going to ask her this very night. I wanted you to know first so that you and Uncle Barnabas can make the necessary arrangements with her father."

There. It was said. His voice had even sounded steady and strong. He felt pleased with himself and now was eager for her reaction.

But there was none. He had expected her to say something. Or at the very least to do something, like turn away. Or walk away a few paces. Or gasp. Or frown. Or something. She did none of these things. She simply stood looking at him with a pitying expression in her eyes!

Behind him, the wooden door creaked as someone opened it. He didn't turn to look, fearful that in doing so he might miss his mother's next reaction. He wanted her approval so badly. But the look of pity in her eyes baffled him. He did not accept it. How could he?

Why should she pity him? Mariamne was a beautiful and loving person. He already knew in his heart that she would accept his proposal of marriage. Why should his mother's eyes hold such a pitying look?

The sound of the wooden door being softly closed came to him. Disappointment mixed with irritation as he watched his mother glance toward the door. A hint of relief filtered across the pitying look in her eyes.

"Forgive this intrusion," his Uncle Barnabas said, coming to them, "but Joseph has arrived. I knew you would want to welcome him to the house, Mary Mark."

"Of course. But first, John Mark has something most important to tell you." She hesitated, looked at John Mark, and waited for him to tell Barnabas the important news.

He shuffled about, glancing at his uncle, then looking quickly away, feeling foolish and embarrassed.

"He wants to marry," his mother interceded. "He wants you and I to make arrangements with the girl's father for a wedding."

"And the girl is?"

"Mariamne. Eldest daughter of Herod Agrippa."

The look that went between his mother and his uncle was one of immediate and private disapproval. He felt a sense of defeat. The look combined sympathetic understanding for his feelings with the harsh recognition that such a marriage would defy custom, tradition, and the realities of living.

To his astonishment, however, his uncle's response belied that interpretation. "Are you in love with her?" he asked.

"I am."

"And she with you?"

"I think so. Yes . . . I'm sure so."

"And how will you support her?"

He looked hard at his uncle. That thought hadn't crossed his mind. He'd just not thought that far. But, of course, it was a perfectly good question. How would he support her?

Barnabas came to him, put his arm across his shoulder, and led him to a bench at the far side of the room. His mother followed.

"A long time ago, John Mark, when I was a lad about your age, I fell in love with a girl as beautiful as your Mariamne. When I asked my father to make arrangements for me to marry her, he laughed at me, called me foolish, and pointed out that the girl's family was from a different class.

They had a different background; they had different customs. They weren't acceptable to my father."

"Did that make you love her less?" John Mark asked on a note of rising defensiveness.

"On the contrary, it made me want to marry her all the more."

John Mark looked to his mother for confirmation.

"Being in love is not easy for any of us, John Mark," she said gently.

"Why didn't you marry her, my uncle?"

Barnabas shook his head, a faraway look in his eyes.

"Our father threatened to disown him," his mother said.

"But if you really loved her . . . " The accusation was clear in his words.

Barnabas, however, took no offense. "Being disowned was not the threat for me that you might think, John Mark."

"But apparently it was for the girl," Mary Mark said. "Or for her father."

"Her father, I think," Barnabas went on. "He was the one who took the threat of my being disowned seriously. He refused to allow the marriage. He sent his daughter away from the island of Cyprus to visit relatives."

"And our father sent Barnabas to Jerusalem for the first time to make trading arrangements with the man who later married me and then, even later, became your father."

"The point we both really want you to understand, John Mark, is that the decision to marry is not yours."

He bridled. "Whose is it?"

"Agrippa's."

"But he's not back yet from Rome," John Mark protested.

"Even if he was, I doubt you'd get his blessing." His mother's voice was soft, compassionate.

John Mark looked from one to the other of them in open disillusionment.

"We both understand how you feel," his mother said,

coming to him. "The heartbreak of such a thing is a deep wound. All that your Uncle Barnabas and I can do is to let you know that we do understand and that we care."

13

As so often happens with unfulfilled matters of the heart, the final decision about whether or not John Mark would marry Mariamne turned on an action totally remote from their relationship. It turned on Caligula's deposing of Agrippa as a king.

The news of Caligula's action caught up with Agrippa at Caesarea–by–the–Sea on his return journey from Rome. His reaction the news came in three stages—astonishment, anger, and fear.

The astonishment came from the fact that his longtime friendship with Caligula meant so little. The anger came when he realized that the demotion was based on a whim. Fear asserted itself with the recognition that the imperial court would no longer have any loyalty toward him. It was the latter that bothered him the most, for without loyalty from the imperial court, he had no assurance that he would even remain as tetrarch. And that meant his wealth as well as his position could once again be taken from him. He had no wish to be poor. That idea upset him beyond measure.

He would have to do something to ensure his continuing wealth. The only satisfactory possibility that came to mind was to arrange marriages for his daughters to the sons of wealthy, ruling families. Since Mariamne was the eldest, her marriage would have to be arranged first.

Until now, he had watched her budding romance with John Mark with approving amusement. The infatuation between the two seemed mutual. There was an innocence about their relationship that called to mind his own first love so long ago. But now Caligula's action changed things. For his own political and financial protection, he must make different arrangements for Mariamne. And he must do so quickly. There was nothing as unwelcome as a deposed king with three daughters to marry off.

As soon as he arrived back in Jerusalem, he sat down with parchment and stylus to personally write to the Parthian court and to the court of the kingdom of Armenia regarding the availability of his eldest daughter as a suitable marriage partner for one of their young princes. The fact that he was outspoken and direct in these letters was neither thoughtless of Mariamne's feelings, nor rudely intrusive to those to whom the letters were addressed. It was simply a matter of expedient necessity. The fact that he personally did the writing, rather than using one of his scribes, indicated the seriousness with which he held the matter of a suitable marriage for his eldest daughter. And the fact that he asked Chuza to personally deliver the two letters and to wait for replies before returning to Jerusalem indicated his need for discretion and secrecy.

"Thaumustus tells me that I can trust you implicitly," Agrippa said to Chuza, handing him the two letters to read before sealing them with the royal signet.

Chuza acknowledged the compliment and read the letters. He remembered what Joanna had told him about John Mark's infatuation with Mariamne and thought what a blow this would be to the boy. But it would be a relief for Mary Mark. He wished there was some way he could let her know. Obviously though, there was not.

"How soon can you set off on this journey for me?" Agrippa asked, eyeing him carefully.

"Within the day, I should think, sire. I shall ask Manaen to take over my duties here at the palace. He knows my job as well as I. And he, too, is a friend Thaumustus trusts, I believe."

Agrippa gave an ironic laugh.

"Sire?"

"It amuses me that you, closest confidante to my brother–in–law Antipas, and Manaen, half brother to Antipas, should turn out to be among my most trusted advisers. Next to Thaumustus, of course."

Chuza gave a slight nod.

"I would have thought you'd hate me, be my enemies. But you've proven in many ways that you serve this court with diligence and loyalty. Why is that, Chuza?"

Chuza's round face shimmered with a smile. The tone of his voice was light, carefully humorous. "Self–preservation, sire?"

Agrippa laughed, wished Chuza a good journey, and ended the audience.

The journey lasted several weeks in spite of the fact that Chuza traveled on horseback with only one attendant and no pack animals. Their mounts were Arabians, intelligent, swift, sure–footed, and blessed with incredible stamina. From Jerusalem, they went southeast through the Judean wilderness, across Edom to the oasis of Dumah in the deserts of Arabia, and then followed an ancient trade route east–northeastward to the beautiful city of Babylon and the court of the Parthians.

Response to Agrippa's letter came quickly from the Parthian king. With it in hand, Chuza and his attendant set out northward through the lush valley of the Euphrates to the city of Edessa and the court of the kingdom of Armenia.

Once again, a response to Agrippa's letter came quickly. And now Chuza and his companion turned southwestward to Damascus, Caesarea Philippi, Tiberias on the shores of the Sea of Galilee, and on down through Samaria to the province of Judea, and finally to the city of Jerusalem.

Agrippa's face beamed with satisfaction as he finished reading the responses from the kings of Parthia and Armenia. "Well done, Chuza! Both royal courts are interested in having my daughter Mariamne and her sisters as well for their royal sons." He turned to Thaumustus. "How quickly can preparations be made to send all three of my daughters on a visit to the royal courts?"

"We can begin at once, Your Excellency."

"Do so. I shall tell my daughters of the invitations sent to them by the kings of Armenia and Parthia."

John Mark did not learn all of this until he met Mariamne in the Agora in the Upper City the next day. At Agrippa's request, Chuza and Joanna had arranged the meeting and chaperoned them from a discreet distance.

"I have been told I must say farewell to you," Mariamne said quietly.

"Farewell?"

"My sisters and I have been invited to visit the royal courts at Edessa and in Babylon."

"Babylon?" John Mark's eyes went wide with disappointment. "That's very far away."

"It will be a very long visit, too, I fear. You must not follow this time." Crystals of tears shimmered in her eyes.

John Mark's heart lurched. Mariamne turned her back to him, as the tears spilled onto her face in tiny shatterings of sadness.

He stepped close to her, so close that the scent of lavender in her hair engulfed him, made him feel weak and yet yearn in desperation to hold her. "But you will come back, won't you?"

With a shake of her head, she murmured, "They will marry me off."

His breath caught in his throat. His dream was ending. This beautiful girl, with whom he'd shared so much of himself, was to be taken from him forever. He moved still closer to her, encircled her waist with his arms, buried his face in the softness of her hair, and let his own tears mix with its exquisite scent. For the longest of moments, they remained embraced in painful sadness, helpless against a custom more powerful than their feelings, hopeless because of a future without each other.

From a nearby arcade in the Agora, Chuza and Joanna watched the farewell with a mix of emotions—regret and relief—that the relationship finally was ending.

"I must go and tell Mary Mark," Joanna said, wiping at her eyes with the corner of her shawl. "You will see that Mariamne gets safely back to her father, won't you?"

She started to move away, but Chuza took hold of her hand, stopping her. "My pet, don't you think it would be best for John Mark to tell his mother about this?"

A startled expression came onto her face.

"As of this moment, the boy has lost everything," Chuza said, his face pale with seriousness in the quickly softening light of the vanishing day. "He needs to be able to tell his mother about his loss in his own time and in his own way. It is his right. It is his need."

The startled expression on Joanna's face altered. "Of course. Of course, he does. And Mary Mark needs to hear it from him, not from me. Of course." She squeezed Chuza's hand and smiled at him. "You're a kind man, my husband, You grow kinder with each passing year."

"I love you for noticing." Chuza let go of her hand. "Come now, we must rescue those young people from each other and return them to their families."

Two days later, the caravan taking Mariamne and her sisters away from Jerusalem departed at daybreak. From a hillock outside the walls of the city, John Mark watched it plod northward on the Damascus road until it was lost to his view. He then turned homeward with a feeling of desolation and the notion that he must now tell his mother. Surprisingly, he found her sympathy and compassion helped ease his despondency. What was more surprising, she really seemed to understand the depth of his misery.

He wondered at it, especially in view of her opposition to the friendship. Finally, he decided that her understanding came from her own experience of losing her beloved with the death of his father. Now that he had experienced something similar, he began to understand how desolate she must've felt all these years. The reason for the loss, by death or by the opposition of custom, didn't matter. What did matter was that such a loss carried with it a new bond of shared experience not easily described. He tried.

Hiding out in a corner of the great storage room one day, he tried to describe his feelings in writing, but it was useless. He was too direct, too blunt, too plain in his use of words. He could describe *things* very well, he decided. But *feelings* . . . ? In disgust, he threw aside the parchment and the stub of charcoal. All the years of study in the School for Scribes' Apprentices were good for nothing more than inventorying merchandise and writing down what others told him. Why had he bothered? Even Dathan and Onan could do that.

More important, why had his mother bothered to cajole and encourage and order him to spend so many years in the school? What a useless expense it had all turned out to be. And what a useless man he was turning out to be!

Barnabas had been right. Even if it had worked out that he and Mariamne could have married, how could he have supported her? At what kind of work could he earn enough to support any woman? He had no trade, except that he could read and write. The business belonging to his mother and Barnabas and Joseph was profitable, but he really wasn't interested. What was his life all about? What was he supposed to do with his life?

He'd asked his mother that question when he told her about Mariamne being sent away. But her answer only confused him.

"The Lord has a job for you to do, John Mark," she'd said. "He has a purpose for your life."

"I wish he'd tell me what it is!"

"He will!" she replied in a serenely confident tone. "He will lead you to what you are to do. But . . . you must be ready to follow him."

Then she'd gone off to join the other women in prayer. It seemed to him they were always praying about something.

He still felt bewildered about his purpose in life. He leaned over, retrieved the parchment and stub of charcoal, got to his feet, and started back across the big storage room to finish counting the latest bundle of pouches brought in from the leather workers. Halfway across the big room, a new thought struck him. This prayer business—it seemed to work for others. It worked for his mother. What would happen if he prayed? He hadn't prayed in a long time, except in a group when he was helping Barnabas with his teaching of new converts. But what would happen if he prayed about his personal problem? What would happen if he prayed in a personal way? A memory of his mother praying came to him. Those prayers were personal. And they were simple, like she was talking to a friend, like she was opening up her heart and mind without fear. When she prayed, she made Jesus seem so real that sometimes he had looked around to see if the prophet wasn't actually there, again in their house sitting on a bench listening to her and talking to her.

She was always alone when she prayed like that. Once he'd asked her why. She replied, "Jesus told us not to make a public fanfare of our praying."

He stopped walking and glanced about. No one else was in the big storage room. He was alone. He listened for a moment, making sure that none of the servants were still sorting bundles somewhere behind the bales of goods. But he heard only a silent, peaceful emptiness. "Lord . . . " he began in a quiet tone, glancing around again, feeling foolish and self-conscious. He cleared his throat and started over. "Lord . . . uh . . . Jesus . . . uh . . . this is John Mark talking to you. You may not remember me. It's been a long time. But . . . uh . . . I need help. I need to know what to do with my life. My mother says you have a purpose for it. I need to know what it is, Jesus."

He hesitated, wondering what else, if anything, he shoud say. He'd stated his need. That would be enough. Now, it was Jesus' turn. Yet the prayer somehow seemed incomplete. He thought for a moment, trying to recall how his mother ended her prayers; and then it came to him. She always used one little phrase: "Praise be to you, O Lord, for knowing my needs and for providing for them out of your great riches." She always said it with such a tone of confidence that he knew she fully expected all her needs would be met.

Now he spoke the phrase aloud, forcing a tone of confidence into his own voice. It reverberated around the big storage room and came back to him as an empty echo. Disappointed, he turned and made his way into the main part of the house.

From the large room near the front of the house, the sound of voices came to him. He went in that direction, curious about who was visiting so early in the day. Two strangers stood in the center of the room talking with Barnabas.

One of the men looked vaguely familiar. He wore a plain brown tunic under a cloak the color of a brindle goat. From the cincture around his waist dangled a scroll pouch, from which protruded a bundle of styluses. A small pouch of charcoal was attached. The other man was a total stranger. John Mark stopped at the entryway, out of their sight, but within listening range.

"This feeling of caution you speak of Barnabas does not surprise us," the stranger said.

"Oh, it is more than caution they feel, Ananias," his uncle replied in an unusually brusque tone. "They feel disbelief and mistrust."

The man who looked vaguely familiar made a sound of protest.

Barnabas faced him. "The apostles simply don't believe you are a changed man, Saul."

Saul? So that's why he looked familiar. Now he remembered where he had seen him—at the stoning of Stephen. But there was something changed about him. A ripple of shock went through John Mark. He moved about to get a better view. The Pharisee was far from handsome. He was small in stature with shoulders and arms disproportionately developed. His head was too large and half bald. His eyes were oddly set. And the dark brows above the eyes were a straight, unbroken line. But what was it that seemed changed about him? In the next instant, he asked himself what difference it made. The man was Saul of Tarsus. Saul! He resented his very presence in his mother's house.

"I didn't believe it either. Not at first." Ananias said, stepping toward Barnabas. "I, too, argued with the Lord when he spoke to me in a vision and told me to help this man. And when the Lord told me that Saul of Tarsus was his chosen instrument to carry his name to the Gentiles and to kings and even to the children of Israel, I could scarcely believe it was the Lord talking to me."

Barnabas looked from one to the other of the visitors, as if judging their sincerity with his silence.

"But on faith, I did as the Lord told me. Now, on faith, I am here in Jerusalem with Saul, or Paul as he now prefers to be known, to help him meet and talk with the Lord's own Twelve."

"They refuse to see Saul for good reason, Ananias."

"But you can talk to them! You can explain to them that the man's conversion is real!"

"I have to believe it myself first."

Saul stepped toward Barnabas. "Can't you take me on faith, my brother?"

The question had the sound of arrogant challenge in it. Impulsively John Mark stepped through the doorway. "Can I be of help, my uncle?"

Barnabas turned in surprise. John Mark went to stand beside him, a little surprised himself. He seldom interrupted when visitors were in the house. And he nearly always tried to avoid confrontations. But in this instance, he felt the need to defend his mother's house and to stand side by side with his uncle against Saul of Tarsus.

Barnabas introduced him and then continued his conversation with the visitors. "Ananias, you honor me by thinking I have enough influence with the apostles to get them to change their minds."

"Then you do take me on faith?" Saul interrupted with persistence.

Barnabas smiled. "No, Saul. But I do take the Lord on faith, just as Ananias has."

"Then you will help? You will meet with Peter and the others on Saul's behalf?" Ananias asked.

"First I will pray about it. Then I will let you know my decision. Where can I get word to you?"

"At the house of Zacchus the cheesemaker in the Lower City."

John Mark followed as Barnabas led the men out of the house, through the courtyard to the main gate that opened onto the street.

As the men stepped through the gateway, Saul hesitated, glanced about and said. "To think, Barnabas, I used to spy on this house with the intention of destroying it."

"What stopped you?"

"At the time, I thought it was the pressure of your friends who are members of the Sanhedrin. Now though . . . I think it may have been a far more powerful force."

He turned and followed Ananias down the street.

John Mark questioned Barnabas with a look.

"Yes, he was talking about the Lord."

"And you believe the Lord protected our house?"

"Absolutely. He still does."

John Mark narrowed his eyes, speculating on the depth of his uncle's faith. He had known for some time that his mother believed that this was true. He'd scoffed when she mentioned it again only a few days earlier. But he'd never even wondered whether or not Barnabas felt the same way.

"Come along, John Mark, and help me to pray about whether or not I should help Saul."

"Me?"

"Why not?"

"I'm not very good at praying."

"You believe in the Lord, don't you?"

"I believe in the man Jesus."

"That's where it all starts," Barnabas replied, turning again toward the house.

By the time evening of the same day approached, Barnabas knew in his spirit what he should do. Taking John Mark with him, he went to the house of Zacchus the cheesemaker, gathered up Saul and Ananias, and took them to Peter's house near the Viaduct.

All twelve of the apostles were there, having just finished a meal together. They were still at the table in comfortable companionship. There was much laughter among them. Their spirits were high, and their greetings to Barnabas and John Mark were warm and friendly. But as they moved around to make room for them at the table, they saw Ananias and Saul. And they recognized Saul. Instantly their attitudes cooled to wariness and suspicion.

"Why, Barnabas?" Peter demanded. "Why do you bring this persecutor into my house?"

"For good reason."

"What reason?" Thomas asked.

"To kill more of us? Like he killed Stephen?" James charged.

The others began protesting all at the same time.

Barnabas stood firm, holding up his hands, trying to quiet them.

Watching, John Mark realized something else new about his uncle. He was a man of courage as well as a man of deep faith.

Barnabas moved forward into the crowd at the table, climbed up on a bench, and finally shouted above their clamor, "Hear me out!" It was not a request; it was an order.

They obeyed. One by one, they ceased their angry talk and most of them reseated themselves. Only Peter, James, and Thomas remained standing.

Barnabas took his time, looked each apostle squarely in the face, and demanded by the look that they settle their anger and listen to his words. "My nephew and I would never knowingly bring harm to any one of you. You should know that. The house of John Mark's mother has shielded you, harbored you and your families for many years. We shall continue to do that, because we, like you, are believers in Jesus and what he taught. But Jesus offered his teachings and his way of living to all kinds of people, Not to just a special few. He even offered the teaching of his word and his way of living by that word to persecutors like Saul of Tarsus."

James started to protest again.

Barnabas stopped him. "Ananias is well known to you. He is one of our own brothers from Damascus. He will tell you of his role in the transformation Jesus has wrought in Saul. It is a miraculous change. This man who stands before you is no longer Saul of Tarsus, a Pharisee, a persecutor. This is a man named Paul to whom Jesus spoke on the

Damascus road. Because of that encounter with the Lord, he is a transformed spirit who now preaches fearlessly in the name of Jesus in many places."

The sincerity of Barnabas' words had caught them all up. Awed silence hovered in the room, as each man recalled his own personal experiences with Jesus, and how those experiences had changed his life. The silence grew. Some of the apostles looked away apologetically as their recollections lengthened.

John Mark straightened and stepped forward. His voice was quiet and sure, the voice of a man. "My uncle and I ask only that you let Paul now speak for himself."

The awed silence turned to astonishment. The apostles all looked at John Mark as if seeing him as a man for the first time. Ananias and Paul exchanged questioning glances. On Barnabas' face was a smile of surprised approval. His nephew had taken a mature, public stand for Jesus for the first time.

But the others were not so ready to accept John Mark's endorsement. Nor for that matter were they ready to accept Barnabas' endorsement of a man who for so many years harassed and threatened, maimed and murdered. The reflective mood brought on by Barnabas' plea quickly melted as the heat of unhappy recall began to rise among them.

"Changing a man's name doesn't change the man," Andrew reminded him.

"And how do we even know that this is truly our brother, Ananias from Damascus?" James questioned. "None of us has ever met him."

"I have!" Barnabas defended.

"It's not Ananias that bothers me," Nathanael charged. "It's that other one!"

Anger and suspicion hovered among them, ready to break forth, barely constrained in spite of their respect for Barnabas.

"Your memory is short, Barnabas," Thomas called out.

Matthew turned to him. "Have you forgotten the hundreds of families that fled because of Saul?"

A general hubbub of protest finally broke the constraints of respect, and many began to recount Saul's acts of persecution. "How could you forget them?" Jude yelled out over the angry noise and comments.

"You and Mary Mark ... and even this boy here ... helped most of those families. How could you forget about them?" Bartholomew charged.

Barnabas held up his hands, trying to quiet them. And though the noise began slowly to abate, the heat of anger and suspicion still was present like a heavy cloak about to bind them all in its restless vengefulness.

Out of this came John's sharp-tongued, acid question. "And how could you forget about Stephen?"

Barnabas snapped around. Paul's face went white. His eyes bulged in anguish, the straight black line of his eyebrows an emphasis to sorrow and regret. Ananias looked as if someone had hit him very hard in the belly and knocked all the breath out of him.

Barnabas turned slowly to once again face the apostles. "I guess I was wrong to bring Ananias and Paul to you. I guess I was wrong to think these brothers from the north would find acceptance. And I guess the Lord must have been wrong, too, to instruct them so definitely to seek you out."

Stunned silence was the response.

Barnabas tugged at the sleeve of John Mark's robe and nodded to Ananias and Paul. "Let's leave this place. If forgiveness is not among those who knew Jesus best, then a man in need must search for it elsewhere." He started for the door.

"Hold, Barnabas!" Peter ordered in his rumbling voice.

Barnabas hesitated. John Mark, Ananias, and Paul remained where they had been.

"There is wisdom in your words. What is past is past. But

what is present cannot be forced down men's throats. You speak of forgiveness, but you forget that some of us find it hard to come by in a quick manner." He turned and looked down at the much-shorter Paul. "That is a fact you must understand, Pharisee. We know we fall short of the Lord's standards, but you must earn our forgiveness."

Paul nodded. "I understand your suspicions. I don't blame you. Were I in your place, I would feel the same."

The humility of Paul's tone and words struck hard at John Mark. He glanced toward his uncle, checking his reaction, but he could not read the meaning of the look on Barnabas' face.

Peter moved back to the table and sat down. One by one, the other apostles followed, reseating themselves and making room for Barnabas and John Mark to join them. "We will hear your witness, Saul of Tarsus," Peter said. "And of course, we have no control over whether or not you stay in Jerusalem. That is between you and the Lord. What is also between you and the Lord is how you act and what you do as well as what you say—wherever you are."

And so it was that Paul gave his witness to the apostles. Then he stayed in Jerusalem for a while and moved about freely, speaking boldly in the name of the Lord. He talked and debated with the Greek Jews. His words angered them. They plotted to kill him.

Kedar brought this news to Barnabas, and within moments Paul himself was seeking admittance at the front gate of Mary Mark's house. "Sanctuary, Barnabas, I really need sanctuary. Can you help me?"

As they had done with so many of the Pharisee's victims in earlier days, the house of Mary Mark now became sanctuary for him until other arrangements could be made.

"We really should see that he gets safely back to Tarsus," suggested Joseph when Mary Mark and Barnabas talked with him about what to do. "We could send him on the caravan that leaves for Caesarea–by–the–Sea. From there, Vitellius would help get him on one of the triremes bound for Cilicia."

"Praise be!" Mary Mark said with a sense of relief. From having had the chance to observe Paul close at hand for two days, she understod why the apostles still reacted with such wariness of him. He was highly intelligent and that very gift made him frightening to many people, as did his devotion to the teachings of Jesus, for the same fanatic energy that had made him so feared before his conversion now fueled his devotion.

But Paul also was responsible for making many converts while he was in Jerusalem. The generally peaceful atmosphere in the region was continuing. Throughout Judea, Galilee, and Samaria, encouraged and strengthened by the Holy Spirit, more and more new converts joined the community of believers. Even beyond Palestine's borders, their numbers increased.

Nicolaos was sent to Antioch to lead and serve the believers there. And Peter began to plan another journey to the coastal cities.

"I need someone to go with me who can record these events when the power of the Holy Spirit begins to move among the people," Peter said one day to the other apostles.

"Why not take John Mark with you?" Matthew suggested. "He's a scribe of good talent."

"He's just a boy!" James scoffed.

"That was no boy who urged us to listen to Paul that night at Peter's," John contradicted.

But James insisted. "Mary Mark would never let him go."

"I'm not so sure about that." Peter thought of the earlier time when Mary Mark had wanted him to take John Mark away from Jerusalem and the girl Mariamne. Now she might want him to go for a far different reason.

When Peter finally went to talk to her, she responded,

"His heartbreak over Mariamne is mending, I think. But the trip would do him much good."

"He could be of real help to me. I need a scribe. I do not write very well. And the teachings of the Lord and the works of the Spirit must be recorded. Someday those of us who knew our Lord will go to be with him, but his teaching must be passed on just as he told us to do."

"I couldn't agree with you more. And by going, John Mark just might find his life's purpose."

"Then, I have your approval?"

She gave a soft laugh. "You have my approval, Peter. But for a decision, you'll have to ask John Mark. The choice is now his."

14

The Year 41 A.D.

Peace lingered in Judea, Galilee, and Samaria through the first half of the year 41, encouraged by three things. First, Agrippa concentrated so keenly on promoting suitable marriages for his daughters that he had no time for internal quarrels or for a power struggle with Publius Petronius. Chuza and Manaen continued to be helpful in these marital endeavors. That fact ensured their positions of prominence and influence with him. In turn, this strengthened the bonds of friendship between the palace and Mary Mark's household, which from a business standpoint was of immense importance.

As Barnabas pointed out, "Let's be practical. It allows us to hate what Agrippa stands for and still do business with his royal court."

For a second thing, the priesthood and Sanhedrin continued to maintain peace throughout the city because the followers of The Way continued to keep their promise to teach and preach and heal only in private homes rather than on the Temple Mount.

But the third reason was the strongest. The Sanhedrin feared reprisals if the peace was broken: reprisals in the form of higher tribute tax for Agrippa. So all remained calm until the middle of the year 41.

Then the uncharacteristic peacefulness was shattered by an event that took place in Rome. It was an event of such significance that it altered the course of the Roman Empire, affecting all who lived within its boundaries. The emperor Caligula was assassinated!

The despotic, unpredictable, emotionally unstable ruler was a victim of his own vanity. Those he trusted most betrayed him. In a public place and in the brightest of sunlight, his closest advisers embraced him in friendship and stabbed him to death. The praetorian guard quickly moved into the breach of leadership and named Tiberius Claudius Nero Germanicus as Caligula's successor.

"They call him Claudius the Clown and they say he's harmless, the idiot of the court, you know," Joanna confided to Mary Mark on the very day the news arrived at Agrippa's palace in Jerusalem. "The praetorian guards found him hiding behind a drapery after Caligula's assassination. On the spot they proclaimed him their emperor and took him to Rome's senate. There was a great deal of argument, we're told. But finally the praetorian guard prevailed, and the senate granted Claudius the Clown all the imperial powers."

"Will the provinces suffer under his rule?"

"Chuza thinks not," Joanna replied. "He believes that Claudius is not a clown at all. He thinks Claudius is wiser than he has ever let on and that he will be an able leader. And Thaumustus tells us that Claudius is one of Herod Agrippa's oldest and closest friends."

"Caligula was supposed to have been his close friend, too, but . . . "

"It may be different this time. The new emperor has invited Agrippa to come to Rome to see him. Caligula never did that."

Mary Mark looked at her in an oddly questioning way.

Joanna tried to be reassuring. "We may all do better with Claudius as emperor. The longer he keeps Agrippa in Rome, the better it is for Judea. Time will tell."

Whether or not time would prove Joanna's words to be true where Agrippa was concerned, it certainly seemed to have beneficial effects for the community of believers. Special success was taking place in the young church in Antioch. A letter to the apostles had come earlier that very day from Nicolaos. They had brought it to Mary Mark's to share with all the others.

"Nicolaos is doing a good job, isn't he?" Mary Mark asked, as Matthew paused in the reading of the letter.

"Does he ask for any of you to come and verify their conversions, like Philip did when he was in Samaria?" Barnabas asked.

Matthew nodded. "The number of Gentile converts is so large that we can scarcely believe them."

"Not that we doubt Nicolaos," John put in quickly, wrinkling his brow with seriousness. "He would not exaggerate."

Mary Mark glanced toward James to see if he agreed. He'd been left in charge of the community's affairs while Peter was away on his trip to the coastal cities. "Do you believe the numbers, James?" she asked, even though she was sure he would say no.

But he surprised her. "However optimistic Nicolaos may be, he would not deliberately exaggerate."

Joseph and Manaen came through the back gate to join the rest.

Matthew waved the scroll in the air. "Good news from Nicolaos in Antioch. He reports many new converts. But there is more. Just hear this news! These new believers have adopted a name for themselves."

James frowned. "A name? What name?"

Matthew straightened the scroll and read, "Because our beliefs are based on Jesus' teachings, and because we believe him to be the Messiah, or the Christos as the Greeks say, we are calling ourselves Christians."

They all looked around at each other, silently sampling the name, individually assessing their personal reactions to it.

"Christians . . . " Manaen spoke the name out loud, as if testing it for each of them once more. "Christos. Christians . . . "

"I like it," Mary Mark said softly. "We are his followers. The name says so instantly."

"But it's not Jewish," James complained.

John poked him with his elbow.

"Well it's not!" James countered.

"Does it matter?" Matthew asked.

"Some of us aren't Jewish, either," Joseph reminded him, "but I don't remember that it ever mattered to Jesus."

Unconvinced, but apparently not willing to argue the point, James went to sit on a small bench near the fountain without further comment.

"What does matter, it seems to me," Joseph went on, "is that there are so many people in Antioch willing to be called Christians and to follow Jesus' teachings." Joseph turned to Manaen. "You have lived in Antioch. Is there such a hunger as this for the spirit of truth among its people?"

Manaen nodded. "There certainly could be. It is one of the three greatest cities of the Roman Empire. It ranks with Rome and Alexandria in size and in the mix of its culture."

Mary Mark watched him, impressed with his knowledge so casually drawn from memory and in the straightforward way he expressed it. He had no affectations and no need for the overtness of action to prove worthiness that so many men seemed to require.

"We should send someone to confirm it," James said.

John agreed. "Just as Peter confirmed Philip's work in Samaria, I think we should confirm the work of Nicolaos in Antioch."

"Can you go to Antioch, Manaen?"

"Regretfully no, Joseph. With Agrippa off to Rome again, I am obligated to certain duties in the palace here."

"What about you, Barnabas?"

"I would be willing from a business standpoint to go. Several of our traders in and around Antioch should be visited. But, with John Mark away on the trip with Peter, I . . . " He looked at Mary Mark.

She smiled back at him, urging him to consider going. "The Lord told us to tell his story wherever we could. And then he sent his Holy Spirit for us to share with others when they are ready to receive him. There must be many Christians in Antioch who are ready, my brother. You can help them. I can manage here for a while."

Barnabas' departure for Antioch came quickly after the meeting in the courtyard. For the next several weeks, Mary Mark found herself managing both household and business affairs almost alone. To be sure, Joseph of Arimathea was in and out from time to time. Manaen was at her beck and call, but with Agrippa absent from Jerusalem, work for him and for Chuza at the palace seemed to triple. He visited her less frequently, though when they were together, he was as attentive as always. Fortunately, Joanna was available and more than willing to help with the prayer groups that still took place regularly at the house.

But the day–to–day routine of managing warehouse workers and household servants fell to her. For the first time in many years she realized how dependent she was on other people. In spite of her perception of personal independence, she realized that nothing she did affected only her. She had to admit to a renewed sense of interdependence. It gave her cause for thought and brought into focus just how much she missed Barnabas and John Mark and her daily visits with Manaen.

She walked slowly through the house, wondering at this unaccustomed sense of lonesomeness. It was a feeling different from the loneliness she had felt just after Yonah died. That kind of loneliness had a sharp, empty quality about it that scourged the far depths of her soul and darkened her vision of every future moment with a black fear.

"Love heals, and faith abides," she whispered, recalling what Jesus had told her when he healed the wounds of her widowhood. And it was true. Never again had she experienced the same painful emptiness. The lonesomeness that now embraced her had only a nostalgic quality, a bittersweet yearning for companionship. It was limited, transitory, bearable. Her wanderings through the house brought her to the main doorway. Beyond in the courtyard, Sallu supervised the work of three gardeners who were pruning the pomegranates and the hibiscus. She stepped out of the house to watch for a moment.

Patches of clouds drifted erratically through the late spring sky, dictating the play of sunlight and shadow and the warmth of the breeze. She tilted her head back, facing the sky, closed her eyes against its brightness, and relished the soft touch of breeze against her face.

"You don't need the sunshine to make you beautiful, Mary of Jerusalem!" With a snap she straightened and opened her eyes. A short distance away, John Mark stood grinning at her. He was taller, tanned, and bearded. Could this really be the boy, her son, who had gone away so many weeks before? And yet, was it possible that he had changed so much in so short a time? Her hand went to her mouth in a gesture of astonished pleasure.

Peter, looming behind John Mark, chuckled. Sallu and the gardeners had stopped their work to wave greetings to the arrivals and stood watching the reunion between mother and son with unabashed interest.

As she started toward him with arms outstretched, he came to meet her embrace. In the next instant, he lifted her off the ground and twirled around, supporting her with arms sinewy and strong. When her feet once more touched the ground, they both were breathless and laughing.

She stood back, holding him at arms' length, taking a good look at him. He was taller, stronger, and bearded, to be sure, but there was something else about him that didn't show quite so clearly, an awareness in the eyes that had never been there before, a gentleness in the tone of his voice that overrode his characteristic bluntness. And there was something else. But what? Was it concern? Was it confidence? Or was it a quality of peace she'd never known him to have?

Peter came up beside them. "Time and distance change us all. But in case you don't recognize him, this is John Mark. I assure you, this is your son!"

"Praise be!

She released John Mark and stood looking at him, delight and happiness racing through her. Then she turned and embraced Peter. "Have you had food?"

"Only a bit of bread and cheese as we walked. We both were anxious to return."

"Then come, let me feed you."

"The young man will eat plenty!" Peter chuckled, winking toward John Mark. "But I must get on to my own house. My good wife will never forgive me if I tarry for a meal."

"Return soon and tell us about your journey," she called after him.

"That I shall." He disappeared through the gate.

Sallu hurried off to tell Rhoda of the young master's return, while the gardeners went back to their work.

"This trip has taught me much," John Mark said as they made their way back toward the house. "My skills in writing and in reading, too, were of great help to Peter. Or so he has told me."

The note of modesty in his voice was unexpected.

"You and Uncle Barnabas . . . " He stopped. "Where is Uncle Barnabas?"

"Antioch." She went on to explain the reason for his trip there as they approached the house.

"He may happen onto Paul up in that territory."

"He already has. According to his last letter, he went up into Tarsus searching for Paul. When he found him, he persuaded him to return to Antioch to teach and preach."

"I hope he'll be careful."

"Your Uncle Barnabas? Careful of Paul?"

He nodded. "Saul was such an evil man for Paul to be such a good one."

"I'm surprised. You stood up for Paul to have his chance to speak to the apostles when Ananias brought him here."

"I know. I did so because of Uncle Barnabas. But Peter still is cautious of Paul, and Peter's wisdom about such a thing should be heeded, I think."

It pleased her to hear the new tone of respect in his voice when he mentioned Peter. At the entryway to the house, a serving girl came toward them carrying a clay water jug to fill the footbath. John Mark stopped, thanked the girl, removed his sandals, and washed his feet.

Mary Mark stood watching him scrub away the street dirt, remembering how many times he had been in too much of a hurry to bother with this sanitary custom and how she and Rhoda both had nagged and scolded him for his carelessness. Those days were probably gone forever. A sudden pang of regret went through her. He had grown up too fast, after all. The boy who went off with Peter weeks before had not come back.

He dried his feet and looked up at her. "Is there food?"

"Plenty." She led the way toward the cooking area and set before him bread, cheese, fruit, and a cruse of wine.

He looked at it and smiled.

She started to turn away. But he reached for her hands,

held both of them in both of his, bowed his head, and quietly said a simple grace.

For all we eat,
For all we wear,
For all we have everywhere,
We thank Thee, Father. Amen.

She knew tears were brimming in her eyes, but she didn't care. They were tears of joy, tears of thanksgiving. If John Mark saw them, they would not frighten him. Now he would understand them.

He let go of her hands and sat down on the bench at the table. "I have much to share with you, my mother."

She sat down opposite him. "You liked being Peter's scribe then?"

He nodded and broke off a wedge from the round of coarse, brown bread. "But I liked even more what he told me about our friend Jesus."

"What did he tell you?" she heard herself ask over the sudden thumping of her heart.

"He told me how Jesus healed his mother-in-law when they lived in Capernaum, how he went up to her and took her by the hand and raised her up, and the fever left her."

A light of intensity had come into John Mark's eyes. Mary Mark wondered at it. It was the same kind of intensity she often had seen in the eyes of the apostles and in the eyes of her friend, Jesus.

"What else did Peter tell you?"

"He told me that Jesus was never too tired to help, that the needs of others always came first with him."

He took a bite of the bread and was silent for a time.

Mary Mark did not move, fearing that to do so would be to break the magic of sharing, yet knowing in her spirit that the depths of what her son had learned these last few weeks could never be completely shared. They were lifetime values that would grow and change and alter yet again as the experiences of years were added to his life. And that was as it should be, she reminded herself, murmuring a prayer of thanksgiving deep in her heart.

"He also told me about Matthew."

"What about him?"

"He was a hated man. Matthew! I couldn't believe it. But Peter said everybody hated him. He was a tax collector. But that didn't bother Jesus. He picked him, anyway, as one of his twelve men." John Mark broke off a bit of cheese, ate it, and then leaned toward her, his elbows on the table. "Matthew even worked for Antipas, just like Manaen did. But it didn't bother Jesus."

She straightened, searched her son's eyes for the familiar look of scornful jealousy. It was not there. In its place was a look of openness and an acceptance she had never seen in him before.

"What I'm trying to say, I guess—" He fumbled with the round of bread, trying to pull another wedge from it, glanced up at her, then as quickly averted his eyes and shrugged. "What I mean is, maybe Manaen isn't such a bad person after all. It doesn't matter that he's Greek. All that matters is that he is our friend."

15

At the close of the year 41, Agrippa returned to Jerusalem from Rome—and he returned in triumph! His title of king had been restored to him, as had all the territories that Caligula had so impetuously taken from him. And this time the endowment of title and territories was in writing and had won the unanimous approval of Rome's senate! Claudius himself had seen to that.

Claudius had considered Agrippa his true friend since boyhood. Now that he was emperor, he wanted to show his loyalty and his affection in a very real way. Restoration of Agrippa's title and territories was the greatest gift he could think of.

Therefore the title of king had been given to Agrippa for his lifetime. The territories over which the title now allowed him to rule would no longer be under the authority of any procurator. For the first time since the days of Herod the Great, no Roman procurator would have any control over the territories of Lysanias, Trachonitis, Aurantis, Decapolis, Galilee, Samaria, Perea, or Judea. Herod Agrippa was now a king in more than title. His power of rule was absolute and all-encompassing.

The effect of receiving all this imperial and senatorial largesse was a restoration of Agrippa's confidence. And he took full advantage of it. He boasted that Rome considered his efforts at marrying off his daughters to the princes of Armenia and Parthia important to its successful rule in those lands. He publicly declared, without the knowledge or agreement of any of its members, that the Sanhedrin considered his kingship the most important political development since the death of Tiberius and the removal of Pontius Pilate as procurator of Judea. He hinted to Jerusalem's priesthood that an increase in the royal tribute tax should be forthcoming at once. He began negotiations with the Sanhedrin for an increased toll to be levied on goods coming into all the territories under his control.

His self–confidence grew into arrogance. He demanded that the Roman commander at Caesarea–by–the–Sea reduce the garrison by one–third to reduce costs. At one and same time, he began to openly denounce the community of Jesus-believers in Jerusalem. He publicly scoffed at the name "Christians" used by the believers in Antioch, and he branded them all as heretics and troublemakers.

"The spots of the leopard remain!" Chuza choked over the words. His round face darkened with frustration. "Agrippa is bent on showing how powerful he now can be. I think he will take action against the believers in Jerusalem on the slightest provocation."

Joseph frowned and rubbed at his beard.

"He is taking himself much too seriously. Who knows? It may even be on a personal basis. Joanna already has warned Mary Mark."

Alarm flared in Joseph's amber eyes. "Not toward Mary Mark herself, surely!"

Chuza shrugged his shoulders. "Who is to say? But I have warned Manaen to take special care about his visits to see her. Agrippa is acting unpredictably. His new power has intoxicated him."

"We will all take care to protect Mary Mark," Joseph said. He rose to his feet. Chuza did likewise and walked with the merchant toward the main gate of the palace gardens. "By the way, my friend, do you know a man named Agabus? A prophet who recently came to Jerusalem from the southern deserts?"

"No, I don't know him. Why?"

"He and two of his fellow prophets came to Mary Mark's house a few days back looking for Barnabas. They'd been told in a vision that Barnabas was a good man and that they should prophesy to him."

Chuza's eyes widened with interest. "Mary Mark, of course, told them he is in Antioch. They thanked her and said they would go on there to find him. But before they left the house, Agabus took Mary Mark aside and gave her the prophecy also." Joseph paused. His amber colored eyes absently searched the air just above Chuza's head.

"Well, what was it? What was the prophecy? Do you know?" Chuza barely kept the impatience from his voice.

"Yes, I know. A great famine is to sweep the land, particularly here in Judea."

Chuza put a hand to his head and gave a moan. "And why not?" With all this new hardness in Agrippa's heart and his greed, a famine would be a just punishment!"

"Too bad that the famine must come to so many. Too bad that it could not come just to the mighty King Herod Agrippa!"

Chuza agreed.

"Is there nothing that you or Manaen can say or do to soften Agrippa's attitude? To get him to balance his lust for power? To put a rein on him?"

The frown on Chuza's face deepened. "Agrippa no longer listens to me nor to Manaen, unless it's something he already agrees with. He does still listen to Thaumustus' advice on most things. But lately, I've noticed that he seems to pay more heed to that man Blastus. I think Thaumustus resents it. I think Agrippa now considers himself above needing advice. He is as jealous of his own opinions as he is greedy for more and more wealth!"

They had almost reached the main gate. Joseph paused, glanced around, and stared thoughtfully across the ornate gardens. "Perhaps there is a way to help ourselves after all, Chuza."

"How?"

"Some of us need to be better acquainted with Thaumustus!"

Surprise filtered across Chuza's face.

"You and Manaen could use another highly placed ally in the royal court, couldn't you?"

Chuza nodded.

"Then, I think we need to help you cultivate that new ally. Perhaps even share a meal with him. After good food and good drink, we might even ask his advice on some matter of importance, like how to deal with Agrippa on the new tax levies or how to put a stop to Agrippa's harangues against the 'Christians' here in Jerusalem."

"But where would we hold such a meal? Surely not in the palace. There are unwelcome eyes and ears everywhere within those walls."

"No, no, outside the palace. The less Agrippa knows about this new alliance, the better."

"I agree."

"What about Mary Mark's house?"

"Would it be safe for Mary Mark and her household?"

"There is no safer house in the whole of Jerusalem."

Chuza looked puzzled.

Joseph chuckled again. "Oh, I forgot you're not one of us yet. You don't know about the shield of the Spirit that's around that house." He clapped Chuza on the shoulder and moved him toward the gateway. "Come with me to get Mary Mark's permission."

Her response surprised them both. "One moment, my friends. We'll need to include the man of the house in this decision."

"Is Barnabas back from Antioch?" asked Chuza.

Mary Mark shook her head. "No, but John Mark is

back from his trip with Peter, and if we do what you're suggesting, he will act as host. He should be in on the decision, don't you think? Let me tell him you're here."

As Mary Mark vanished through the doorway, Chuza looked toward Joseph in astonishment. "I heard the boy had changed," he whispered, "but to call him the—"

"Man of the house?" Joseph shrugged. "If his mother thinks he's mature enough for that job, she's right to turn it over to him."

At that point, Mary Mark returned with John Mark. He greeted Joseph and Chuza and listened with careful respect to their ideas about cultivating a better relationship with Thaumustus.

"It's as simple as this, John Mark," Chuza concluded. "Manaen and I need another ally in the palace. We think Thaumustus is an ally, but we need to make certain that he is."

Without hesitation, John Mark agreed. "Besides, it will be helpful to us, too, Chuza. To Joseph, Uncle Barnabas, my mother, and to me. The trading business can always use more allies."

A look of approval crept into Joseph's eyes. He bowed. "Then you will host a dinner for us?"

"Gladly, sir."

Joseph gave a full salaam, which John Mark quickly returned. Chuza, trying to hide his perplexity at this change in John Mark, hurried to do the same.

And so it was agreed. Plans for the dinner were made. Invitations were prepared and hand-delivered to the small select group. Attending were Thaumustus, of course, Manaen, Chuza, Joseph, Nicodemus the banker, and Peter. With John Mark as host, there were seven of them.

Mary Mark, with Rhoda's help, personally supervised the menu, the cooking, the cleanliness and beauty of the house, and the comfort of the seating arrangements. As she and Rhoda withdrew from the room to supervise the servers, she whispered, "The rest is up to the men — and to the Holy Spirit."

Rhoda clucked her tongue. "I never dreamed I'd see the young master hosting such important people."

Mary Mark gave her a hug. "He's a man now, Rhoda. I can hardly believe it either."

The friendliness of the atmosphere was noticeable from the outset, since all present, except Thaumustus, were friends of such long standing. But as honored guest, even Thaumustus quickly entered into the easiness of mood. "My thanks to you for your cordial hospitality, Master John Mark. I thank you for inviting me. This is my first opportunity to be a guest in a Jerusalem home."

While the fact had not entered into their planning, it was obviously important to Thaumustus that he finally had received a social invitation. Joseph and Chuza exchanged a covert glance of satisfaction.

"And our thanks to you, sir, for accepting our invitation. We all want to know you better." John Mark picked up his wine goblet in a gesture of salute and sipped from it. The others followed his lead.

With the toast completed, Joseph leaned forward and said, "Another toast may be in order also, Thaumustus."

"And what might that be?"

"A toast to his excellency, Agrippa, concerning the matter of the restoration of his title of king over a sizable number of provinces."

"Ah, yes. It is by providence itself that such an occurrence should have come about." Thaumustus raised his wine goblet before anyone else could. And then he added in a jovial tone, "Or, if not by providence itself, then by Agrippa himself was this all brought about, wouldn't you say?"

His candor startled them. The suspected resentment Chuza had reported to Joseph apparently was more real than imagined.

"I sound facetious," Thaumustus went on, "but I am seriously concerned at how m'lord Agrippa has changed since the restoration of his title and his power."

The hesitant silence lasted only a few seconds, for John Mark bluntly asked, "In what way do you think King Agrippa has changed?'

"Politically. And in a competitive way."

"With whom?" asked Peter.

"Publius Petronius, for one."

"Why Petronius?" Nicodemus asked.

"As you know, Publius Petronius is still the governor of Syria. He still holds great power. And he, too, has the full confidence of the new emperor. Now however, since Agrippa has been named king over the northern border provinces, he feels that Petronius' ruling authority should be diminished and that Petronius should begin paying certain . . . uh, shall we say . . . uh . . . homage to him." He paused and looked around at the group. When no one offered a comment, he continued. "But then he believes that the kings of Tyre and Sidon should begin paying him a certain homage too! If he pushes for this, I am fearful for what might happen."

Thaumustus' openness and candor was totally unexpected. A surprised silence again drifted through the room. His remarks deserved some kind of response. But everyone recognized that even though the atmosphere was cordial and Thaumustus seemed very sincere, they had no assurance that their words would not be carried back to Agrippa and used against them at some future time.

"Perhaps you worry needlessly, Thaumustus," Manaen said in a guarded manner. "It would seem to me that Agrippa would want Publius Petronius for a friend. And the kings of Tyre and Sidon, too. They are not as influential as Petronius, but a man like Agrippa needs friends everywhere, I would think."

"I agree with you, Manaen. But Agrippa remembers how stubbornly Petronius tried to follow Caligula's edict about placing that statue in the Temple. And he still remembers what it cost him personally to get the edict changed."

"But now he has his title and his territories back," Joseph inserted. "If he handles it right, Petronius can be of enormous help to him."

"Of course, he can," Thaumustus agreed.

"And the fact that Manaen has such a strong friendship with Petronius should be considered a real asset by Agrippa."

"I agree with you again, honorable merchant. But . . . " He hesitated and made a sweeping gesture that included everyone. "I am rude to bring my doubts about my king into the conversation here. I beg your indulgence."

"No apology needed," John Mark quickly offered."

"Indeed not," Joseph confirmed. "We appreciate your position. We have felt the change in Agrippa's attitudes about the tribute tax and about tax levies on caravan goods."

Nicodemus spoke up. "Most recently he has asked the Sanhedrin for a portion of the interest charged by bankers."

"Perhaps there will be some way these men can be of help to you, Thaumustus, in the days to come," Manaen put in.

Thaumustus raised his wine goblet in an appreciative salute, and the conversation shifted to less serious matters. As course after course was brought in, the talk flowed more and more freely among them with an enjoyment that matched the quality of the food. The hour grew late, and finally John Mark asked Peter to tell about his visit to the coastal cities.

"To tell it all would take a great deal of time, so I will

tell you only what I reported to my Jewish brothers on my return to Jerusalem. They were critical of me and of John Mark, because we had gone into the houses of uncircumsized men and had eaten with them."

"I have been wondering all evening about that, since I am uncircumsized and don't particularly believe in your Jesus," Thaumustus inserted. "How did you explain that to them, Peter?"

"I will tell you, as I told them, simply what happened. I had a vision of this very large sheet being let down from heaven by its four corners. In it were all the four-footed animals of the earth and the birds of the air. Then I heard a voice telling me to get up, kill, and eat. I remember replying, 'Surely not, Lord.'

"But the voice from heaven spoke again telling me that anything that God has made is clean. Three times this happened, and then the sheet was pulled up into heaven, and the vision was over. Immediately after that, men came from the house of Cornelius in Caesarea–by–the–Sea saying the Holy Spirit had brought them to me and that I should go back with them to save all the household. We went.

"And as I began to speak in that house, the Holy Spirit came on that household as he had come on all of us at the beginning." He hesitated as if remembering every detail of this latest vision and the comforting presence of the Holy Spirit. His hesitation lengthened into a pause.

"And then what happened in the house in Caesarea?" Thaumustus prompted.

Peter straightened and chuckled gently. "Well, as I said, the Holy Spirit came on them. And I remembered what the Lord had said about John baptizing with water, but that we would all be baptized with the Holy Spirit. And it seemed to me that if God gave them the same gift as he gave us who believed in the Lord Jesus Christ, then who was I to think I could oppose God? That's what I told the brothers here in Jerusalem."

"They had no other objections, then. They understood that God has granted even the Gentiles repentance unto life!" John Mark's voice brimmed with enthusiasm. Pride for Peter beamed in his face. Faith in the reality of what he had experienced with Peter shone in his eyes.

Behind a curtained screen at one side of the room, Mary Mark had been standing for some time, listening to the conversation. Now at John Mark's comments she caught her breath. Tears of joy sprang to her eyes. Her son truly had come home—not only physically and mentally a man, but spiritually as well. The guests' reaction to Peter's story and to John Mark's assessment of it was a thoughtful silence. Each man sat absorbed in his own interpretation of what he'd heard, each considering the impact on his own soul.

Thaumustus finally moved, giving each of the others a look of dismay. "This no doubt enrages Jerusalem's Jewish leaders," he said.

John Mark glanced at him as if surprised he would say such a thing.

Peter straightened. "I am Jewish. It does not enrage me."

Thaumustus shrugged. "Of course not. You believe in this Jesus who, I am told, also ate with publicans and sinners."

"That is true," Peter confessed. "He did that. And I do believe in him and in his practices."

"Otherwise he would not have shared this meal with you," John Mark asserted.

Thaumustus reddened.

Manaen tried to smooth over the bluntness. "Of course, you're right about people like Jonathan, or Gamaliel, or Zechariah, or any number of other Jewish leaders. They are not as liberal in their thinking as Peter and those others who follow the teachings of the man from Nazareth."

Thaumustus reached for a grape, held it between his thumb and forefinger and inspected it. "I understand he was quite a political issue while he was alive. I hope he doesn't become a political issue again after having been dead for so long."

Every man in the room stared at him, wondering if the comment carried an implied threat.

Manaen breached the startled pause. "In any event, I would doubt that Agrippa would ever make an issue of such a point. He seems to me to be a man of tolerance for others' religious beliefs."

Thaumustus disagreed. "With m'lord Agrippa, religious tolerance is a matter of political strategy. There are more Jews in his territories than those who call themselves 'Christians.' Thus Agrippa will do whatever is necessary to keep the Jews happy. That means that the Christians in Jerusalem should be cautious. They're in the minority. You, sir, for instance." He pointed to Peter. "You should be especially cautious. With his strange new aggressiveness, m'lord Agrippa is quite unpredictable."

In the uneasy silence that followed, Thaumustus reached for another grape, popped it into his mouth, washed it down with the remaining wine, and got up. The rest followed, making their farewells. From behind the curtained screen, Mary Mark stood unmoving as the familiar and unwanted sense of foreboding crept over her again. Had the dinner been a mistake? Would Thaumustus become an ally of Manaen and Chuza? Or was he not to be trusted after all?

When she thought all of the men had left the room, she stepped from behind the curtain calling for Rhoda to have the other servants come and clear the tables.

Manaen was waiting for her. "I couldn't leave without seeing you."

Startled, she turned, her hand flying to her mouth in a defensive motion.

"A thousand apologies," he laughed, coming to her and embracing her, "but ever since you told me about the change in John Mark's attitude toward me, I will make more excuses than ever to be with you."

"What about Thaumustus?"

"Let him get his own woman!"

She blushed. He grinned and gently kissed her.

"Does he know about us?"

"Does it matter?"

"It might." She pushed away from him. "Considering his warning of caution to Peter and John Mark just now."

Rhoda and two serving girls came from the other side of the room and started removing food bowls and goblets.

Mary Mark turned and led the way out into the small courtyard at the back of the house. The night air was cool. Manaen put his arm around her shoulders and pulled her close to him for warmth as they walked. "I'm frightened, Manaen. Ever since Agrippa had Antipas banished, I have feared him. Oh, I suppose at first I thought I just didn't like him because he was so bold. But it's more than dislike—it's fear. I'm frightened for John Mark, and I'm frightened for you."

He squeezed her reassuringly.

"Does he know you are one of us?" Mary Mark asked.

"I don't think so. It's true he doesn't like James, but he hasn't made a single move toward him, or toward anyone else who is a believer. In fact, he may not know the identity of any other believer except for the apostles."

"What if Thaumustus tells him about Peter's witnessing tonight? Won't he be suspicious that other believers were in the group?"

Manaen stopped walking and turned her toward him. "We calculated that risk beforehand."

"And . . . ?"

He shrugged. "We were all invited by Joseph the merchant. He's your business partner, and you're both above suspicion, at least so long as Agrippa keeps getting fat tax money off of your caravan goods and special discounts for merchandise he buys for his palaces."

She lapsed into silence. Money was important. She knew that. But could it really protect them all from an aggressive, inquisitive, power-hungry man like Agrippa? She doubted it. The reasoning seemed weak somehow. And certainly it didn't dispel the lingering sense of foreboding that had come over her just moments before.

16

"It's news from Uncle Barnabas," John Mark shouted, running toward his mother across the big storage room and waving the parchment scroll over his head.

Excitement coursed through her. She turned from the task of checking the quality of the newest wool shipment. Barnabas had been in Antioch almost a year. She had missed him. "Read the scroll to me, my son."

John Mark broke the seal and unrolled it. "My dear sister and nephew. The work here in Antioch continues to go well. Daily many people come to us to begin their praise and worship of the Lord. There is much hunger for his truth. Nicolaos is a good teacher and true shepherd to his flock. He sends his love to you both. The prophecy of famine that Agabus and the others brought to us has resulted in an ingathering of great quantities of foodstuffs for Jerusalem. Paul and I will bring this love offering to Jerusalem for our brothers and sisters who are in need. By time you receive this letter, we will already have started our journey. May the Lord bless you and keep you. Barnabas." John Mark rerolled the scroll and handed it to her. "It will be good to have Uncle Barnabas back."

She agreed, took the scroll, and stuffed it into the pocket of her robe. She would read it herself later and savor the look of Barnabas' precise script.

"There's just one thing, my mother," John Mark said, glancing around the big storage room that bulged with foodstuffs as well as with goods. "I hadn't realized we were having a famine."

"It will come, no doubt. It is the prophecy of Agabus."

"And of other prophets as well. This very day on the Temple Mount, I heard it discussed three different times by three different rabis. They were urging people to be saving of their staple food."

"And how did the people react?"

"They were more concerned over this." John Mark reached into the fold of his sash, drew forth a small leather pouch, opened it, and poured a few coins into the palm of his hand. He sorted through them with his index finger. "Ah, here it is."

She looked carefully at the coin he put in her hand. It was newly minted and bore the likeness of Agrippa's face on one side and his name and title of king on the other. For some reason, it did not surprise her. It seemed quite natural, in fact, that Agrippa would take full advantage of his current state of grace with imperial Rome. On the other hand, she could understand the concern of the people, since traditional Jewish custom considered graven images a sin.

"Manaen thinks Agrippa has made a mistake," John Mark said, watching her careful inspection of the coin.

A riffle of pleasure went through her. It always pleased her when John Mark quoted Manaen. It meant he truly saw something of value in his opinions. And it meant he was establishing a friendship with him.

"Manaen says Agrippa's flaunting his authority and the Sanhedrin and preisthood resent it."

"Do you agree with him?"

"Yes, I think I do." He cocked his head and grinned at her. "You're glad for that, aren't you?"

"I'm glad you don't dislike him as you once did." She handed the coin back to him.

"He's changed."

She smiled, but said nothing about the changes that had

occurred in him in recent months. No need to make him self-concious. It was best to leave well enough alone.

John Mark returned the coin to the leather pouch. "Manaen also told me that Agrippa lets his pride get away from him. He had his own coins minted because his grandfather, Herod the Great, minted his own coins. And since Agrippa now rules as much territory as his grandfather did, he thinks it proper to emulate him in every way. He may even build another wall for the city."

"A new city wall? Where?"

"Around the northern part of the Suburb." He put the leather coin pouch back inside his sash and returned to his work at the far side of the storage room.

Mary Mark went back to checking the wool shipment, but her thoughts were on Agrippa's growing arrogance and the effect it would have on the community of believers. Good or bad, it would have an effect. The whims and attitudes of rulers always had an effect on those who were ruled. Her thoughts were also on the developing friendship between John Mark and Manaen. She welcomed that.

It was strange how the two unrelated subjects seemed to be warp and woof of the same thought–fabric. Perhaps it was because she and Manaen so recently had talked of them both and shared their feelings at a time and place away from the responsibilities that normally commanded their attention.

Riding two of Manaen's beautiful Arabians, they had gone west from the city up into the hills toward Emmaus. The day was still young enough for coolness, but the sky's hint of brassy sheen portended another day of heat.

When they came to an obscure trail that seemed to lead toward a grove of pines and poplars and cedars, they followed it. It led into a small tree-shadowed glen. Along one side of its secluded greenness, a brook traced a thin, shallow course. Huge rocks shouldered protectively along the opposite side. At its far edge in front of them, the ground rose abruptly to form a natural cuplike boundary.

Mary Mark reined her horse to a standstill and looked at the tranquil beauty of the place. Primrose and mallow, white, pink, and softest yellow, peeked shyly from among taller reeds and grasses. The clean pungence of cedar and pine came to her. She closed her eyes and breathed deeply of their fragrance.

"You understand. I can see it." Manaen held his arms out to her to help her dismount.

"What is it I am to understand?"

"The reason I like this place so much."

"You've been here before?"

"Many times. I just happened onto it by accident one day when I was out riding. I found it so peaceful that I've come here often, when I've been discouraged or have had some weighty matter to give thought to."

"When have you ever been discouraged?" She teased him gently and let him lead her to a grassy knoll spreading out smoothly from the base of a tall poplar.

"I'm discouraged now." He sat down next to her.

"Your face is not one of discouragement."

"That comes from hiding my true feelings so often, I suppose."

"From whom?"

"Agrippa. Blastus. And anyone else in the palace I don't trust."

Surprised at the seriousness of both his tone and his words, she turned and searched his face.

"I'm particularly discouraged about Agrippa," he went on, without prompting. "His demands have grown impossible. Not only is he a king—and quite serious about it, as Thaumustus complained at the dinner at your house—but now, he's put on the white shoes, as well."

"The white shoes?"

"The white shoes of a Roman consul. He's become a consul. The emperor Claudius has made him a consul! Can you imagine such a thing?"

It meant nothing to her. The Romans had many titles of which she knew nothing, but if Manaen felt this was important, it must be so. She waited, knowing he would continue and wanting him to.

"Consul to the emperor ranks higher than Rome's senators, Mary Mark! It's a title given only to the most favored. Not even Agrippa's grandfather achieved such an honor."

"And a consul's rank is shown by the wearing of white shoes? How odd!"

"No more odd than the phylacteries worn by self–righteous Sadducees."

She conceded with a nod of understanding. The trappings of office were always odd and always in the way. They were symbols of pride, nothing more. She could remember a time, though, when she thought they did mean something more.

Manaen picked at a blade of grass and crushed it between his fingers. "The awful part of it is that people we need as allies for this kingdom are jealous. They're suspicious of this latest honor for Agrippa. King Aretas, the heads of state of Parthia and Armenia, the kings of Tyre and Sidon, Publius Petronius—they all feel threatened by this occurrence."

"And it will affect our political relations with them, won't it?"

"More than that. It will affect our trade with them." He tossed aside the crushed blade of grass.

The uncomfortable feeling going through her crystallized into the realization that she would be affected personally. Up to this point, her concerns had been for her friends Manaen, Joanna, and Chuza. But now . . . She wondered if Joseph knew of this development. She would wager he didn't. Then she wondered why Joanna or Chuza had not alerted them. "Manaen, did you learn of this just recently?"

"Only last night. Agrippa himself told us. Called us to his private chambers rather late, as a matter of fact. A packet of directives from the emperor had arrived from Joppa at dusk. This appointment of his was among them."

She felt a sense of relief, and immediately following came a sense of guilt. Was her trust in her friends so shallow? Or was it that her self-interest in the trading business was so aggressive? She turned away, pretending to be busy with the picking of a yellow primrose so that Manaen would not see any hint of mistrust or guilt in her face. But his next words caused her to turn back to him with a startled stare.

"The fact of the matter is, Mary Mark, I'm seriously thinking of moving away from Jerusalem. I'm seriously thinking of returning to Antioch."

Her heart stood still. She scarcely breathed. She was flabbergasted. "Move away?" the words came out in a whisper. And she knew the shock must be showing on her face, for as he watched her, the look on his face softened. He began to smile. He picked up her hand and held it with gentle firmness between his own hands.

"You understand, don't you?"

"No. I think not."

"A real man will take only so much. I don't like it when Agrippa makes me look foolish in front of others."

"No . . . you must not go . . . "

"I don't like being told that I offend people when I speak to them or being asked to do trivial things and then being laughed at behind my back. I don't like being asked to help and giving it and then being ignored."

"Agrippa has done that to you?"

"A man should not have to take that."

"Nor anyone." she said sympathetically. "But, Manaen, you must not leave Jerusalem. Not now. Not under such a circumstance."

He ignored her plea. "I've had my fill of Agrippa. He's earned nothing in his life, except by stealing and cheating and lying. Where is the justice in that? Where is the justice in having to serve such a man?"

Now it was she who took his hand in hers. "Manaen, my dearest Manaen."

He gave a heavy sigh and looked away, stared out across the shallow brook beyond the trees to the distant hills of Judea shimmering in the day's growing heat.

"I'm sorry you are so troubled. I wish I knew the words to console you. To give you comfort and bring you peace."

"You could come with me to Antioch."

Startled, she let go of his hand.

"The idea is not so unthinkable," he protested. "I truly care for you."

What was he thinking? What had happened to this man she thought she had grown to know so well?

"I have great love for you, Mary Mark."

She ducked her head, not wanting him to see the tears of disappointment welling up. His angry disillusionment with Agrippa was one thing, but to have him talk of running away and to suggest that she run with him diminished the maturity of their relationship—and just when John Mark was no longer a hindrance.

"I would marry you, of course. We would not just . . . just . . . " He groped for words. "We would not just run away!"

Her throat seemed sealed. Her hands trembled.

"Oh . . . I've gone about this in the wrong way, haven't I?"

Still she remained silent.

"I've expressed my love for you in the most awkward

way." He reached out, brushed away the wetness of her tears, and pulled her close.

She did not resist, liking, as always, the feel of his arms about her—solid, strong, comforting.

"I apologize, Mary Mark. I do apologize. Vanity has no gender, has it?"

By the time they had returned to the city, nothing had been resolved. But they both had their emotions under control and simply talked of things of a much less personal nature. Many months would pass before they would speak again of the happenings of that day. But for Mary Mark, one thing was certain. If Manaen sincerely wished to marry her, he would have to do so because he found something of value in her—not just because he wished to escape Agrippa.

She pushed the memory away and finished sorting through the bales of wool, called for one of the servants to come and finish the inspection, and went off into the house to find Rhoda and Sallu. With Barnabas coming home, preparations of welcome needed to be made. And preparations needed to be made also for the foodstuffs he and Paul were bringing with them. Extra helpers would be needed for unloading and sorting. Sallu could find them among the community of believers. Extra storage space would be needed. She would have to call on Joseph for that. But before she could return to the storeroom, she saw Rhoda open the main gate and usher Joseph across the courtyard toward the house. Quickly she went to greet him.

"I was just on my way to your house. I have wonderful news," she said as he came into the house. "Barnabas is coming home."

Joseph's face brightened.

"Paul will be with him. And they are bringing gifts of foodstuffs because of the famine prophesied by Agabus and the others."

"Ah, good. It will be good to have Barnabas back here

with us again. I have sorely missed him."

"As have I." She moved back into the main room of the house and motioned for Joseph to be seated. "We shall need extra storage space for the gifts from Antioch, don't you think?"

He agreed. "And extra workers, too."

"Sallu can arrange for that among our community."

"He'd better hurry," Joseph frowned.

"Hurry? Why? It will be many days yet before Barnabas and Paul arrive."

"Because of Agrippa."

She pulled her chair closer to Joseph. "What has he done now?"

He leaned toward her. "Our worthy king has taken it upon himself to conscript workers for his new construction project."

"What construction project?"

"A new city wall."

"City wall—oh, yes, John Mark told me of that just a few minutes past. But he spoke as if it was some plan for the future."

"To begin with, it was a future project, at least from what I'm told by Chuza and Manaen. But all this talk about the coming famine that Agabus has prophesied has stirred people up. If there's going to be a famine, they want to leave Jerusalem and go where there is no famine. And of course, if they do that, if a large number leave, there won't be as many people to pay taxes or to buy the sacrificial animals needed for the Temple rituals, or . . . "

She didn't often interrupt Joseph, so great was her respect for him. But this recital of basic economics was unnecessary and quite unlike him. "The point being that the money coming into the palace coffers will be reduced."

"Exactly. So Agrippa has decided that there shall be no mass exodus. He will hold people here by conscripting workers to build his new city wall. Then they can't leave Jerusalem. They will be under conscription to his service."

Mary Mark shook her head in disbelief.

"What is worse," Joseph continued, "is the size and the scope of this project."

"How do you mean?"

"Agrippa is so proud of the fact that he rules as much territory as his grandfather did that he has determined he now shall match Herod the Great's building programs."

"He's not enlarging the Temple, too!"

With a chuckle, Joseph shook his head. "Not yet. But this new city wall is designed to be higher and stronger than any of those sections built by Herod the Great!"

"Oh my . . . "

"Oh my, indeed. Agrippa soon enough will demand more taxes. And I think there is going to be serious trouble with the rulers of surrounding kingdoms."

"They're already upset over his having been made a Roman consul, aren't they?"

"Indeed. And now Manaen thinks that Publius Petronius will see this building of a wall as a threat of war."

"War?"

"In the future perhaps, but war nevertheless."

"Oh, my . . . "

"Once again, whether there is war or not, this kind of unrest and likelihood of more taxes jeopardizes our trading agreements and trade routes. I am concerned about how we protect them this time." With a tired sigh, he leaned back in his chair and stared moodily across the room.

She folded and unfolded her hands, wishing she could help him and understanding his fatigue. He must be well into his seventh decade and he had worked hard all his life, fought for what he believed was right. None of it had been easy. But at least when Antipas was tetrarch, the protection of the trade routes and the caravans had never been a problem.

"Are men like Agrippa sometimes trapped by their own vanity, Joseph?" The question was tentative, related narrowly to an idea gradually beginning to form in her mind.

He glanced at her with curiosity. "Sometimes. What are you thinking?"

"I was just wondering . . . " She groped for the right words. "Does the emperor Claudius know about Agrippa's wall?"

"Hard to say. Why?"

"I wonder if he would perceive it as an aggressive act? The same way Petronius does?"

A slow smile slid onto Joseph's face. "Are you suggesting that we can in some way influence Rome against Agrippa?"

She folded her hands in her lap and cleared her throat. "Not we, but Petronius might."

"He, too, is very close to the emperor. He, too, is a Roman consul," Joseph agreed. "But he would not be foolish enough to go on a direct attack against Agrippa. At least, not all by himself."

"What about the other rulers? What if they sided with Petronius? Would he then take a direct complaint to the emperor?"

Joseph shook his head. "I doubt it. I doubt Petronius would ask such a favor of the other rulers. There are too many other political situations involved."

"Could you get the support of the other rulers for Petronius?"

Again, he shook his head. "My influence as a merchant is not that strong in this situation. And while we could ask Manaen to speak with Petronius, he has no influence with the other rulers."

She nodded. "But Agrippa might."

Joseph arched an eyebrow.

"What I mean is, Agrippa's poor standing with all these other rulers might be used to influence Rome against him, and without his even realizing what is happening."

"So that's why you asked if a man could be trapped by his own vanity?"

She nodded hesitantly. "What if Agrippa hosted a great party for all of these rulers at his palace in Tiberias with the purpose being to cultivate better relations with all of these men? You know, the same idea as the dinner you used to cultivate a better relationship for Chuza and Manaen with Thaumustus. Why can't the same idea be used in this instance?"

Joseph began to nod, understanding what she was leading up to. "But what will show up at this palace party that had no part in our dinner is Agrippa's vain and bragging nature. Am I right?"

She nodded, uncertain and still questioning whether her logic made sense to her old friend.

But he went on. "Your belief is that Agrippa will further alienate himself from his peers and influence them to complain to Rome as a group. Is that what you're thinking?"

"Yes. And that way, Agrippa himself has caused the complaint. Whatever retribution follows, there is a certain safety in numbers."

"And of course," Joseph concluded, "having all those rulers together at one time and one place will give me the opportunity to visit with them about trade routes, tax levies, and other business considerations."

As they had done so many times over the years when strategy was important to them, they sat looking at each other silently calculating the risks and carefully considering the advantages. The house had grown very quiet. Not even the muffled voices of the servants could be heard.

Joseph stirred at last. "It is a plan worthy of consideration. I want to talk to Chuza and Manaen. Then we'll meet again." He stood up and smiled at her. "Yonah would be as proud of you as I am, Mary Mark."

She blushed and led him to the doorway, across the court-yard, and out the main gate.

The next morning, on his way to the Temple Mount for a meeting of the Sanhedrin, Joseph stopped at her house. "Chuza and Manaen like the idea, and have planted the seed with Thaumustus and Agrippa."

Within a few days, Joanna came to Mary Mark with the news that Agrippa was planning a great celebration for all the heads of state of the neighboring kingdoms and territories. The event was to take place at the palace in Tiberias, and she and Chuza and Manaen had been instructed to go there in advance to oversee the preparations. At what appeared to be the last moment, Joseph decided to travel with them on the pretext of needing to see his trading contacts in Galilee, particularly the one in Tiberias, a man named Justus Romanus.

A mixture of satisfaction and regret went through her. "Barnabas will be disappointed when he learns that the four of you are not here for his homecoming."

"But he will appreciate the reason for us being away," Joanna said with a wink.

And, indeed, that was exactly his reaction when several days after the four friends departed for Tiberias, he and Paul arrived from Antioch. Their very large caravan contained the generous gifts from Antioch's Christians to those living in Jerusalem. Before anything else was done, the caravan was unloaded, carefully divided into much smaller units and discreetly stored away in a number of different places arranged for earlier by Joseph.

Then excitement reigned. Barnabas was home. Friends came from all over Jerusalem and the surrounding area to welcome him. Paul was greeted with somewhat less enthusiasm, but even he was welcomed. The merriment went on for days. Mary Mark's house brimmed over with people coming and going, with the preparation of food, with the serving of many meals, and with groups of both men and women sending up continuous prayers of thanksgiving to the Lord.

When at last the pace abated, the time came when the family could sit down privately and share with Barnabas all that happened in his absence. In turn, he shared with them the wonders of evangelism in Antioch and his growing respect for Paul as a preacher and evangelist.

"There is only one piece of news I bring from Syria that will not please you, John Mark."

"About Mariamne?"

"Have you already heard?"

"No, it is just that she is never very far from my thoughts. But tell me, is she well? Nothing's happened to her?"

"She is married, my nephew."

A pained expression crossed his face. Mary Mark's heart cried out for him.

"She was married to her cousin, the young Archelaus."

He looked away.

Mary Mark went to him and put her arms about his shoulders. "I am sorry, my son. Truly sorry. Even though we knew it would happen. Even though we know it's best, I am still sorry. For your pain."

He hid his face in his hands. "I shall always love her. Always."

17

James, son of Zebedee of Capernaum and older brother to the redheaded apostle John, felt he had found his true calling in administration of the business aspects of Jerusalem's community of believers.

"Peter takes care of the spiritual things," he often said. "And I take care of the details."

But there was one part of his work that tried both his patience, of which he had very little, and his sense of forgiveness. It was tax collectors. He simply could not abide them. The only one he'd ever met that he could first learn to tolerate and then grow to love like a brother was Matthew, but, by and large, tax collectors irritated him beyond measure.

Like the one standing in front of him now. And what made this one more irritating than usual was the fact that he had brought in one of the newly minted coins with Herod Agrippa's visage engraved on it. James twisted the newly minted coin in his fingers, inspecting it with distaste and watching Agrippa's image distort before his very eyes. The longer he watched it, the more distorted it became, and the more intense became his feelings of irritation. From his first meeting with the ruler, he had felt instinctive dislike for him. And though during the years, he had met him face to face only on one other occasion, the intensity of the dislike had not waned. If anything, it had increased because of the repeated contacts he'd had with his tax collectors. The one who stood before him now was watching him watch the coin he twisted in his fingers.

"It is a coin of rare beauty, is it not?" the man asked, completely misreading James's interest in it. "Soon, it will be the new coin of the realm, even replacing the Roman denarius. In the kingdoms ruled by King Herod Agrippa, at least."

"Oh, at least." James flipped the coin back to the man.

Across the room, Matthew looked up from where he was at work reconciling the inventories of the gift caravan from Antioch.

"All the money–changers in the city have a plentiful supply of the new coins," the tax collector volunteered. "They will exchange all your Roman coins for you."

"At what price?"

"Only a nominal charge." He glanced at a small parchment in his hand. "On second notice, I see you will pay a slight bit more for the exchange."

"Why?"

The man glanced up questioningly. "You do represent the group now known as 'Christians'?"

"I do."

"Then the money–changers will require a slightly larger fee from you. It is a new policy of King Agrippa." He gave a thin smile.

Resentment rose inside James, but he checked it, determined that he would not provoke an argument.

"There is another more important matter that I came to see you about, though."

"What could be more important than m'lord Agrippa's new coin?" James hid the acid of sarcasm behind a thin smile of his own.

"Oh, I didn't mean to say that the king's new coin is not important," the man nervously recanted. "It's just that I came to see you about another matter, too."

"And that is?" James pushed.

"Your tax levy."

"What tax levy? We've already paid. Our record with you should be good."

The man gave a nervous cough. "There is a new tax you have not paid."

"On what?"

"On the caravan that recently came to you, with goods for your people."

A fresh wave of resentment went through James and clearly showed in the flare of redness in his face. Gifts were never taxed, only goods to be sold. It was the law of both the Romans and the Jews. James glanced toward Matthew, debating how they should deal with this and feeling the constraints of conscience very strongly. To speak the truth in this situation would be to give away, to Agrippa, as much as a third of the gifts sent from Antioch for the needy, but to lie, of course, was to violate the teachings of Jesus.

Matthew got to his feet and came toward them. "What caravan of goods do you mean, sir?"

"The big caravan that came from Antioch a few days ago."

Matthew feigned an expression of puzzled ignorance.

"It was an enormous caravan," the tax collector insisted. "Didn't it come to this house?"

James made a gesture with both hands, palms up, and looked about the room with a pitiful expression.

The tax collector began to nod in agreement, and a rueful smile came onto his face. "It is a very small house. That I see. But you might have stored the contents of the caravan in many places all over Jerusalem."

"That is true," said James.

"In fact, that would be a very smart thing to do, wouldn't it?" Matthew put in.

"No, not really. Eventually, we would find it, and the tax would have to be paid by the holder of the goods."

"Sir, who ever told you that such a caravan has come into Jerusalem?" James asked.

"And who told you it was meant for the 'Christians'?" Matthew added.

The tax collector looked momentarily befuddled. "Why, as a matter of fact, it was the king's own close counsel, Thaumustus. He told my superior, and my superior told me."

"Thaumustus?" James repeated in spite of himself.

The tax collector nodded.

Matthew shook his head in mock regret. "As you can see, there is barely room in this rude house for the three of us and table and bench."

"It will be hard to tell my superior he is wrong."

"Yes, I imagine it will be."

The man scratched at his head with the parchment.

"Have you been to see the high priest, Jonathan?" Matthew asked, leading the man to the doorway. "Possibly he can help you discover where the caravan from Antioch is located."

The man folded the parchment, stuffed it into his sash, and stepped out of the house. "I shall go there now." He salaamed and moved off down the street.

When he was completely out of sight, James said, "We must warn Joseph and Mary Mark."

"They have the goods distributed in such small amounts they can never be traced," Matthew reassured him, "but I am concerned for Manaen. And Chuza and Joanna, for that matter. They must be told about this. And about Thaumustus' part in it. They were saying only a day or so ago that they feel they are making a real friend of this Thaumustus. Can we get a word of warning to them in Tiberias?"

James thought a moment. "What about asking John Mark to carry the warning?"

"Of course."

They turned at once and made their way to Mary Mark's house in the Upper City. Barnabas opened the front gate for them. Quickly they told him about the situation and their idea of sending John Mark to Tiberias with the warning for Manaen and Chuza. They must be very careful of what they said in front of Thaumustus or anyone else who would want to know where the Antioch gifts were stored.

"He's as good a messenger as any, and better than most since he hosted that dinner for Thaumustus."

Inside the house, they found Mary Mark and told her of their plan. She agreed as quickly as Barnabas and went into a small side room calling for John Mark to come and join them.

"I'd like to go," he said. "I can leave at once."

"I'll have the servants prepare food for you to take." Mary Mark thanked James and Matthew and hurried off toward the cooking area.

Barnabas went off to prepare a horse for the journey while John Mark received full instructions about the warning he was to carry to Manaen and Chuza in Tiberias.

It took two days for John Mark to reach Tiberias. And when he did, he found his entrance into the palace blocked by unyielding guards. Since Agrippa's royal party from Jerusalem had arrived and so had most of his distinguished guests from all parts of the surrounding empires and kingdoms, even the public rooms of the palace had been closed to the casual visitor. "Security, son," one of the guards explained.

"Security?"

"Against Zealots. His majesty wants no disturbance while he entertains these important people."

John Mark peered around the guard into the enormous hall just inside the entry. It was crowded. Important–looking people stood about in groups of two or three talking. Others strolled around looking at the beautiful hall in seeming appreciation. And he realized that each head of state had brought a large entourage with him — ministers of trade, viziers of royal households, and chancellors, counselors, even a high priest or two. No wonder they needed to be careful about who came and went.

He wondered how he would ever find Manaen or Chuza. If he insisted on getting in or asked to be announced to Chuza or Manaen, it would simply draw attention to his being there. If they called Thaumustus, he would recognize him. So would Agrippa. And he had no intention of arousing any curiosity about the purpose of his visit here. It would be better to be patient, he decided, and find a more obscure way to get into the palace. He thanked the guard and turned away.

To his left, the Sea of Galilee glistened in he morning sun. He went in that direction. Beyond the corner of the palace wall, his view of the sea became unobstructed. It was the color of lapis lazuli flecked with silver and gold shimmerings. The size of it surprised him, even though he so often had heard it described by Peter and Barnabas and by his mother.

"It is a beautiful place, my son," she said as he was leaving Jerusalem. "I would like to be going with you. It is the land of our Lord, where he performed so many miracles."

He shielded his eyes, trying to make out the foothills that formed a backdrop to the area Jesus had known so well. Magdala. Taglitha. Capernaum. Bethsaida. But the haze of distance intervened, veiling the northern shoreline and its foothills.

He rubbed his eyes, ridding his vision of the after–effect of glare, and glanced down toward the piers and quays jutting out from the foot of the palace grounds into the water. The royal barge was tied alongside the largest quay. A group of men appeared to be about ready to embark. A larger group milled about doing things to the barge, loading on baskets of refreshments and making other preparations.

He started to turn away when suddenly he recognized Agrippa and Petronius. Both men were wearing the insignia of Roman consuls—white shoes. Manaen and Chuza were there, too. But how could he attract their attention without attracting the attention of the others?

As he stood surveying the situation, a group of servants carrying additional refreshments came from the palace and went toward the quay. On impulse, he followed, using them as a shield. Within moments, he found himself aboard the royal barge. Its rich trappings and fittings made him pause. Great, soft rugs covered most of the shining teak of the forward deck. Comfortable couches and chairs were covered with skins. A great long table with side rails of gleaming brass held a sumptuous assortment of food and drink. Shading it all were gold, royal red, and crisp white linen canopies. The luxury dumbfounded him. But within another moment he regretted the impulsiveness that had brought him on board. He was unfamiliar with boats except in a very general way, and it abruptly occurred to him that there appeared few places to hide on this luxurious craft.

The group of servants he'd followed had disappeared below deck somewhere while he had been ogling the barge's rich trappings. The dignitaries were beginning to move along the quay preparing to come aboard. The barge captain and the banquet master, standing quayside, straightened to welcome their king and his guests. Below him, he heard the oarsmen moving about.

Heart racing, sweat breaking out in the palms of his hands, John Mark glanced about for a hiding place. Across from him on the aft deck was an enormous coil of rope. It seemed unattached to anything; it was just there. And it was tall enough for him to crouch behind. In the moment before he made for it, however, the servants who'd led him on board reappeared from a doorway near the main mast, which had been hidden from his view. They were followed by the helmsman and a group of sailors As soon as they were clear of it, he made for the doorway, went down the steps inside, and found himself in an open area on a middle deck. The sounds of the oarsmen still came from below him. Above, the planking of the main deck creaked as the royal party came aboard and the crew prepared to cast off.

John Mark went forward along a narrow passageway. At its end, it narrowed even more. He realized he must be at the very prow of the barge. A small trapdoor was cut in the planking above his head. It was slightly open, propped by a wooden dowel, as if to give ventilation to the passageway along which he had just come. But as he examined it, he discovered that the opening also allowed him to hear the conversations taking place on the main deck. He recognized Manaen's voice and that of Chuza and Agrippa. He could hear them clearly. For the first part of the voyage, the amenities were observed by Agrippa and his visitors. Toasts and compliments accompanied much moving about. There was particularly heavy action in the area where he remembered the table of food was positioned. There was much laughter and joking. Someone dropped a goblet of wine. Its splashings found the opening of the trapdoor and John Mark's upturned face.

But the farther they sailed into the heart of the Sea of Galilee, the more serious became their conversations. Food and drink did their work. The cadence of the oarsmen matched the rhythm of the waves. The peace of a tranquil sailing lulled the human soul. And in his hiding place beneath their feet, John Mark dozed.

Sometime later, Agrippa's voice roused him. Strident, harsh, boastful, it came tumbling down through the trapdoor's opening. "Of course, I shall be successful!"

"But that is a very great undertaking," said one of the visitors unknown to John Mark.

"My grandfather was a great builder. So shall I be! The new city wall is already started."

"And does the work go forward quickly?"

"With efficiency, Publius. With efficiency!" Agrippa answered.

"Considering that he's using conscripted labor, there is no reason for the work not to go forward with efficiency," King Aretas said in his clipped, staccato Nabatean dialect.

"Conscripted labor?"

"It's a very cheap way to add to my slave holdings," Agrippa laughed.

"I thought Jewish law prohibited that."

"But Roman law does not, Publius."

There was a momentary silence.

"I like the Roman law. It's a very efficient method of gathering manpower. And now, since I am king, I may use Roman law if I choose. Emperor Claudius has decreed it."

Dismay began to rise inside John Mark, matching a longer silence of disapproval that settled over the royal party above him. He wondered if they, too, found Agrippa's arrogance as threatening as he did. His own reaction could stem from the fact that he once held Agrippa in such high esteem because of Mariamne, he reminded himself. Reactions from the visiting dignitaries might be different. They were men of maturity, experience; they were leaders of other men.

"Did the emperor Claudius also decree that you should mint your own coin of the realm?" asked Publius Petronius.

Agrippa gave a laugh of surprise. "Did I need his decree?"

"No, I suppose not. I'm sure he must have implicit confidence in you, Agrippa."

John Mark felt the barge give a small shudder. It came

about. The wind shifted. A freshet of air came through the trapdoor with such abrupt force that it knocked the wooden dowel loose, and the trapdoor fell shut with a thud.

Quickly he moved away from it and slipped back down the passageway to hide behind one of the larger supply baskets. For the rest of the voyage, he stayed hidden there. Not until the barge was once more tied up at the quay did he make his way back up to the main deck, mingling with the sailors and servants and waiting for his chance to get to Manaen or Chuza.

The chance finally came as the party of dignitaries disembarked. Chuza and Manaen waited until all of the visitors were safely back on the quay. Then when they stepped forward to disembark, John Mark went to them and caught Manaen's sleeve. "A word, Manaen," he said in a low tone.

Astonished, both men turned to him.

"I have a message for you from Jerusalem."

Without prompting, Chuza and Manaen positioned themselves so that John Mark was totally hidden from the group of dignitaries proceeding along the quay toward the palace.

"The message is be careful of what you say to anyone about the caravan from Antioch. Please warn Joseph, too. And Joanna. Thaumustus sent a tax collector to James."

Manaen waited a moment, his eyes searching John Mark's face. Then he asked, "Is there more?"

"Be especially careful. James fears that Agrippa or Thaumustus may try to trap you both."

"But what about James? What about the tax collector?"

"Matthew distracted the tax collector. Sent him to Jonathan. Told him the priesthood might have received such a caravan, if there was one."

Chuza and Manaen grinned at each other.

"Were you on the barge with us?" Manaen asked.

"I was. Though hiding was no easy matter."

A look of new respect filtered into Manaen's eyes.

"And I'll have to hide again," he said, looking over Manaen's shoulder. "Your friend Thaumustus is coming back."

Chuza casually turned away to intercept Agrippa's counselor.

"Where can I find you later?" Manaen asked.

"At the home of Justus Romanus. He and his family have worked with my mother and Joseph for many years. Do you know his house?"

Manaen nodded. John Mark turned, went back to his hiding place below deck, and stayed there until he could hear no more sounds of people moving about and the cover of night had turned the hiding place black as pitch and uncomfortably cool. Then he made his way back to the house of Justus Romanus.

Manaen, however, did not come to join him until a great deal later, but the news he brought was worth waiting for. Publius Petronius, aroused by Agrippa's arrogance and considering him a threat to himself and to Rome, had written a private letter to Emperor Claudius telling him of the new city wall Agrippa was building and about the new coins he had minted with his image on them. He warned Claudius of Agrippa's overweaning ambition to outbuild his grandfather, Herod the Great. And he quietly sugggested that such ambition was a threat to the peaceful rule of Rome.

"And he has already sent a special messenger to Rome this very night," Manaen concluded. "Joseph wants your mother to know that especially."

John Mark looked puzzled.

But Manaen gave no explanation. He simply smiled and said, "Safe journey home, my friend."

18

The Year 44

The time it took for messages from the eastern provinces to reach Rome depended on whether the message was carried overland or by sea—and then upon the fortunes of weather. By land, the travel time depended upon whether the messenger rode alone on horseback or if he joined a caravan with its slower moving pack animals. The trip overland from Tiberias to Rome could be as swift as six weeks or as lengthy as five months. By sea and with favorable winds, the time required for the journey could be as short as three or four weeks.

The letter from Publius Petronius to the emperor Claudius went by fast horse from Tiberias to Caesarea–by–the–Sea, and from there, on the morning tide aboard one of Rome's infamous triremes, ships of war that carried both sails and oarsmen. In peacetime, they served as fast–moving packets to and from Rome and the coastal perimeters of its empire. By using this route, the letter from Petronius was delivered to the imperial palace a mere three weeks after it was written.

But once there, it met one delay after another. Narcissus, Claudius' first secretary, was far more concerned with messages arriving from Britannia where fighting continued around the walled city of Londinium, than he was about a message from a governor of an eastern province. And so the letter of Publius Petronius lay unopened and neatly stacked with many other missives for several additional weeks.

Meanwhile in Jerusalem work on the building of the new city wall began. The huge quarry situated in the hills just north of the city was reopened. It had been the source of the stones used by King Solomon's builders in the creation of the First Temple. Centuries later, Herod the Great used the same quarry as his source for stones for the building of the Second Temple. When Herod Antipas succeeded his father as ruler of Judea, he used stones from the same quarry to complete the work on the Temple and, as needed, to maintain the Temple Mount and its massive wall. General use of the quarry, however, had been prohibited.

But now the great quarry was once again open. Hundreds of quarrymen, loaders, hod carriers, and stonemasons were employed or conscripted. Engineers and surveyors were pressed into service to plot the location of what had become known as "Agrippa's Folly." Men with picks and shovels were conscripted to dig trenches in the rock–strewn surface of Jerusalem's outskirts for the foundations of the wall.

The work was hard, the pay was small—two mites a day plus a midday meal of goat's cheese and stale bread. The weather was unseasonably hot. Drinking water was limited. James went daily among the workers, sharing water from his own goatskin and talking to them. But the more he talked, the more the workers asked the overseers for water and for rest time. And the more they asked, the more demanding the overseers became. Tempers flared. Fights broke out. Roman soldiers and palace guards broke up the fights and imprisoned many of the workers.

In fact, they imprisoned so many that, at Joseph's insistence, the Sanhedrin finally called a special emergency session to put a halt to the imprisonment of the wall workers, except for those who might have committed the most severe of crimes. The Romans agreed almost immediately, for they realized that dwindling prison rations would soon leave them with only prisoners dead of starvation. But getting the agreement of Agrippa to change the local law was to take a good bit longer, for he still lolled in the relative coolness of his seaside palace in Tiberias.

"It is criminal," James fumed to Mary Mark and Barnabas when he came to bring a report on the community's foodstuff inventory. Matthew, Thomas, and Simon Zelotes were with him. "There must be something we can do beside wait for Agrippa to change the laws about imprisonment."

"We're already sending food baskets to the prisoners," Mary Mark reminded him. "Distribution to the prisoners has simply been added to the daily distribution of food to the widows."

"But are we doing enough?" James challenged.

Irritation went through Mary Mark. What else did he expect them to do? He could be such a thorn sometimes. His attitude had become so pugnacious in recent months. She only hoped he didn't turn rabble–rouser. If he did, that would bring down the wrath of the Romans, the priesthood, the Sanhedrin, and the palace against the community of believers. "What else would you like us to do, James?"

"Well, *you've* certainly done enough already, James," Matthew said in an unusually critical tone. Mary Mark and Barnabas looked at him in surprise.

"Matthew's right," Simon Zelotes agreed. "James *has* already done enough!"

"What has he done?"

"What did I do that was so terrible?" James flared.

"You incited a riot," Thomas charged

"A riot?" Mary Mark's eyes went wide.

"Thomas is right, James," Matthew confirmed. "If you hadn't done all that talking to those men a while back, there wouldn't have been any fighting in the first place."

"And nobody would've been thrown in prison." Simon Zelotes shook his finger in James's face.

Astonished, Mary Mark and Barnabas looked from one

to the other of the apostles. They had occasionally heard them argue among themselves before, but never like this. They actually seemed angry with each other. And the charge of inciting a riot was as serious as any that could be made—except for murder.

"Are you responsible for those men being thrown into prison?" Barnabas demanded in alarm. "What did you say to them?"

James remained silent.

Matthew spoke up. "He told them they shouldn't put up with the working conditions. That's what he said."

"And I was right!" James flared. "You know I was right."

"Right or not, it was none of your business," Thomas reminded him. "Simon and I both told you at the time to leave it be, to let Joseph and the Sanhedrin handle it."

A look of angry embarrassment flooded onto James' face.

Angry herself, Mary Mark walked away and sat down on a nearby chair, leaving the solution of this to the wisdom of Barnabas. As strong a leader as James was administratively for their community, he was neither diplomatic nor clever in his dealings with people who did not believe as he did. He was idealistic. Too idealistic. Rigidly, inflexibly idealistic. This was an example of how misplaced his helpfulness could be: giving the workers water with his hands and planting the seeds of sedition with his mouth! There was no question that the treatment of the men who were working on Agrippa's wall was dreadful, but James' rabble-rousing was worse. The results of his efforts were harmful to the very people he had hoped to help. And to think they never knew about it until now.

"What's already been done, we can't undo," Barnabas said in a tone of controlled quiet.

"That's about the only thing we can all agree on where this incident is concerned," Matthew inserted.

"What we do from this moment forward, though, becomes extremely important. Do you agree, James?" Barnabas waited for a reply. None was forthcoming.

"Like the rest of us, you have never liked Agrippa," Barnabas went on "but you cannot let personal prejudice blind you to the safety of the whole community."

"Besides, James," Thomas spoke up, "we're still a minority in Jerusalem. In spite of our growing numbers over the past few years, we're still a minority. And it just doesn't make sense for us to be the cause of a public riot."

"Even if we were in the majority, it wouldn't make sense," Simon Zelotes charged. "Agrippa's been accusing us of being troublemakers ever since he got his title of king back. Now you've proved him to be right about us!"

"But the treatment of those workers was wrong. What were we to do? Stand idly by and see that awful injustice go on?"

"That's just what you should have done, my brother," said Barnabas in a flat tone. "Injustices go on every day of the year, and we stand idly by. And why do we do it?"

"We do it out of self–preservation," Matthew said, going to James. "You know that as well as the rest of us. But your hot temper . . . and your idealism . . . got the best of you."

James moved away from him.

Matthew followed. "As your friends, all we're asking is that you don't try to change the world by yourself."

James turned and looked at each of his brother apostles with an unrelenting hardness. Then he glanced at Mary Mark and Barnabas. "I'm obliged for your guidance." He turned and without waiting for the others, left the house.

Mary Mark regretted the strain developing among the apostles because of James' stubborn attitude. It was true, he no longer agitated publicly. Peter had ordered him to stop. But he continued to do so privately with every person he met. His actions were divisive. When the apostles began coming to the house one by one to talk with her and with Barnabas about the situation, they placated them as best they could, urged tolerance, reminded them of James' abilities and courage, encouraged forgiveness of his poor judgment, and led them in prayers.

But to Joanna and Manaen, who finally had returned from Tiberias with Agrippa's entourage, she confided her worry and a new sense of foreboding. "It will take more than listening and soft words to settle this. Not since the stoning of Stephen have I felt such a strong sense of disaster."

"Those of us who live in the palace feel equally unsettled," Joanna replied as the three of them walked together in the palace gardens. "Agrippa grows more jealous of his powers daily. He is sensitive to every remark and comment. We walk around on tiptoes and speak to each other in whispers lest we offend him in some way."

"The thing I'm so impatient for is an answer to the letter Publius sent to the emperor," Manaen said. "It has been months since the letter was sent. I felt sure the emperor would not like it that Agrippa was building his new wall and would take immediate action to stop it. But . . ."

"Perhaps the letter never arrived in Rome," Joanna suggested.

"Or if it did, perhaps the emperor never received it," Mary Mark added, pulling her mantle more closely around herself, feeling an abrupt coolness in the air as the sun slipped behind the western foothills. Shadows enveloped the gardens, muting the individual brilliance of flowers and shrubbery with a common grayness. At the far end of the gardens, servants came to the palace entrance bearing great torches, which they placed in wall stanchions. The smoky orange flames delineated the entrance to the palace and darkened the surrounding shadows. "On the other hand," Mary Mark wondered out loud, "is it possible that a response has been received and we just don't know about it?"

Joanna and Manaen stopped in their tracks, looking at each other in surprise.

Mary Mark continued walking another two or three paces before realizing they had stopped. She turned, went back, and peered at them through the shadowed twilight. "You mean that is possible?"

It was Manaen who recovered first. "Of course, its possible. But probable? I think not." He thought for a moment. "If that were the case, you'd think Agrippa would give himself away. In some little way."

"How do you mean?"

"He means that since Agrippa is living with his emotions out in the open most of the time," Joanna replied before Manaen had a chance to answer, "receiving a message from the emperor would be something he'd brag about.'

Mary Mark looked to Manaen for confirmation. "In some way, Agrippa would have shown that a message from Claudius had come."

"Or Thaumustus would," Joanna added.

"But I have noticed nothing from either of them," Manaen said with a shake of his head. "And since Agrippa is back in Jerusalem and plans to stay here for a while, you will do well to warn James again to be more discreet, Mary Mark."

"I'll do what I can," she agreed. "In the meantime, what has Chuza been able to do about a meeting with Agrippa for Joseph and Jonathan and Gamaliel and the other leaders of the Sanhedrin?"

"He has it arranged for three days from now," said Manaen.

"We must get relief for those men who've been imprisoned. But unless Agrippa consents to free them, the Romans will continue to hold them. And to think that James is the cause of their imprisonment!"

Manaen came close and slipped his arm around her. "It will all be set right, Mary Mark. You must believe that."

But in spite of Manaen's assurances and in spite of the agreement reached between Agrippa and the Sanhedrin's representatives three days later, all was not set right. To be sure, the prisoners were released. Those who could returned to their work on the new city wall. Those too weak from the experience and the families of those who had died in prison were cared for by members of the community of believers in fulfillment of what they considered their obligation. But the havoc created by James' agitation was to have still more far-reaching effects.

As the Feast of Unleavened Bread approached in the year 44, abrupt word came from the royal engineer to the overseers at the construction site that all work on the new city wall was to be halted! Workers were to be sent home. Platoons of Roman soldiers accompanied the royal engineer when he made the announcement. Whether their presence was one of protection or enforcement was unclear, for no reason was given—only the order to cease work.

News of this surprising occurrence spread throughout the city like sand blown by strong wind. Preachers and teachers on the Temple Mount were interrupted by the news. Strangers stopped in the narrow streets of the Lower City to compare reports. In the Upper City, residents surged into the Agora avid for details.

A breathless John Mark brought the news to his mother and uncle only to find he was not the first to do so. Manaen was already there. So were Joseph, Joanna, Peter, James, John, Matthew, Rhoda, Sallu, and Kedar. They were gathered in the small courtyard at the back of the house.

"The order to stop work actually came from the emperor Claudius," Manaen explained from his place on the stone bench alongside Mary Mark.

"That means the message from Publius Petronius really did get through then," said Barnabas.

"Apparently so," Manaen went on, "because the message from Claudius accuses Agrippa of treasonous acts."

"And did he specify the reasons for his suspicions?" Peter wanted to know.

"I'll wager they were the same as those listed in the letter from Petronius," Joseph inserted.

"The very same," Manaen said. "But the emperor also told Agrippa that the only way he could prove he was not a traitor to Rome was to stop the building of the wall and release the workers from their conscription!"

Joanna gave a gleeful laugh. "As of this morning Agrippa did as he was told. He sent the royal engineer to the construction site to stop the work."

"But under the watchful eyes of three platoons of Roman soldiers!" Manaen added.

The laughter that followed gave way to a small celebration; they hugged each other and everyone talked at the same time. Agrippa finally had been forced to give an accounting of his actions! For the briefest of moments, Mary Mark even thought rather kindly of the Roman emperor Claudius.

Manaen put his arm around her shoulder and pulled her close. "I told you all would be set right."

As she turned to look at him, she caught sight of James standing just beyond the bench next to Peter and John. The expression on his face puzzled her. It was not exactly a frown. Nor was it a look of satisfaction, though under this circumstance, it certainly should be, she told herself. Instead, it was an expression of dismay, of indecision, of calculation.

"Didn't I tell you all would be set right?" Manaen repeated, pulling her even closer.

Laughing at his exuberance, she nodded. He stood up, pulled her to her feet, and gave her over to the embraces of John Mark and Joseph.

By the time she could once more look for James, he had disappeared from the courtyard. The sense of foreboding that had come upon her so many weeks before abruptly focused itself on him. The peculiar expression on his face evoked it. She shivered and turned to Barnabas.

"What's wrong? You're pale," he said.

"It is James."

Peter and John came up. "What about James?"

"He left. Too quickly. And with such a strange expression on his face that I fear for him."

The farther he got from Mary Mark's house, the faster James walked. By the time he reached the Viaduct, he was practically running. Excitement charged through him as he thought again of the work on the wall being stopped. An injustice had been halted! Relief had come for mistreated men. And the community of believers now had the chance to claim public praise for the part they had in this victory for justice! What others thought or said didn't matter. What did matter was that all Christians who felt as he did could take credit for a victory over Agrippa.

He hurried across the Viaduct, took the steps leading up onto the Temple Mount two at a time, and made his way through crowds of pilgrims toward the spot on Solomon's Porches where Nathanael, Bartholomew, and Jude were teaching. So intent was he on his own mission that he failed to notice Gamaliel, Jonathan the high priest, and another ranking member of the priesthood in conversation just at the edge of the group being taught by Jude.

Without the ceremony of courtesy, he interrupted Jude by placing his hand on his shoulder and kneeling down beside him.

"Ah, Brother James! Our greetings to you," said the imperturbable Jude. He turned back toward those listening to his teaching and introduced James. "This man, too, is one of us who knew Jesus and shared his public ministry. We consider him a leader of our community along with Peter and John."

The group acknowledged the introduction with nods and smiles.

"Have you come to help me teach" Jude asked.

"I have come to make sure you know of the good news about the building of the wall being stopped."

"Yes, we all know of it," Jude said.

"Good. And do you know also that we Christians are the ones that got it stopped?"

Jude looked at him in surprise, as did most of the people gathered around. Since James had not spoken quietly, Bartholomew and Nathanael and even the groups they were teaching a short distance away also heard this boastful statement. Nor was it lost to the ears of Gamaliel and Jonathan.

"It is true," James defended against their looks of surprise. "Our protests over forced labor had a great deal to do with stopping the construction of this unneeded wall."

Dismayed silence was the response from all within hearing distance.

James stood up. "Our protests were heard as far as Rome. And Rome ordered Agrippa to stop work on the wall."

Jude tugged at the arm of James' robe and implored, "Sit down, my brother. Sit down. You don't mean that!"

But James pulled away and with a thin laugh said, "To those of you just learning about us Christians, be aware that we can fight as well as pray!"

Across the moment of stunned silence, Gamaliel turned to look directly at James. He was a tall man with a beard as white as the linen cassock he wore. His moderate views and careful declarations caused him to be greatly respected throughout Judea, Perea, and Idumea. He had, on more than one occasion, pleaded for lenience toward those who followed Jesus. And, in fact, in two instances, he had persuaded the Sanhedrin not to put Peter and John into prison.

Circling the group of wide–eyed students, he moved to confront James. "The Sanhedrin will be gratified to know of your actions in this matter. We had no notion of the power of your influence with Rome."

It was James' turn to be surprised. Until now he had not noticed Gamaliel nor the high priest Jonathan, who also was coming toward him. But surprised or not, he had no intention of recanting his belief that his agitation over poor working conditions, in spite of what resulted thereafter, did, indeed, have an effect on closing down construction of the wall.

"Had we known such influence was yours, we would've asked your assistance in many of our dealings with the emperor." The tone of Gamaliel's voice was bland enough, but his words implied a taunt.

"We've assisted you in many ways already," James asserted, straightening. "but you have never thought any of us worthy of your respect."

"Respect?" The normally passive Jonathan blurted out the word. "Respect? For men who follow a dead heretic?"

James' temper flared. He fought to control it but felt it flame into his face anyway. Jude stood up. Bartholomew and Nathanael came to stand with them against whatever happened next. Some of the students, though, got up and walked away. Beyond the portico, a flash of sunlight glinted briefly from the helmet of a Roman soldier patrolling on the watchtower of the Fortress Antonia.

"I suppose you'll tell us next that Emperor Claudius and King Agrippa are also followers of Jesus the heretic!"

"No, priest, he'll not tell us that," Gamaliel intervened. "Nor will he tell us which members of Agrippa's court follow the heretic."

A fearful sensation of danger momentarily overrode James's prideful anger. The realization struck home that his efforts could truly imperil other believers. A sinking feeling went through him. He never meant to do anything that would expose the identities of other believers, especially not the identities of Manaen and Joanna.

"But you can be sure there are many followers of The Way in Agrippa's court," Gamaliel continued, carefully surveying the four apostles for the slightest change in facial expressions. "How else could simple fishermen from Galilee have any influence over anything?"

Again James' temper flared. "We had enough influence to stop mistreatment and injustice. We got the building of the wall stopped. You self-righteous Pharisees didn't do it!"

"And you want public credit for it?"

"I do."

Jonathan resisted. "First he wants respect. And now public acclaim?"

"That should not be hard to give them, honored priest." Gamaliel countered the resistance in a tone that was far too calm.

The priest looked stunned and glanced at him for affirmation. Jude, Bartholomew, and Nathanael did likewise. But James appeared to be taking Gamaliel at his word. An expression of satisfaction bordering on smugness came onto his face. He nodded ever so slightly as the great teacher turned and walked away with Jonathan, protesting anew, following.

"That was foolishness, James. Absolute foolishness," Jude admonished when the Pharisees were out of sight.

"You let him trap you!" Nathanael declared.

"He'll go straight to Agrippa," said Bartholomew.

Jude caught James by both arms and swung him around. "You and your temper! No wonder Jesus called you a son of thunder! Don't you know Agrippa will retaliate?"

19

Retaliation was not long in coming. In fact, it began the very next day, one day before the Feast of Unleavened Bread. Since that was one of the most important celebrations for the Jews and since the Jews were politically important to Agrippa, he had always respected their traditional religious holidays. If he was to respect this one, he must take his revenge on James quickly or else put it off for several days.

Under the present circumstance, he had no patience for delays. The edict from Claudius had been humiliating. His face still flamed just from the thought of it. Now James' public claim that the Christians had caused it to happen added unforgiveable insult to the humiliation. And so, on this day immediately preceding the Jew's festival of Passover, he set in motion his acts of revenge.

Even the elements of nature seemed to sense the tragedy about to happen, for the day came in stealth, its sunlight shimmering through great banks of clouds for only a moment. The grayness that followed cast a pall of shadows over Jerusalem's preparations for Passover. There was a forbidding uncertainty in the air. Even the hills beyond the city walls gave up their claim to springtime colors and accepted the mottled drabness of thousands of pilgrims' tents—gray, white, black, and tan.

Inside the walls, the pilgrims were equally colorless and mottled. They clogged the streets and did nothing to lift the sense of foreboding, representing, as they did, slow-moving clusters of humanity bent on sacrifical celebration.

Inside the palace, the uncertain grayness of the day met its match in Agrippa's dark, brooding anger. His retaliation had begun. Orders had been issued to harass anyone known to be a member of the community of believers. No matter who they were or where they were to be found, they were the targets for the king's men.

"But of most special interest to me," Agrippa told the captains of the guards, "are the leaders of Christians, Peter and James. Particularly James. I want him captured and brought here to me. As for Peter and the rest, throw them into prison."

The search began. Every house suspected of harboring Christians was included. They found many of those houses strangely empty, as if the occupants had already been warned. The house near the Viaduct where Peter lived with his wife and mother-in-law was broken into and ransacked. So was the house occupied by James and John and the other apostles. But in the Lower City, several other houses, including that of Zacchus the cheesemaker, where Paul was staying, yielded up victims. Paul barely escaped by crawling through a drainage ditch and covering himself with trash and other household debris.

When the squad searching houses in the Upper City came to Mary Mark's, the captain showed reluctance at battering down the gate and forcing entry. He remembered that one of the king's daughters had been a friend of John Mark's. And he also remembered that Manaen was a friend of John Mark's mother. He decided that under such circumstances, he dared not force his way in. Instead, he rapped loudly at the gate seeking admittance.

Kedar opened the gate. Manaen was with him.

Startled at seeing Manaen, the captain quickly bowed. "Your pardon, Honored Counselor, we seek two men. One named James of Capernaum, and the other named Simon Peter of Bethsaida."

"There are no men here by those names," Manaen said. "Sir, I do not doubt your word," the captain apologized, "but I am ordered by the king to search inside all houses within the city."

Manaen glanced past the captain to the squad of guards. "How many men do you have with you?"

"Twenty, sir."

"You don't need that many to search this one house."

The captain started to protest.

Manaen interrupted. "You can search with two or three of your men. For that, I give you permission to enter."

Reluctantly the captain agreed and motioned three of his men to follow as Manaen led the way back across the courtyard toward the house. It began to rain. Kedar ignored it and remained at the gate, holding it open, but blocking the entry so that none of the other soldiers could enter. Manaen, the captain, and the three guards disappeared into the house.

Mary Mark came toward them and accepted Manaen's explanation of why the guards were there without comment. She glanced out at the rain, a pensive look coming into her face as if tears of a deep inner sorrow were mingling with it and somehow finding no solace against a dreadful disaster. But when she turned back to give a nod of permission for Manaen to lead the guard on through the house, the pensive look was gone.

Had the captain of the guards been a more observant man, he might have noticed her changing expressions or wondered at how calmly she seemed to accept the news that she was suspected of harboring fugitives. Instead, he and his men trailed along after Manaen rather passively. They looked only into the rooms on the main floor of the house he showed them. They asked no questions about alcoves, or if there were other rooms on the floor above, or if there were storerooms attached to the house. And they either did not see, or paid no attention to, the small back courtyard with its stairway leading to the upper room. As a result, the searchers returned to the main room of the house in a very short time. The captain thanked Mary Mark and Manaen and left the premises.

Kedar bolted the gate and rushed back into the house. Sallu and Rhoda appeared at an inside doorway. Other servants came up behind them. All questioned Mary Mark and Manaen with wide-eyed looks.

"Your presence here did make them careless, sir, as you suspected it might," Sallu said to Manaen. "They searched no corners. They asked no questions."

"But they also may come back," Manaen warned.

"If they do, it would almost be welcome," said Mary Mark, "for it would mean they had not captured Peter and James wherever they are out in the streets."

James had come to Mary Mark's in the darkest twilight bringing with him all the apostles except Peter, whom he could not find. He was now fully aware of the danger in which his confrontation with the Pharisees earlier that same day had placed them all, and the boldness of his impulsive anger had turned to fright—not for himself, but for the others.

For help, he sought out Mary Mark's household where a survival plan was devised. The main goal of the plan was to get all of the apostles out of Jerusalem as quickly and discreetly as possible. For all he knew, Agrippa's men might already be searching for them.

John Mark was sent back to Peter's house to wait for him, to warn him of what had so recently happened, and bring him back to the safety of the upper room where his wife and mother-in-law already had come. They were a regular part of the customary prayer group and had come to Mary Mark's early in the day to help make preparations for a special Passover supper in memory of Jesus.

Sallu was sent to fetch Joseph of Arimathea. His counsel was needed. He came quickly. Uncertain about whether or not Manaen, Joanna, and Chuza had yet learned of this newest danger, Joseph sent Kedar to the palace to alert them and, if possible, to bring all three of them back to Mary Mark's house. But only Manaen and Joanna returned with Kedar. Chuza remained behind rather than draw suspicion by his absence.

A while later, John Mark returned with Peter and the planning began in earnest. It was a simple plan. Posing as pilgrims, all the apostles were to leave Mary Mark's house by twos and threes. They were to walk the short distance to the Gate of the Essenes and leave the city through it. They were to cross the far western end of the Valley of Jehoso-phat. There they would be met by the merchant Justus Romanus of Tiberias, who, with his family, had come to Jerusalem to celebrate Passover. His tents were situated near the western end of the valley; and it would be there that the apostles were to wait until Joseph and Manaen could arrange for horses to be brought to them about daylight. Then, again by twos and threes, they were to scatter in different directions.

"The church at Antioch will welcome all of you," Barnabas said as John Mark left the room to go and make all the arrangements with Justus Romanus.

"And there are many brothers living in Samaria who also will welcome us," John added, clapping James protectively on the shoulder.

James gave a wan smile. "But I cannot go."

"Not go?"

"I must not. I am the cause of all this. If I run away, the entire community of believers will suffer for it!"

"No, James! No!"

A clamor from all the rest supported John's protest. Mary Mark shuddered at the truth James spoke.

Finally, Peter held up his hands for silence. "Then I must stay, too, James."

Shock was the response.

"You and I are the leaders of the community of believers. We are the shepherds, you for the practical, I for the spiritual. If we leave, the flock will be scattered. We both must stay."

An argument ensued. Strident, adamant, emotional. Once again, Peter held up his hands to silence them. Reluctantly, they subsided, realizing that no amount of arguing would change the mind of either Peter or James.

"Pray with us, my brothers and sisters," Peter said. "And pray for us!"

They knelt together, all of them. Clasping hands, they began to pray.

Our Father in heaven,
We give our hearts to you willingly and sincerely.
We ask for strength to do your work,
We thank you for your love and comfort and guidance.

Later when John Mark returned to report that Justus Romanus was waiting for them, all the apostles said their farewells to Mary Mark's household with the certain knowledge that they might never again see each other.

And so it was that by the next morning when Agrippa's squad of soldiers actually came to search Mary Mark's house, the apostles, with the exception of Peter and James, were well on their journeys to freedom.

Accompanied by Joseph, Barnabas, and John Mark, Peter and James went quietly about the city warning believers of the impending harassment and persecution. To warn as many believers as possible, they split up and went in separate directions. It was more dangerous for Peter and James, but they knew that those believers who were not warned would become victims of bodily harm and imprisonment.

As dawn made its stealthy, uncertain entrance and pilgrims began crowding into the streets, they were forced to slow down in their efforts to alert all believers. None of them wished to attract the attention of Agrippa's guards or the Roman soldiers, who by now patrolled the streets in great numbers because of the crowds of Passover pilgrims. By the time the rain began, most of the houses in the Suburb and the Upper City had been warned. But in the Lower City where James was carrying the warning, only a few houses could be reached because of the crowds and the soliders.

At last, James gave up the effort, pulled the hood of his robe more closely about his head, and with regret turned back toward Joseph's house where the others would be waiting for him. It had been agreed that he and Peter would hide there for the time being, not wishing to further endanger Mary Mark's house. The shortest route to Joseph's was a path leading up a sharp incline to the western end of the Viaduct. As he approached the top of the path, someone above him cried out, "Thief! Thief! Stop him!"

James looked up just in time to see a young man about John Mark's age hurtling down the path toward him. Instinctively, he stepped into the middle of the path and blocked it, steadying himself to sustain the impact of the thief's body against his own. Even so, the blow staggered him. He went down onto one knee, dragging the thief with him. Together, they tumbled a short distance down the rain-slick pathway. As their struggling bodies came to a stop, James lay panting, trying to catch his breath. In the next instant, he felt the thief being pulled off and away from him. One instant more, and he felt himself being lifted to his feet.

The rain came harder now. In trying to steady himself as he stood up, he glanced down to find better footing and saw the heavily laced, open-toed sandals of the man who had helped him to stand.

Fear paralyzed him. The man helping him was a Roman legionnaire. Daring not to show his face, James made a pretense of brushing at his robes. Then he mumbled a word of thanks to the solider and accepted his help in the climb back to the top of the incline. Another legionnaire and one of Agrippa's palace guards followed, dragging the struggling young thief between them.

As they reached the pavement of the street, a crowd gathered around them, and the man who had been robbed stepped forward. James turned to leave, fearful that someone in the crowd would recognize him.

"A moment, sir," the helpful legionnaire said. "You stopped this thief. There may be a reward in that!"

The legionnaire grabbed the hood of the thief's robe and threw it back to reveal his face.

From Agrippa's guardsman came a gasp of astonishment, followed by a cynical laugh. "Why, I know this man. He's the son of the royal baker. His name is Onan!"

Neither the face nor the name meant anything to James. He turned again to leave, a fearful anxiety pushing at him.

The legionnaire began to search through the thief's robes and withdrew a large money pouch.

"That's mine! That's mine!" the thief's victim asserted, quickly stepping forward. As he did so, he brushed sharply against James in such a way that the hood of James' robe was dislodged. For the merest moment before he readjusted the hood, his face was in open view.

But it was long enough for the thief, Onan, to recognize him. He gave a shout, pointed excitedly, and exclaimed, "James! James of Capernaum! James, one of the leaders of the Christians! King Agrippa searches for him. Grab him!"

20

I t was Chuza who brought the word to those assembled together in the house of Mary Mark that James was dead.

"After his capture at the Viaduct, he was brought before Agrippa for sentencing, then taken to a small alcove near the palace stables. And there, in the presence of Agrippa and three leaders of the Sanhedrin, he was beheaded."

Mary Mark felt suddenly sick. She turned away and sank down onto a nearby bench. Joanna went to comfort her. John Mark, his face white as bones bleached in a desert sun, stood stiff as a statue at a far table.

For Joseph, Barnabas, and Peter, the sharp edge of shock had been dulled by their earlier fears for James. Together they waited quite a long time in Joseph's house for him to rejoin them. When he did not, they suspected that he had been captured. Together they had returned to Mary Mark's only moments before Chuza brought the news of his death. And now grief made them stand apart from each other in the big room, each man an island of sadness, as if distance from each other somehow made it all more bearable.

"It was foreordained. Agrippa's grandfather killed the innocents when he heard of the birth of Jesus," Joseph said quietly, his eyes full of tears. "Antipas beheaded John the Baptizer and did not stop Jesus' crucifixion. And now James is Agrippa's victim. The blood of all the Herods thrives on cruelty. It was foreordained. We should have known."

"But to be killed by the sword . . . " Manaen's face paled as the reality of it came to him. He clenched his fists against the idea.

Mary Mark got up and walked to the far side of the main room to a window opening onto the small courtyard at the back of the house. The rain continued its steady downpour. The grayness of the day had deepened even more as the evening closed in. Mary Mark stared into it, sick at heart, feeling a kind of desperate desolation and questioning in her mind why God had let such an awful thing happen.

As if reading her mind, Peter came to her. In a voice that shook with the agony of loss, he said, "God does not deserve credit for this dreadful act."

She turned and searched his face, remembering that he and James had been friends for most of their lives. They'd played together as boys, worked together, shared homes together, endured the hardships as well as the joys that their loyalty to and love for Jesus had caused them to experience. And now she had to marvel at his reaction. There was no bitterness in his face, no hatred in his eyes, no disillusionment about God's protection for his friend. Why?

"I will miss my friend James," Peter went on, "but, I know his spirit lives. He is yet with us. I know that for a truth. It allows me to accept what has happened without disbelieving the greatness and goodness of God because of the meanness and the cruelty of man."

Outside in the courtyard, the bougainvillea covered gate creaked gently. Mary Mark turned and watched as a number of believers came through it in single file and climbed the stairway seeking sanctuary and prayer in the upper room.

"Still they come to you," Peter said. "And it is right that they should. Long since, the Lord chose this house as a sanctuary for his people. James' death has not changed that. The believers here in Jerusalem now need your strength, Mary Mark, and your faith and steadfastness more than ever."

She turned away from the window and went back to her place beside Joanna.

"What have they done with James' body?" Manaen asked, going to Chuza.

"It lies there where it fell waiting to be claimed."

"Who should claim it?"

"Someone powerful enough not to fall into Agrippa's trap." Chuza responded in a voice which still shook with revulsion. "Whoever claims the body will be suspected of having ties to the community of believers." He paced back and forth across the room, thinking hard and rubbing his hands nervously together. "I can't tell you how dangerous a mood Agrippa is in. Killing James by the sword has highly pleased the Pharisees and the Sadduces. Agrippa now seeks Peter. Then he will seek the other apostles. He intends to destroy all the leaders of the community in Jerusalem and then the community itself." He stopped his pacing directly in front of Joanna. "My pet, I fear for you and your friends. Agrippa has written to Emperor Claudius that he intends to rid Palestine of all Christians. It is his effort to regain his place of favor with the emperor."

"In that case," John Mark said, "we shall have to see that doesn't happen."

Everyone looked at him in surprise.

He turned to his mother. "So far as the claiming of James' body is concerned, Joseph will have to claim it. He's the only one of us with that much power. And as one of his business partners, I want to go with him."

A protest rose in Mary Mark's throat; but she stopped it before it could be uttered, in respect for her son's maturing sense of responsibility. Dangerous as their situation now was, he already was deeply a part of it—as a man of character and responsibility should be, she told herself rather sternly.

A halfhearted smile came onto his face. "Besides, Agrippa will remember that I was once in love with Mariamne. He will suspect me of nothing except being a foolish young lad wanting to be of help to Joseph.

Mary Mark glanced at Joseph, half hoping that her old friend would refuse to let John Mark go with him. Instead, he welcomed John Mark's offer with approval and respect glistening in his eyes.

Mary Mark got up, embraced John Mark, and held him close for a long moment. "Protect our friend Joseph. And see that James is buried with all the proper reverence we hold so important."

"I will, my mother. You can be sure I will."

When the gate in the back courtyard creaked softly shut behind them, Barnabas turned to Peter. "We must find a safe hiding place for you."

Peter gave a heavy sigh. "The running and hiding and running again is just beginning, isn't it?"

"I'm afraid it is, my friend," Barnabas agreed.

"The persecutions we saw at the hands of Saul will be nothing compared with what is to come. My spirit feels it." Peter hesitated and looked at Barnabas. "There may not be a hiding place left for me in Jerusalem."

"There are two houses I can think of that might be safe for you Peter," Manaen offered.

"Which houses are those?"

"Your own house. And the cheesemaker's house in the Lower City."

Peter and Barnabas looked at him in obvious disagreement. The others began to protest.

But Manaen persisted. "The guards have already searched both places. It is unlikely they will search them again. And also, both houses have hidden exits. Yours has the better one, Peter. At least, it's not a drainage ditch!"

"What do you think, Chuza?" Peter asked.

"I think it's unwise for me to advise you. As unwise as it would be for me to know where you really do hide, my friend." The round little man shrugged sadly and looked at Joanna. "It's even unwise for my wife to know where you hide. As I said, Agrippa's mood is ugly and unpredictable. If he should ask either of us, it is better that we don't know."

Out of the thoughtful silence that followed came the realization that sharing and openness among them might be coming to an end. It was not a happy realization. It had something to do with loss of trust, a violation of discretion. Until now, their mutual ties to Jesus had caused them to transcend the limitations of occupation and age, position and wealth. Secrecy and isolation among them had been put aside, as had the suspicions caused by differences of class, color, and geography. They simply stood together through peace and persecution by virtue of an open sharing of information and a bond of mutual belief.

Now, though, Chuza's reminder that he was not one of them emphasized the danger. As Joanna's husband and friend over the years to all the rest of them, the distinction had seemed to make little difference. But with danger so close, he himself brought the distinction clearly into focus and, by doing so, proved his friendship to them as a community and as individuals.

Joanna got up from the bench beside Mary Mark and went to him. "Thank you, my husband, for caring about our friends. You are right, of course." Hesitantly she took his hand. "I shall return with you to the palace at once."

Mary Mark walked with them to the courtyard, embraced them both, and watched as they slipped through the gate pulling the hoods of their robes close against the rain.

When she returned to the main room of the house, she found only Rhoda there. "Where are the others?"

"Manaen has returned to the palace. Barnabas, Sallu, and Kedar have gone to tell the rest of the community about James' death."

"And Peter?"

Rhoda rubbed at her eyes with the sleeve of her tunic. "Peter has gone off by himself to find a hiding place."

Unfortunately, his efforts to hide were not successful. In an attempt to get to the house of Mary and Martha in Bethany, he was caught by an alert Roman sentry at the Dung Gate in the city's wall. A shout brought the Temple guards, who took him to the prison beneath the Temple Mount and there chained him at the wrists and ankles.

Word of his capture pleased Agrippa, yet he feared that Peter might escape from the Temple guards' prison. Therefore, he asked the Roman commander to assign his soldiers to bring Peter to the prison deep within the Fortress Antonia and keep him there until he could be brought to public trial after Passover.

The Roman commander obliged. He assigned four squads of four soldiers each to the task. Once inside the fortress prison, Peter was chained at the wrists, and two soldiers stayed with him.

Barnabas brought the news of Peter's imprisonment back to Mary Mark. He had seen the soldiers taking the big apostle into the Fortress Antonia as he made his rounds telling believers about James' death. The Passover supper now included prayers for Peter's safety and release, as well as the prayers of thanksgiving for Jesus and his resurrection. And when the Passover supper was completed, a prayer vigil for Peter's safety was begun by many believers.

So Peter was kept in prison. But the community of believers was earnestly continuing to pray to God for him.

The night before Herod was to bring him to trial, Peter, bound with two chains, was sleeping between two soliders, and sentries stood guard at the entrance.

Suddenly an angel of the Lord appeared, and a light shone in the cell. He struck Peter on the side and woke him up. "Quick, get up!" he said.

The chains fell off of Peter.

"Put on your clothes and sandals," the angel said.

Peter did so.

"Wrap your cloak around you and follow me."

Peter followed the angel out of the prison, but he had no idea that what the angel was doing was really happening. He thought he was seeing a vision.

They passed the first and second guards and came to the iron gate leading out into the street. The iron gate opened for them by itself, and they went through it. When they had walked the length of one street, suddenly the angel left him.

Peter came to himself and looked around. He was at the eastern approach to the Viaduct. The darkness of the night was deep and still. It seemed that all in the city, friend and foe, were sleeping. In the heavens, the shimmering stars looked close enough to touch. He looked down at himself, checking to make sure he was not dreaming. The sandaled feet were his. The cloak of good Galilee homespun was also his. He crossed his arms, feeling his shoulders, flexing the muscles in them, and then he touched his face, letting his fingers explore brow, nose, and beard. He felt every touch. He was not dreaming; this was no vision; he was awake. He was very much alive and physically standing at the approach to the Viaduct. Behind him loomed the forbidding bulk of Fortress Antonia and beside it the awesome heights of the Temple Mount.

"Now I know without a doubt that the Lord sent his angel and rescued me from Herod's clutches and from everything the Pharisees and Sadducees were planning." He breathed deeply of the night air. As the joy of freedom raced through his spirit, he whispered a prayer of thanksgiving to God.

His next thought was of his friends and family and their safety. When his escape was discovered, there would be no safe place anywhere in Jerusalem for him or for anyone who knew him. Of that he was certain. The joy of his own freedom gave way to the urgency of concern for the others. He turned, went across the Viaduct into the Upper City, and made straightway for Mary Mark's house.

He went to the front gate, out of caution for the safety of the obscure back entrance that led so directly to the upper room. Going in the front gate might be more dangerous because it opened directly onto the street, but it seemed to him the best thing to do. He rapped on it, quietly at first, wondering if the house was being watched again. Beyond the gate in the courtyard, all was still. Nervousness began to creep up inside him. He pushed at the gate, hoping to open it without assistance, but it was barred from the inside. He rapped again, hard enough this time to make his knuckles hurt and loudly enough to awaken the deepest sleeper. He glanced about, suspicious now that every shadow might contain unfriendly ears and eyes.

Just as he was about to rap for the third time, he heard the sound of footsteps on the other side of the gate, stealthy, hesitant.

"Open the gate, Let me in." He said it in a half whisper.

"Peter?" Rhoda's voice came back to him from inside the gate. "Peter, is that you?"

"It is. Let me in."

"But . . . it can't be . . . it . . . " The sound of her footsteps hurrying back toward the house finished her sentence. It also confirmed her astonished disbelief.

Peter felt disbelief himself. He pushed at the gate. It was still barred. "Rhoda, how can you do this?" he muttered, pushing harder at the gate. "Come. Let me in! Rhoda! Rhoda!" In disgust, he slumped against the gate and sighed heavily. "It appears the angel of the Lord left me too soon," he said to himself, making a fist and pounding at the gate insistently, demandingly.

Once more the sound of footsteps in the courtyard came toward the gate. In another instant, he heard someone lift the bar out of its couplings, and the gate swung open.

Mary Mark, a small clay lamp in her hand, peered out at him. An excited Rhoda stood close beside her.

Mary Mark's eyes widened. "It is you! It really is you!"

"I know it's hard to believe, but yes, I am Peter!"

She stepped aside, making room for him to come in. He did so quickly, closed the gate and secured it once more with the bar, then followed Mary Mark into the house and up an inside stairway to the upper room. Rhoda trailed close behind them.

When Peter stepped into view of the believers who had assembled so many days before to keep a prayer vigil for him, they all got up onto their feet at once. A respectful hush then fell across the room. It was as if they momentarily doubted that he really could be standing before them. Had they prayed with such intensity that their vision was still transcendent? Or had they prayed with such wavering faith that they were astonished at its power to help free him? Whichever it was, their respectful silence extended until Barnabas and John Mark came to him, shaking his hand in welcome.

His wife and mother–in–law came forward to embrace him. Tears spilled from Peter's eyes as he returned their embraces and held them close. The others now came forward, some rushing, all talking at once, expressing their joy at his escape and asking for details about how his escape had occurred. With his hand, Peter motioned for them to be quiet, and he described how the Lord had sent the angel to bring him out of prison.

His listeners looked at each other, some believing, but most of them astonished. And in their delight, they began to murmur fresh praises.

"Remember what Jesus told us?" Peter asked them. "Over and over again, he explained to us that men may find certain things impossible to do, but God doesn't. With God, all things are possible. And because of God, I stand here before you."

As he finished, he turned to Barnabas. "Will you send word to Capernaum to James, the brother of our Lord, that he must now be our shepherd here in Jerusalem? I must leave this city and go to some other place. The Holy Spirit is telling me to go."

"Of course, Peter, I will tell him what you said."

"And when you can, tell the brothers, too, of my wish in this matter."

Again, Barnabas agreed.

He turned and looked at his wife and mother–in–law. "I shall miss you. And I shall send for you as quickly as possible." Fresh tears glistened in his eyes.

His wife moved closer to him and gently brushed at the tears with her strong, brown hand. "Whoever leaves house or family for the sake of Our Lord or for his gospel will receive a hundred times as much in house and family, love, and honor," she reminded him in a half whisper.

He smiled at her and turned away as John Mark came forward and extended his hand. Peter ignored the hand and instead pulled John Mark to him and gave him a bear hug. "I shall miss you, young master scribe. I ask you to remember one thing. 'Many that are first will be last, and many who are last will be first.' If our friend Jesus was here tonight, that's what he'd say to both of us. Don't be sad for me. We will meet again."

John Mark blushed with the emotion of the farewell.

"Mary Mark," Peter said coming to her and taking both of her hands in his, "I can never thank you for all your kindnesses, and for the love you have shown to all of the brothers and to my family. May the Lord bless you and keep you."

"And may the Lord give you peace, my friend. We will watch after your wife and mother–in–law. Go in safety. And return here someday in safety."

Peter turned to the assembled faithful. "I bid you all farewell. May the Lord make his face to shine upon you."

With Peter's departure, the prayer vigil came to an end. Believers began to leave by twos and threes to return to their own houses. For the first time in many days, Mary Mark found her house temporarily at rest and quiet.

But she also found the quiet to be an uneasy one. She was suddenly very tired. Her grief for James was still too fresh. Her regret at Peter's having to leave Jerusalem gnawed at her, and the sense of foreboding, while dispelled to great degree by all that had already happened, still remained with her. She made her way to her own chambers, wondering what would happen next and if she would be able to cope with it.

21

In the morning, there was no small commotion among the soldiers as to what had become of Peter. The two soliders who slept in the cell with him awakened to find themselves guarding nothing but a set of empty wrist chains. The big man who had constantly prayed to his God and who had repeatedly tried to convince them that Jesus was still alive had vanished. He was nowhere to be seen, either in the cell or outside it in any of the other wards of the prison deep inside Fortress Antonia. He simply had vanished. So had his clothes.

"Somebody had to have helped him!"

"But who could have?"

"Somebody had to. He's gone!"

The two guards outside the cell heard the argument and came running to find out what had happened. After their initial astonishment, they hurried to the iron gate at the prison entrance. The chain and padlock were in place, as they had been when the guards last checked it the night before.

"Impossible!"

"It's as if some angel spirited him away," said one of the cell guards in a half whisper of awe.

"Don't be a fool! He's got to still be somewhere inside the prison."

"He's gone, I tell you."

"Look again! Search everywhere!"

Search again they did, but to no avail. The prisoner, Simon Peter of Bethsaida, leader of the followers of The Way, was nowhere to be found.

"What will we tell the captain?" Fear masked the guard's face.

"And what will the captain tell the commander?"

"And what will the commander tell King Herod Agrippa?"

No one had any choice but to tell the truth. Peter had escaped. They didn't know exactly when and they certainly didn't know exactly how he had done it, but he was gone.

Agrippa's reaction was one of angry frustration. As he had done before, he ordered another citywide search for Peter. Only this time, the Roman legionnaires were ordered to assist his palace guards. That put four times the number of soldiers into the search. And, in reality, he would have liked to have had four times more that number. The order for this search included every house in the city.

"Not just those suspected of harboring Christians, but every house in the city!" he shouted.

The Roman commander looked stunned. The order was an unrealistic one. It would take weeks to go through every house in the city. The prisoner would have long since escaped Jerusalem altogether.

Chuza and Manaen exchanged a look that held not only astonishment, but fear. The houses of Mary Mark and Joseph, until now immune to anything but a cursory search for James, would come under the rough scrutiny of the Romans.

Thaumustus' face held a look of surprise, too. But like the others, he said nothing.

Agrippa pushed out of his chair and strode the length of his chamber and back again to stop face to face with the Roman. "The Jews' Temple guards could have done a better job keeping a prisoner."

Embarrassed resentment flooded the man's face.

"I want to cross-examine your guards myself. Bring them here to the palace at once."

When the commander returned with the four guards and their captain, Agrippa questioned them personally, but he received from them no more information than their commander had initially reported to him. The situation added to his angry frustration. Then and there, using the power of his position as a consul to the emperor, he ordered the four Roman guards and their captain executed!

Heavy pressure and harassment now came against all the citizens of Jerusalem. No one was immune, but those suspected of being Christians received the most brutal treatment. Houses were ransacked. Cabinets and storage chests that were large enough to hide a person were bashed in with the butts of Roman lances. Many householders were thrown out into the streets. Many others were thrown into prison on the flimsiest of charges. And still others who were bold enough to resist the searchers were either bludgeoned to death or condemned to crucifixion. People fled from Jerusalem by the hundreds.

But hundreds of others made their way to the house of Mary Mark and the sanctuary of its upper room. They had done this for so many years that they did it now out of familiar assurance. They dismissed the notion, if they even thought of it, that her house, too, would be subject to search, or that it was dangerous for them to be there, or that there was danger for her household as well.

Mary Mark accepted them without hesitation, refusing to bar the gates and the doors, her only requirement being that those who sought sanctuary must become part of the new prayer vigil for all the citizens of Jerusalem. "It makes no difference now," she told them, "whether they are Jews or Gentiles, believers or Pharisees, the people of Jerusalem need our prayers. And God needs to know from us that we reject Agrippa's evil!"

Chuza and Manaen did not share Mary Mark's courage nor her perception of faith in action. While they may have agreed with her in principle, they also knew for a fact that soldiers would come and search every inch of her house. That would result in disaster. They began to consider how they could forestall such a thing.

"There is only one person I know who can help us," Manaen finally spoke up.

"Who?"

"Thaumustus."

"Thaumustus?" The surprised look on Chuza's round face was followed quickly by one of disapproval. "Why should he help us?"

"Consider these things," Manaen replied. "His attitude toward us both has been more open and friendly ever since the dinner in Mary Mark's house. That's one thing."

"Yes, but that means nothing. It was after the dinner that he told the tax collectors about the Antioch caravan."

"I think it does mean something when put together with his more recent reactions."

"Such as?"

"He's jealous of Blastus and Agrippa's promotion of him from personal servant to court chamberlain."

"What else?"

"He was as revulsed by the beheading of James as we were. And he opposed the way the search for Peter is being done."

Chuza leaned back in his chair, considering what strength there was in all of this for motivating Thaumustus to help them, doubting that they could trust him at all.

"And one more thing," Manaen added. "He doesn't hate Christians any more than he loves Jews. Like you, Chuza, he's a religious neutral."

"Then, if we ask his help, it must be on a very practical basis? Is that what you're saying?"

Manaen nodded.

"And what if he's offended by our request?"

Manaen shrugged. "Then we know he's an enemy to be wary of. But what is new in that?"

Chuza got up and paced. By the time he returned to his chair, he'd made his decision. "Very well. Let's ask his help."

They found Thaumustus alone in his own chambers. Chuza broached the subject with discretion, careful to reveal as little as possible about who had what religious beliefs. He simply described the citizens who sought refuge in Mary Mark's house as friends who had known the family a long time or business associates who had become frightened at the brutal way the Romans were making a search of all houses. "You have been a guest in that house, Thaumustus. You know the quality of its hospitality. The mistress of that house will not turn away anyone. But . . . "

"But if the soliders find such a large group there when they search," Manaen interrupted, "they will jump to the conclusion that all are these so-called Christians and do something dreadful."

Thaumustus sat with his hands folded across his belly, looking first at one and then the other of them for a seemingly endless moment. A feeling of heaviness settled in the room.

"You know, of course, that I cannot stop the soldiers from searching," he said.

"But there must be some way to divert them," Manaen insisted, going to him. "You're the king's high counselor. You have influence with the Roman commander."

Thaumustus shook his head. "Not in this matter. He takes his orders directly from Agrippa. Remember, Agrippa is still a Roman consul. The emperor may have stopped the building of the wall, but he did not take away Agrippa's consulship."

The three of them settled into silence, considering the problem. Outside, the wind made a sudden whirling gust, changed directions, and whirled again before letting the sandy debris it had claimed settle earthward once more.

Thaumustus straightened in his chair. "Of course, I could instruct the soldiers to leave that house for my personal inspection, couldn't I?"

The heaviness in the room vanished.

"I would need help, though."

A thin smile began to play at Manaen's lips. Chuza's eyes narrowed in wary interest.

"Could you two give me that help?"

"We could," Manaen hurriedly agreed.

Thaumustus stood up. "I shall inform King Agrippa that I have chosen to do this because of the household's association with the merchant, Joseph, and because of the friendships with many here in the palace."

Chuza stiffened slightly. Manaen shifted uneasily.

Thaumustus took note and said reassuringly, "Have no fear. I know you, Manaen, are attracted to the woman Mary Mark. That is none of my concern. My concern is for the goods and foodstuffs belonging to that house. That will be Agrippa's concern, also. He will not want them destroyed, or confiscated, by the Romans. His greed will see the sense of having me search that particular house instead of the Romans."

Both Chuza and Manaen relaxed.

"I shall inform Agrippa at once and send the message to call off the soldiers. Then I think we should all go at once to Mary Mark's. Wait for me at the side door."

Chuza and Manaen proceeded in that direction. But within two or three steps, Chuza said, "I must tell Joanna. She has been so worried about Mary Mark." He turned away and hurried off to his private apartment. Joanna, however, was not to be found in the spacious living quarters. Nor were her two maidservants. Chuza frowned, trying to remember if she'd told him she was going out. He was sure she hadn't.

If she had, he would have ordered her not to go. The streets were very unsafe now, even the streets of the Upper City. He went back down the long corridor, through the side door, and out into the gardens where Manaen sat on a bench waiting. Thaumustus was nowhere in sight.

"Well?" Manaen questioned.

Chuza sat down, puffing a bit from hurrying. "She was not in our chambers. Nor were her two serving girls." He paused frowning more deeply. "Nor, for that matter, were my manservants." Fear came into his eyes. "And they're all Christians!"

Manaen straightened. "Agrippa's seized them? Is that what you're thinking?"

Chuza nodded.

"But, he wouldn't believe Christians were working in his palace!" Manaen objected.

"He said he'd rid Jerusalem of all of them. Wherever they were to be found!"

Before Manaen could make another reply, Thaumustus came out from the side door, motioned for them to join him, and led the way through a small, private gate in the south wall of the palace and out into the street. There he stopped to report that Agrippa had given his approval for him to personally search Mary Mark's house. Other than that, none of them spoke during the short walk.

Manaen marveled at Chuza's composure, knowing how he adored Joanna, recognizing how worried he must be, and realizing that he must be more suspicious than ever of Thaumustus. Not that he blamed him. It was quite unlike Joanna to go out of the palace without telling him. Something must have happened, something serious.

As they rounded the corner and went toward the front gate to Mary Mark's house, a squad of legionnaires approached from the opposite direction.

"It looks as if we have not come a moment too soon,"

Thaumustus said, continuing past the gate to hail the leader of the soldiers.

Manaen and Chuza stopped at the gate and watched as Thaumustus talked with the soldier. It was obvious the man did not believe what Thaumustus was telling him. He began to argue and continued to do so until Thaumustus pulled from his robes a slip of parchment and a small pouch of coins. He held the parchment up for the soldier to read. But the man waved it away, as if the writing on it meant nothing to him. When he realized that the pouch of coins was for him, though, he stopped arguing. A moment later, he saluted Thaumustus and ordered his squad of soldiers to withdraw.

Manaen let out a sigh of relief and rapped at the gate.

By the time Sallu opened the gate, the soldiers had disappeared from sight. Sallu greeted Manaen and Chuza, looked suspiciously at Thaumustus, and led the way into the main room of the house. Mary Mark and Barnabas were in conversation with a visitor. Manaen looked hard at the man, recognizing him.

"Forgive this intrusion my friends," he said, going to Mary Mark.

She glanced beyond him to Thaumustus. Wariness flashed briefly in her eyes. And though she spoke her usual words of welcome, the tension in the air belied the words.

Manaen couldn't help but wonder if the unexpected appearance of Thaumustus was the total cause of the tension or if the conversation with Paul, the other visitor, was partly responsible. He knew that Paul's aggresssiveness sometimes irritated Mary Mark, and he abruptly remembered that she was opposed to his most recent efforts to get Barnabas to return to Antioch with him. He wondered if his arrival had interrupted another discussion of that subject.

Barnabas introduced Paul to Thaumustus and to Chuza.

"Paul is a maker of tents," he smoothly explained. "We often buy from him."

When the introductions were acknowledged, Manaen turned again to Mary Mark. "Thaumustus is here to personally search your house.

Her eyes widened.

"You mean before the soldiers come?" Barnabas asked.

"Instead of the soldiers, sir," Thaumustus replied.

"Oh?"

"None of us wanted the soldiers in your house, Mary Mark," Chuza said. "Thaumustus succeeded in getting the king's permission to do the search himself. In respect to the amount of goods and foodstuffs that might otherwise be . . . ah . . . damaged, you might say. You know, of course, the Romans are ransacking everything."

A troubled look came into Mary Mark's eyes. "We have heard a great many stories about destruction and brutality."

Barnabas studied Thaumustus. "You'll be required to report all that you find here to Agrippa, I suppose."

Thaumustus smiled. "Not necessarily. Your friends who have come to you for sanctuary will be of no interest to the king."

In spite of themselves, Barnabas and Mary Mark exchanged looks of astonishment.

"We told him," Chuza quickly inserted. "Manaen and I. We told him that your business associates and many old friends, frightened by the Romans, have sought sanctuary with you."

"I'm a practical man," Thaumustus said, giving a side glance toward Paul. "Destruction of a city over religious differences is not practical. I don't believe in it."

The tension in the air abated but did not totally disappear. "Where would you like to start your search, sir?" Mary Mark offered.

"Wherever you say m'lady."

She led him through the various rooms on the ground floor, deliberately avoiding a small pantrylike alcove off the cooking area where a door to the big storage room was located. Her natural reluctance to expose the household's wealth was matched by caution. Joanna, those people she'd brought with her from the palace, and several dozen other Christians were hiding behind the bales and baskets. She also avoided any mention of the small courtyard at the back of the house and the stairway leading to the upper room. The latter had been masked rather effectively with baskets of reeds and tall grasses.

With equal reluctance, she hoped she would not have to show Thaumustus the rooms on the second floor, even though care had been taken to hide several important features. The door that led directly into the upper meeting room had been covered by hanging a huge lion's skin over it. And only a few of the community remained in the big room in a prayer vigil. All the rest were hiding on the flat roof of the house. This was what concerned her the most about taking Thaumustus to the second floor. If the refugees were moving about, the noise could be heard in the rooms on the second floor. And even though Thaumustus claimed no interest in the refugees, Mary Mark was not willing for him to see that several hundred of Jesus' followers were hiding in the house.

By the time they completed going through the entire ground floor of the house, Thaumustus hesitated at the foot of the stairs and glanced upward.

She held her breath, praying that he would not ask to search there, too.

"What's up there? Storage?"

"Sleeping rooms," she answered, hoping her voice sounded steady and even.

He nodded, gave a short bow, and turned again toward the main room.

"Paul and I have finished our discussion of tents. And of other things, as well," Barnabas said, glancing carefully at Mary Mark. "Come, Thaumustus, and have some refreshments with us."

Thaumustus and Manaen took chairs. Chuza drew Mary Mark aside and told her about Joanna being missing from the palace.

She gave his hand a reassuring squeeze. "She is here. And she brought with her all those from the palace who believe as we do. Not to fear, my friend. They are all well hidden."

"Even if Thaumustus changes his mind? Even if he asks to see all your friends and business associates?"

"Even if he changes his mind." Her words sounded more reassuring than she felt.

She excused herself and went into her own rooms in a far corner of the house. The strain of the search had tired her. This would not be the end of it. She had no assurances that it would be otherwise. Chuza had brought that possibility into focus with his comment about Thaumustus changing his mind. He could. Of course, he could. But more likely, it would be Agrippa who would change his mind. Still in an ugly and unpredictable mood, he could order the house destroyed in the blink of an eye.

She thought of all the people sheltered in the house. She remembered the look on Peter's face as he bade them all farewell. And she remembered James—idealistic, impetuous, rash, quick-tempered. And dead at Agrippa's hand. With John, his brother, leading the other apostles to safety away from Jerusalem, the community of believers was left without a leader. It would be many weeks before James, the brother of the Lord, could return from Galilee and head the church.

She closed the door to her room, needing privacy, needing a time to think. To put things in perspective, to pray to the Holy Spirit for guidance. Hard days were yet to come.

"Ecclesia." She said the word softly, remembering with a special fondness the first time she'd heard Manaen use it. The Greek word for "a gathering together." The gathering. The church. "Ecclesia!"

What would become of it now? Suddenly she realized that it was her house, her brother, and herself who were holding together the believers in Jerusalem. But for how long? How long could they withstand Agrippa's persecution? Was there nothing she could do to help make things better?

22

The answers to Mary Mark's prayers, meditations, and questions came to her sometime during the velvet hours of the night. Perhaps the answer that was most responsible for spurring her to action was the remembrance of something she had heard Jesus say many times. "Seek out every opportunity to turn danger into peace and disaster into victory. Go forward with faith. Fear not."

By the time the sun made its appearance above the heights of the Mount of Olives, she had slipped through the bougainvillea covered back gate without anyone seeing her and made her way to the palace of Herod Agrippa. The hood of her robe pulled close about her, she announced to the sentry at the palace gate that she had come to minister to the wife of Chuza. He gave her immediate admission, not realizing that Joanna lay safely at slumber in Mary Mark's own house.

Once inside the palace, she saw a servant girl polishing one of the beautiful mosaic floors. Pretending to be a servant herself, she asked directions to the apartment of the honorable Manaen. The girl pointed the way and gave a knowing giggle. Mary Mark felt the heat of embarrassment come into her face as she realized what the servant was thinking.

But without looking back, she hurried on in the direction the girl had indicated. Moments later, she opened a great wooden door and let herself into the apartment. It was large, airy, and furnished in a style befitting a person of high standing. Manaen was lying asleep on a couch of Roman design. No servants were in the room. She went to him and gently shook his shoulder.

Almost in one continuous action, his eyes flew open, and he sat up. "Mary Mark! What . . . why . . . "

Gently, she cupped her hand over his mouth. "Please, don't call your manservant. I want no one to know I am here but you."

He pushed her hand away from his mouth. "Nor do I!"

"Until later, that is."

"What do you mean, until later?" Disapproval of her being in his private chambers clearly showed in his face. "Did anyone see you come in here?"

"Only a servant girl."

"The palace will buzz with talk of it."

"Let it buzz." She walked away.

He rubbed at his head, as if trying to rid himself of sleep's lingering mists. "I don't like it. I don't want the reputation of my future wife to be—"

A small gasp of surpise escaped from her.

"Why do you act so surprised?"

She stared back at him, almost forgetting the real reason she had come here. Since his profession of love for her on the day they had ridden out of the city to the secluded vale on the Emmaus road, he had never again spoken of his feelings for her or of his intentions toward her. In the intervening time, so many serious occurrences had involved them both that she'd decided their special friendship was all there would ever be between them.

And she'd come to terms with that belief. She valued the friendship. She was comfortable with it, even to the point of laughing at herself for ever worrying about whether or not John Mark would be a hindrance to their relationship. Of course, he no longer was. But to hear Manaen refer to her as his future wife now shocked her in an oddly unexpected way.

Manaen pulled his robe from a nearby chair and shrugged into it. "You know I love you. I've shown it in a hundred ways. Why should you act so surprised when I mention that I think of you as my future wife?"

She did not answer.

He studied her for a moment, then cinched the robe tightly around his waist, walked to one of the narrow windows in the suite, opened its lattice, and looked out. "The light of the morning is barely with us," he exclaimed, turning toward her. "What are you doing here, anyway, and at such an unaccustomed hour"

"I need your help."

"For what?"

"To see Agrippa."

His mouth gaped. He stared at her. "Why should you want to see Agrippa?"

"I must talk with him."

His look turned hard, suspicious.

"It is most important that I talk with him," she insisted, realizing how foolish she must sound, yet not daring to explain what she hoped to accomplish. Nor could she divulge the full reason she had come. No conventional wisdom would sanction what she had in mind. But she had not come here as a result of logic or of conventional wisdom. She had come simply because she could not ignore the still, small voice of the Holy Spirit. This was an unconventional visit for an unconventional purpose, and that is what finally convinced Manaen to take her to see Agrippa. "I cannot ignore the voice of the Holy Spirit. I must speak with Agrippa."

The sun now fully penetrated the corridors of the palace with shafts of new light. As they approached the royal chamber, its ornate gilt doors flew open. Agrippa came striding through them, shouting obscenities at two servants awkwardly scurrying backwards before him. One of the servants stumbled. Agrippa kicked at him, shoving him out of the way. Chuza hurried up from the interior of the royal chambers to dismiss the servants and to placate Agrippa. At that moment and at the same time, they saw Mary Mark and Manaen standing in the corridor. Both men came to an astonished halt.

Chuza gasped her name out loud. She nodded to him respectfully. "I have come to see King Agrippa. The matter is urgent and very important."

Chuza looked to Manaen for an explanation, but he only gave a resigned shrug in response.

"I am told you are a man of high intelligence, sir," she said to Agrippa.

He remained motionless, apparently intrigued by the novelty of a woman coming unsummoned and unannounced to his royal chambers, especially this woman.

"I have also been told that you can be a man of compassion. Is that true?"

A look of faint amusement slipped onto his face. "What is it you want, woman?"

"Peace. Peace for Jerusalem is what I want."

The look of amusement disintegrated into one of arrogance. He started to move away from her.

"Such peace is a matter of prosperity, Your Excellency. Your prosperity."

He hesitated and glanced at her.

"Unfortunately, prosperity is being destroyed by all this persecution."

He turned fully toward her, folded his arms over his chest, and stared at her with new interest.

"Your prosperity can be much better served by peace in Jerusalem. Besides, your house–to–house search for the man called Peter is a useless one. And it is an evil one."

The fact that Agrippa stood listening to such criticism of himself mesmerized Chuza and Manaen. They had never known him to accept such bluntness, not even from Thaumustus. That he would accept it from a woman was inconceivable. They knew he would strike back, yet they found themselves unable to move or speak in Mary Mark's defense.

"Whether or not Peter is still in the city, which I doubt, your soldiers will never find him."

Anger glinted in Agrippa's eyes.

"In the meantime, they kill and maim and imprison hundreds of innocents. And if you care nothing for that, let me remind you that they also make spoil of goods and foodstuffs that could better bring shekels into your own treasury. That is an insult to your intelligence, Your Excellency."

Stepping toward her, he made a cursing sound. "And what about your treasury? Yours and Joseph's?"

She stood her ground. "Your treasury is the important one. You are the king of many kingdoms. Your popularity and your strength is dependent upon the size of your treasury. Or so you thought when you married off your daughters."

At the mention of his daughters, the tiniest trace of regret slipped into his face. He unfolded his arms and turned as if to leave. Instead, he walked to a marble bench nearby and sat down.

Mary Mark followed, seating herself on the other end of the bench.

He rubbed at his forehead and repositioned himself so he could look at her directly. "You speak boldly, woman. Do you pride yourself on your honesty and directness?"

She waited, suspicious of a trap, for only now did she realize just how boldly she had been speaking.

"Well, do you?"

Manaen held his breath.

"I insist on an answer," Agrippa continued. "Tell me how honest you are and how much pride you take in it. Otherwise, I shall have to test your honesty."

She remained silent.

"Very well. Then test your honesty I will."

Still she said nothing.

"Are you what they call a Christian? If you are, you cannot lie about it. Or so I hear." He leaned toward her, pressing for an answer. Sunlight streaked his breastplace and fired a brilliant reflection up onto the sardonic set of his mouth and the look of cruelty in his eyes. "Well, are you one of these Christians?"

"I am," she nodded without hesitation. "Jesus the Nazarene is a very good friend. And I believe him to be the Christ, the Messiah that our people have awaited for so many, many years."

The frankness of her response took him off guard. He stared at her for a long moment, apparently trying to assimilate what she had just admitted. It was blasphemy, of course. She admitted to being a Christian. He could have her strung up and quartered for such an admission. And she had sat there calmly, admitting her friendship with a dead heretic as if he was not only her friend, but her hero, her savior, and as if he was alive! He looked up at Manaen. "She takes me for a fool, doesn't she? How can you have a liking for a woman like this?" He turned. "And you, Chuza, why do you allow your wife to be a friend to such a one as this? Are you all Christians, too?"

Neither man made a response.

Agrippa rubbed again at his forehead. "What do you want from me, woman?"

"I want you to stop the persecutions."

"You're mad."

"Call off your soldiers."

"I should call them here to cast you into prison!"

"Give Jerusalem her peace. Stop the persecutions."

With a curse of disgust, he stood up and paced back and forth in agitation, obviously wanting to leave this strange encounter, yet for some reason unable to do so.

Mary Mark remained unmoving and silent. Her part was done. The plea for peace had been made. All else now was in the hands of the Holy Spirit.

A half dozen feet away from where she sat, Agrippa suddenly stopped his pacing and stared at her with demonic intensity. "Peace for Jerusalem?" he shouted. "That's what you want? That's what you shall have. By the gods of Rome, that's what you shall have!"

Manaen and Chuza stood thunderstruck.

"You shall have your peace. For seven days. Tomorrow I leave for Caesarea–by–the–Sea. I will absent from Jerusalem for seven days. And for those seven days, I shall declare a truce. No more searches, no persecution, no harassment. For those seven days."

Chuza's eyes were round with stupefaction. Manaen's showed utter dismay.

Mary Mark sat with hands folded in her lap, waiting for Agrippa to finish. He was a master of politics. She knew there would have to be a trade–off. He had not yet mentioned one. But when he began to pace again without saying anything further, she asked, "And what do you want from me for this seven–day truce?"

He spun around. "I want Jerusalem to be rid of you!"

She reeled inwardly. Leave Jerusalem? Leave her house? It was the symbol of everything worthwhile in life. Yonah. John Mark. Barnabas. Jesus and his men. The spirit–filled Pentecost. Joanna, Chuza. Peter, John, James. Joseph. Manaen. And the other believers. Those hundreds and hundreds of people who believed in the living Lord as she did and who sought shelter in her house. Leave all that? Leave her house? How could she leave it?

Only the greatest of restraint kept her from looking at Manaen. She dared not, knowing how easy it would be to yield to the temptation of wanting the protection of his strong arms, knowing that if she did look at him all the fear and pain rising inside her would be exposed to full view. That would give Agrippa comfort. And he must never know how sharply his words frightened her. Their confrontation was not yet over. She dared not let him see fear in her eyes or give him any hint of the depth of anguish tearing at her heart.

"No one but fools would believe in a dead prophet like this Jesus of yours," Agrippa stormed. "But you say you believe in him. You act as if he's alive! Well, if he is, he's a threat to me and to my power. And I'll have him crucified again! So, I give you this truce of seven days. In that same seven days, you are to make preparations to close your house permanently and leave Jerusalem forever."

"And you will extend the truce?

"You are never to return," he evaded.

"And if I decide to stay?" She asked it over the pounding of her heart.

"I will destroy your house, and all within it, and all who are associated with it!"

Later that same day, she explained how she felt to Joseph and John Mark and Barnabas, Manaen, Joanna, and Chuza.

"I've never thought of myself as a sacrificial lamb. But I know now how it feels."

Joanna began to cry. Chuza attempted to comfort her.

"I'm not the first, of course, nor will I be the last," Mary Mark went on, fighting back her own tears. "Jesus tried to explain it to all of us a long time ago, but only now do I feel I really know what he meant."

John Mark came to her and put a steadying arm around her. Barnabas followed, supporting her, too, so that the three of them stood linked in the tight bonds of family love and reassurance.

Five days later the news came from Caesarea–by–the–Sea that Herod Agrippa had been struck down by sudden illness and had died.

"I was there," Joseph's courier reported to them. "I saw him stricken. He was wearing his royal robes and had just finished delivering a public address from his throne. The crowd shouted, 'This is the voice of a god, not of a man.' King Agrippa loved the applause. He accepted all their plaudits of his godlike qualities. And that's when he was stricken."

The three of them exchanged looks of astonishment.

"You know sir," the courier concluded, turning to Joseph, "it was as if an angel of the Lord struck him down because he gave no praise or honor to God."

For several minutes after the courier departed, the three of them had little to say. Each was lost in personal thought. Agrippa's death changed everything. Organized searching for Peter, already halted by the seven days of truce, was forgotten by the Romans. Persecution of the Christians remaining in Jerusalem ceased. Payment of recently added Temple taxes was deferred. And once again, a procurator would be appointed by Rome to govern the lands of Herod Agrippa until his son came of age.

For Mary Mark personally, it was a turning point of destiny. Agrippa's one–sided truce no longer mattered. The decision she'd already made would never have to be acted upon, unless she chose to do so. Her house was no longer a target for destruction. With the Herods out of power, fears for her friends subsided, and the strange, oft–repeating sense of foreboding disappeared.

But it was not until many days later that the full perspective for her future became clear. She, John Mark, and Barnabas had just returned from Agrippa's funeral memorial. They had invited Manaen, Joseph, Joanna, and Chuza to come home with them for refreshments, and they were all gathered in the small courtyard at the back of the house. Household servants moved in and out among them, serving them and seeing to their wishes.

"His bier was impressive," Joanna said. "Gold. Wrought with jewels. He would have liked it."

"He would have wished for a bigger crowd, though," said Chuza, reaching for a sweetmeat.

"But all of his children came," said Joseph. "I am glad for that."

"I saw Mariamne," John Mark said.

Mary Mark looked quickly at her son, thinking she heard a touch of wistfulness in his tone. But he smiled at her, reached for a goblet of new wine, and sipped at it.

"Mariamne is still very beautiful," Joanna said.

John Mark nodded. "But it's really best that she married a prince."

Joanna looked at him quizzically. Rhoda, who was about to serve a basket of bread, gave him a similar look. But from behind her, Sallu grinned at Mary Mark as if they shared some wonderful secret. Then he stepped to the doorway and motioned for all the other servants to come out into the courtyard.

John Mark noticed and paced his next words accordingly. "Yes, it's good she married as she did. In fact, it was really the right thing for her to do. She would have been unhappy as the wife of an itinerant scribe like me."

Manaen glanced at him, startled. "An itinerant scribe?"

Joanna and Chuza stared in astonishment. Rhoda cast a concerned glance toward Mary Mark.

"In the last few days, John Mark has made a very important decision," Barnabas said.

"Indeed he has," Mary Mark confirmed with satisfaction. "My son has finally found his purpose in life."

"He's putting his talents to work for the Lord," Joseph added with an approving chuckle. "In fact, he's decided to go to Antioch with Barnabas and Paul when they leave next month."

There was a pause the length of a gasp as the reality of the news settled in their minds. Then Joanna, Chuza, and the household servants crowded around him, congratulating him with hugs, slaps on the back, and words of encouragement.

But Manaen slipped out of the crowd and went to Mary Mark. He leaned toward her, his deep–set eyes searching her face, his craggy brow furrowed.

At this nearness, her heart gave a funny thump. She suddenly wished there were no people crowding the courtyard so that he could put his arms around her and hold her close.

"Are you going to Antioch with them?"

She shook her head. "My future is here, in Jerusalem, in this house. There will be more and more new believers. Many of them will need help." She glanced about. Memories good and bad, happy and sorrowful crowded through her mind, tugged at her heart with a nostalgia born of love and of promises now fulfilled. "I may even enlarge this house. What would you think of that?"

"If I speak to Barnabas and John Mark about my intentions toward you as my wife, what would think of that?"

Her throat felt suddenly dry.

"Would it be pleasing to you?" Manaen asked.

She smiled up at him and gently carressed his oddly imbalanced face until her voice could slip past the dryness in her throat. "It would please me. Very much," she whispered, closing her eyes and saying to herself, "Praise be to you, O Lord, for knowing my needs and for providing for them out of your great riches."